Murder On The Floodways

Life and Death on a Small Cotton Farm in Pemiscot County Missouri

Harold G. Walker

Published by Dragonfly Publishing, Inc.

Cover design: William Pack
(www.williampack.com)

Cover photo: Grey Horse Lake, 1917 - Courtesy of Missouri State Archives (600
West Main, Jefferson City, MO 65101)

ISBN: 978-0692455784 (soft cover)

Printed in the United States of America.

First Printing, 2014
Dragonfly Publishing, Inc.

To the memory of Verlan Raymond Busby
February 14, 1944 - March 6, 2014

and

To those who work the fields

Acknowledgements

This endeavor has been a trip through my childhood in a very special part of Missouri, the Bootheel, where cotton was king and the rugged Floodway system was my playground. The killing that happened when I was twelve years old has never been far from my consciousness and this book has been a labor of love for the people and the place.

First and foremost, I wish to express my gratitude to my wife, Kathleen, for her support and encouragement, without which, this book would not have been possible.

I want to recognize my deceased parents, Fred and Glenda Walker, with whom I lived through this tragedy and who allowed me, as a child, to hear their assessments of the crime, the funeral and most importantly, the people.

Furthermore, I want to convey my eternal thanks to my brother, John R. Walker and his wife, Helen Acom Walker, who assisted me with their memories and made it possible for me to locate and interview individuals.

A special thanks goes to my childhood friends: The late Verlan Raymond Busby, his wife, Helen Robinson Busby and Billy Joe Busby for sharing their memories and family pictures with me.

I want to thank Arlena, Alma Faye and Charles Robinson who shared their memories and family photographs with me.

I want to thank Ms. Sallie Huddleston Pratt, half-sister of Harry Leslie "Fats" Shell who shared her memories and family pictures.

I want to thank Jerry and Lanny Crane, sons of Junior Herbert Crane and Junior's grandson, Scott Crane, current pastor of Tatum Chapel, who shared their memories and pictures of their father/grandfather with me. Also, a special thanks to the membership of Tatum Chapel for their hospitality when I attended services there, a very special place.

I want to thank Maria Chamberlain, daughter of Dr. Wayne Wood for sharing her memories and a picture of her father with me.

I want to thank Charles R. Faris, retired Chief Deputy and former Acting Sheriff of the Pemiscot County Sheriff's Department, who shared his memories with me of having responded to the scene of the murder along with the late Deputy Sheriff, Junior Upchurch. Thanks also to Captain Ryan Holder of the Pemiscot County Sherriff's Office for his help when searching for records associated with the murder investigation.

Thanks also to Mary Riley, Malden Missouri for her invaluable help in locating individuals.

Thanks to Stephanie, at Hoggard & Sons Funeral Home, Piggott Arkansas for her research.

Thanks to, "findagrave.com," that led me to the December 13, 1957 Caruthersville Argus newspaper article reporting information taken from the original Sheriff's report.

Thanks to William (Tony) Byrd, Dunklin County Genealogy Society, for finding a December 9, 1957 Daily Dunklin Democrat newspaper article about the killing.

Thanks to former close neighbors to our family farm, Barbara Holloway Jones and Wilma McMahan Reed, for their recollections.

Thanks to Griff Walker, Pastor, First Baptist Church, Wardell, Missouri for his insight and encouragement.

Thanks to Dr. Rick Hollinger and the Saint Charles Writer's Group, affiliated with the St. Charles, Illinois Public Library, for their support and always constructive criticism.

A special thanks goes to my editors: Jean Monfort (University of Chicago); Joni Holderman, WritePros, Surfside Beach, South Carolina; Bruce Steinberg, Esq. St. Charles, Illinois.; Lucas J. Walker, Esq. Ottawa, Illinois; James Riley, Orland Park, Illinois and Kevin Moriarity, of Waterline Writers, Batavia, IL.

A very special thanks goes to Calvin Chambers, Batavia, Illinois, a gifted artist and illustrator who, by working with witness memories was able to illustrate the moment of the murder.

In addition to those listed above, there are many other individuals who have helped make this memory a reality through their support in various ways. To those go my sincere and heart-felt thanks.

Foreword

by

Bruce Steinberg

There is something magical about the Southern voice throughout the history of American literature. Samuel Clemons expertly crafted its vernacular in the thoughts and observations of Huckleberry Finn. Nelle Harper Lee's Scout discovered the unexpected power of her morally strong father steeped within old prejudices. Bailey White, and her Mama, mined humor and wisdom from observations of the Southern human landscape. Done well, the Southern voice not only earns the acceptance of Southern ears, but also draws in readers from all parts of the continent, and the world, to experience a culture simultaneously foreign and familiar. With confidence, I say Harold G. Walker's *Murder on the Floodways* possesses such a Southern voice. Only time will tell its final stature in the world of books. For me, though, the tale captured my Northerner's attention from its opening moments: the fate of a benign cat, Ol' Tom, at the hands of Hokey. It's a moment that defines the man's demonic character as well as a community living in fear and the need for humanity to rescue it from the edge of civil war.

It is possible that Hal and I could have been born and raised in more different backgrounds, but not much more different. He grew up in the Missouri Bootheel, steeped in old-style cotton farming and Baptist traditions. I was raised in a Chicago suburb where Hanukkah candles filled bungalow picture windows in December while a Christmas tree was a rare sight. Yet now I consider Hal my friend and, I believe, the feeling is mutual. We bonded over literature, each of us authors of books birthed from unique tragedies that defined our lives and shaped our perspectives. From my own experiences, an author undertaking such a story must be expert at listening, dedicated to research, and patient with fellow witnesses to the events. Hal Walker, with *Murder on the Floodways*, proves without doubt that he possesses these qualities. As a result, the pages unfold with respect for the reader, presenting a well-paced story that is both true and captivating.

After the demise of Ol' Tom, we meet the defining geography of the land as though we are spying out the window of a slowly descending spacecraft, witness to the country, the state, and the county, until the nooks and crannies of a culture become revealed. The landscape itself is its own character, shaping the lives of the Busby and Shell families, and all the families around them, including the Walker family from which a young Harold Walker observes these people living within a 1950s, hardscrabble cotton farming environment.

From the start, there is no hiding the fact that Donald "Hokey" Busby will kill his best friend, Harry "Fats" Shell, both young men with the world of possibilities before them. As frightening as Fat's murder unfolds, and as inevitable as Hokey's fate becomes, the strength of the story flourishes within a unique Southern culture and what these deaths mean to its people: the lines that are drawn between the family and friends of the killer versus the family and friends of his victim, for no one can carry on as a bystander; the building pressure within the community already leaking lava, a fighting word away from erupting into widespread violence. Yet the Bootheel, the Floodways more specifically, also embraces the Baptist faith, and denominations of the Baptist faith ,not only held dear by the citizenry, but also woven into its fiber. In a scene both unimaginable yet true, the depth of faith is tested, and the best of faith arises not through the words of its preachers, but from the hearts of two women, both of them giving as well as forgiving. Together they make it clear that if the community is to avoid further bloodshed, their faith, true and unadulterated faith, must also survive.

The mystical resolution in *Murder on the Floodways* places a final stamp on this cotton belt, Floodways culture, long since bulldozed off the American landscape by modern times. Sad, perhaps, but also hopeful, that even in the most difficult times, people can and will survive, if only they have faith in each other.

Murder on the Floodways is a Southern tale told in a Southern voice, set in a Southern place. Its story, however, proves universal. For all of us need faith, at least in each other.

* * *

Bruce Steinberg is the author of The Widow's Son, *grand prize winner of FirstNovelFest2000;* River Ghosts, *a Kirkus Star Review literary mystery and Amazon.com Hot New Release;* My Occasional Torment, *both the novel and the stage play; and* An Assassinated Man, *based on a true story. He is a criminal defense attorney, a former freelance writer for the Chicago Daily Herald and other print newspapers and the "Footloose" slice-of-life columnist for the monthly sports magazine* Silent Sports. *He has been a member of the Geneva Night Writers Workshop and the St. Charles Writers Group, where Hal Walker one day entered to say, I've got a true story to tell y'all . . .*

Author's Note

In this book, I have presented the facts of the killing and the bucolic life style found on my family farm in the mid-1950s. Although much of the dialogue is predominantly made up, it is done so with a deep cultural understanding of the people, the events being depicted and the era. As for the thoughts of others, I created internal thoughts that reflect the documentable situation being described. This genre is generally known as "literary non-fiction."

THE STATE OF MISSOURI

IOWA

IL

KS

OK

ARKANSAS

Bootheel

TN

MS

N

Illustration by Cal Chambers

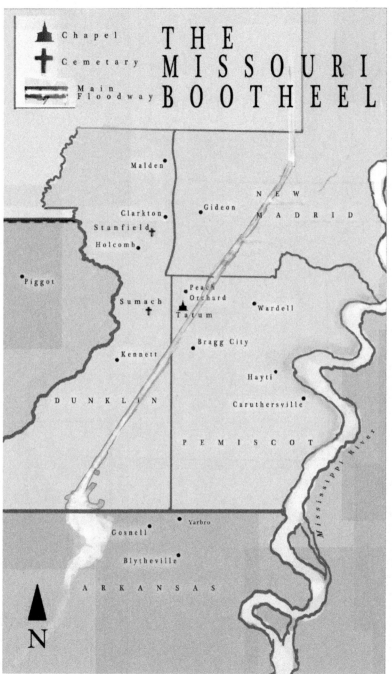

Illustration by Cal Chambers

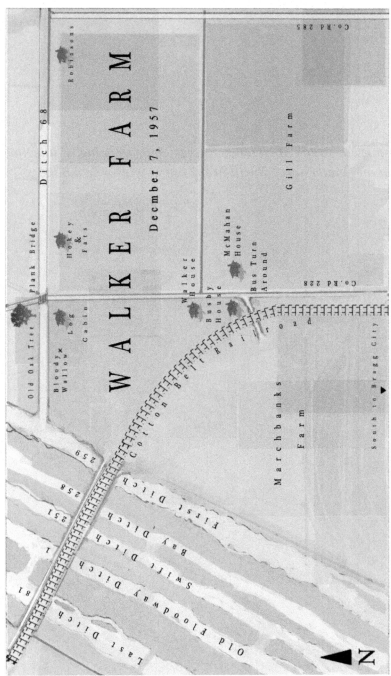

WALKER FARM

December 7, 1957

Ditch 68

Plank Bridge

Robinsons

Hokey & Fats

Old Oak Tree

Log Cabin

Bloody× Wallow×

Walker House

Busby House

McMahan House

Gill Farm

Bus Turn Around

Co.Rd 285

Co.Rd 228

Cotton Belt Railroad

First Ditch

Bay Ditch

Swift Ditch

Old Floodway Ditch

Last Ditch

259

258

257

1

81

Marchbanks Farm

South to Bragg City

N

Illustration by Cal Chambers

"There is a great streak of violence in every human being. If it is not channeled and understood, it will break out in war or in madness."

—Sam Peckinpah

1

Fall 1955

Ol' Tom, an orange tabby and a common sight around the farm, bore a chewed up left ear, a faded right eye and numerous scars from territorial battles. Only moments before, he was bellowing for attention before finding himself flung into the air by an angry hand. He tried to right himself for a safe landing through a series of proven aerobatic twists and turns. His instinct, upon tumbling to earth, had always been to stay low to the ground and scurry away from the danger as fast as possible, to get to the plank bridge. There, he would crawl up into the familiar oak support beams where he always found safe harbor.

The sculpted steel hammer was tripped. An ounce of steel shot, traveling at 1,100 feet per second, met Tom at the highest point of his trajectory. A high-pitched scream escaped his lungs only to end in less time than a cat's heart can beat. A pinkish mist replaced his middle. His eyes dimmed. Scarlet pieces of Tom were driven toward the old oak tree that stood by the plank bridge, some 20 feet beyond. The shot ripped off a pie plate sized piece of bark and impaled scarlet pieces of Tom into the tree, marking it for the remainder of its days.

An angry voice cried out, "Goddammit, I told y'all to keep that damn cat quiet while I'm trying to sleep!"

Fifty-one-year-old Bill Busby, whittling on a stick while sitting on the front porch of his family's small tenant house, was stunned by what he saw. He cringed, stopped whittling and looked down at his feet. He liked Ol' Tom but knew he mustn't make a sound. Say nothing, don't look in the direction of the voice. In the kitchen washing dishes, his wife, Ruth, age forty-four, heard the blast and the high-pitched human-like scream. A spontaneous tremor gripped her body; she denied her instinctive need to rush to the door, toward the sound. Instead, she closed her eyes tight as a tear escaped down her cheek. What did Ol' Tom ever do to you? What made you hate him so? Eleven-year-old Raymond, standing in the hard-packed dirt yard near his twenty-year-old brother, Hokey, said nothing, turning his head away. Li'l Joe, the youngest of the Busbys' three boys, at age five, cried out in fear. Ol' Tom had run afoul of Donald Ray "Hokey" Busby for the last time.

* * *

Whether states' borders follow twisting rivers or surveyors' stakes, straight and true, there seems to be at least one identifying border characteristic making many states immediately recognizable by their shape alone. The Texas panhandle, the Oklahoma panhandle, the boomerang shape of California, the notch in the Northeast corner of Arkansas, and the Bootheel of Missouri are prime examples of such characteristics.

The magnificent Mississippi River churns and twists its way southward through more than 2,000 miles alongside the borders of ten states on its way to the Gulf of Mexico. Three hundred miles of that journey make up the eastern border of Missouri, the last 50 miles of which are alongside what is called the Bootheel.

The Bootheel is an oddity, a stepchild to Missouri and an orphan to Arkansas. In its infancy, it was Arkansas Territory. Yet neither Arkansas nor Missouri saw any particular benefit to having 980 square miles of uninhabitable swamp. Geologically speaking, the Bootheel is a natural basin into which runoff water from the foothills of the Ozarks and floodwaters from the Mississippi collected for eons, creating a great swamp.

The swamp was identified as the lowlands, the Upper Mississippi Delta, and more contemporaneously as Swampeast Missouri. It has been described by historians as a wild and dark region, an impenetrable morass, a no-man's land, and a hideout in which disease was carried by every gnat, fly, and mosquito. Bears, bobcats, panthers, venomous vipers, poisonous plants, and berries flourished in that dark region. Unrecognizable quicksand pits lurked inside of and around each bend that could, in moments, swallow up a man or horse with no signs remaining. Liquor stills and highwaymen sprang from the mud in that treacherous and forbidden land.

In 1907, a group of wealthy visionaries met to establish the Little River Drainage District and began planning a reclamation project. What eventually came of that initial meeting would be hailed as the world's largest drainage system.

Between 1914 and 1928, huge steam-powered dredges moved more earth than was moved in the creation of the Panama Canal. Eons of mud and muck were ripped and chewed from the swamp, following a blueprint laid out in a perfect grid by an army of surveyors. At completion, near a thousand miles of canals and ditches reclaimed land that would be favorably compared to the Nile Valley Delta.

By-products of the digging process were ditch-dumps, elongated miniature mountain ranges composed of excavated material dumped alongside each canal and feeder ditch as high as the canal or ditch was deep. In years to come many of those ditch-dumps, piled along the southern side of the feeder ditches, became rutted field roads surrounded by fields of cotton and soybeans.

The feeder ditches were like the fingers of a giant hand, funneling water from the fields into the five large canals heading south through the Bootheel to the Mississippi River. Where the canals came together side-by-side, like the wrist of a giant hand, the canals and associated ditch-dumps measured a quarter mile wide.

An extensive Bootheel railroad system, known as the Cotton Belt, connected every small crossroad community that had a cotton gin or grain elevator. The railroad tracks, built upon a high roadbed, became a well-trodden walkway from community to community for those with no cars, or for everyone when county roads were impassable. On occasion, adventurous souls challenged the trains by driving their cars on the tracks. At times, when those dare-devils came face-to-face with the lumbering old engine coming round the bend, the cars were forced to freewheel into the ditches that ran alongside both sides of the tracks. Usually, the only damage done was to the egos of the drivers.

From Peach Orchard to Bragg City, the Cotton Belt ran due east and across the five big canals on five giant trestles. Each trestle was some sixty feet high. These spans allowed people access into the heart of the Floodways, and by so doing, the waterways became inextricably interwoven into the social lives of the communities surrounding them.

During the week, twice a day, sometimes more, but never on Sunday, the big diesel engine made its way back and forth through the Bootheel, huffing and puffing with bales of cotton, grain, and freight. The last car was always a red caboose where the brakeman sat, grinning and waving at children gathered to see this welcomed bit of excitement. To the added delight of the children, the friendly brakeman sometimes tossed out candy and newspapers.

Occasionally, a penny placed on the rail ahead of an oncoming train became a treasured souvenir to be shown to friends as evidence of a grand adventure. On Sundays, the Floodways were as busy as downtown on Saturday night. Folks in their Sunday best made their way around and over fields of cotton to enjoy the serenity and beauty of the slow-moving streams: to fish, to swim, or to just stroll with good friends.

The Floodways were also an incubator for young imaginative adventurers, giving rebirth to old legends and hauntings by ghosts, dark spirits or specters, collectively called "haints[i]."

2

I was three years old in 1948 when my dad, Fred Walker, moved our family to a small, one-hundred-twenty-acre cotton and soybean farm on land reclaimed from the great swamp. It was Mom and Dad's first big gamble, taking a mortgage on what once was a vast shallow lake called Grey Horse. The lake was surrounded by gum, hickory, and oak trees. Cypress trees flourished in the stagnant waters, their knees gathered round the base of the cypress, like lost children. It was a piece of land on which the first two mortgage holders went bust, helping fuel the general truth that the Bootheel was the poorest region of Missouri.

The farm was tucked into a remote northwest corner of Pemiscot County, the southeastern-most county of Missouri. The name Pemiscot came from the Native American word *Pem-eskaw,* meaning "liquid mud," a most appropriate description of that land before the reclamation.

The farm was bordered on the north by Feeder Ditch 68 and on the west by the five big canals. Running east-southeast across the southern border was the Cotton Belt Railroad that ran between Peach Orchard and Bragg City and beyond to Pascola, Hayti, and Caruthersville. Together, the steel rails of the Cotton Belt and the majesty of the Floodways formed a man-made corner into which our small farm and my whole world were nestled.

There was no electricity, no phones, and no modern plumbing. The county roads were little more than muddy lanes.

The families who lived and worked on the farm were the Busbys and the Ladens. The work was from sun-up to sundown in the harshest of conditions: syrupy heat, swarms of mosquitos, and the occasional angry pit viper during the summer and freezing rain in the winter. At age thirty-nine, Mom, my eighteen-year-old sister, Glenda Mae, and my eight-year-old big brother,

Johnny, worked as hard as Dad, age forty-two, alongside the Busbys and Ladens.

To be a farm family in Southeast Missouri during that era required uncommon grit found in the pioneering spirit of Americans who crossed the plains in covered wagons. Just like the pioneers, Mom and Dad, and others like them, were starting a new life on new land as farm owners.

The work required physical strength and stamina along with skill sets as disparate as sharpening a hoe to a razor edge, and crimping a blasting cap onto a fuse and inserting it into a stick of dynamite to blow apart stubborn stumps. The only day of the week when work wasn't performed was Sunday, the Sabbath, unless, as the Bible allowed, "The ox was in the ditch." As the years passed, the new land began to take on the look and feel of a miniature cotton plantation, similar to the ones Dad recalled from deep-seated memories of Mississippi when he was a small boy.

His farming success led him to lease more farmland from the Little River Drainage District that lay between Canals 258 and 259, known respectfully as First Ditch and Bay Ditch. The fifty-yard-wide field stretched a half mile north and a mile south of the Cotton Belt. A shack, looking like an 1880 homestead with a small lean-to barn and a fenced pasture area, came with the lease. It was here where Dad allowed his prized mules, Tom and Jerry, to eventually retire in a serene environment.

Johnny beamed with joy when he got a dream job from the Little River Drainage District as the first official gauge reader on the Floodways. The job called for him to record the depth of the water in the five canals each day of the week. A measurement plank was nailed to one of the big pilings on each of the five railroad trestles across the canals. This plank bore big black numbers from zero to sixty feet. He recorded the level of the water every day, no matter the weather, receiving the princely sum of five dollars a month. That job made him a permanent fixture on the Floodways where his many adventures became legendary.

A swimming hole, created by a concrete spillway between Canal 1, called Old Floodway, and a dry ditch that ran alongside the east side of Old Floodway, was used by the more adventuresome who knew the location. Johnny knew the locations of all the swimming holes and guided a group of his friends, one of whom couldn't swim, to that hidden pool. Kenny, the non-swimmer was cautioned not to wade into the pool as the others jumped and splashed into the eight-to-ten-feet of water. He came too close.

As Kenny floundered and was going down for a second time, Johnny came to his rescue, cheered on by Don Gill and others in the group. A nearby fisherman, "Coots" McCurry, noticed the emergency and headed for the pool. Johnny, after trying to drag Kenny back to the bank with his arm around Kenny's neck and armpit, found that the rescue couldn't be made in this manner as Kenny clung to him so tightly that they were both in danger of drowning. Johnny's quick response was to shoot to the bottom, slipping from Kenny's arms, planting his feet on the sandy bottom of the pool. He grabbed Kenny's legs between the knee and ankle and held him tight, giving Kenny a solid rock to stand upon and have his head above water. That solid rock was Johnny, going for a record time of holding his breath. Coots arrived and pulled Kenny into the boat. When Johnny felt Kenny being pulled up he let go and, as his lungs were about to burst, pushed off the bottom and shot straight up. His head rammed into the bottom of the boat. He fought off the darkness of unconsciousness and wheeled about, seeing the light above. He surfaced and was also dragged into Coots' boat, to forever be hailed as Kenny's savior by most everyone, especially Kenny and his mother.

On another occasion, Johnny killed a big water moccasin that was coming at Mom while she fished from the bank of Canal 259. The shot from his hip with a single-shot lever-action .22 rifle struck the reptile square in the head, flipping it over as pretty as you please. The current took the snake away with a trail of blood following behind.

He had set a high standard for family marksmanship, one I could never duplicate. When Dad heard the story, he grinned, his gold tooth glistening, and said, "Johnny's a regular Dead-Eye Dan." That was the absolute best that could be said about marksmanship in our family. Johnny's presence on, and knowledge of, the Floodways and the people who called the Floodways home were his legacy. His adventures became blueprints for me to follow in my coming adventures.

3

Like most farm families in the Bootheel, our family was self-sufficient. On days when Mom and Dad finished working in the fields, mom would sometimes say to Dad, "Fred, get us a chicken for supper."

Mom would boil up a bucket of water and place it in the yard for when Dad came from the barn. As he walked back to the house, he'd grab a strolling chicken, grip it by the head and, while not missing a step, wring the chicken's neck. The body of the chicken would fly off while the chicken's head remained in his hand. As he continued to walk, he'd throw the head of the chicken out into the cotton patch while the headless body, blood flying, flopped all over the place. Once the chicken's body quit hopping around, Dad held the chicken by its feet and pushed it neck first into the boiling water loosening up the feathers so it could be easily plucked.

Mom would then carry the bare chicken into the kitchen, gut it and throw the innards into a slop bucket. Normally, either me or Johnny would take the bucket to the barn and dump it in the slop trough for the hogs. Mom placed the chicken parts, coated in a mixture of flour, salt, pepper, and seasoning, into a frying pan coated with lard. Hot biscuits were browning in the oven and green beans from a Mason jar were coming to a boil. She could whip up a complete dinner in just a few minutes. Nothing tasted better than Mom's meals.

I continued to "grow like grass," as Mom would say. Sis left home for college at Arkansas State in Jonesboro. After a semester or two, she quit and married Bill when I was seven and in the second grade. She left for Arizona after a big church wedding at the First Baptist Church in Kennett. It was a new beginning for her and her husband. Her leaving devastated me. I hardly ever saw her again.

The farm flourished under Dad's sound management principles: "A day's pay for a day's work," and the most important ingredient, good cotton weather, hot nights, and slow spring rains. In keeping with a southern tradition, Dad felt strongly that the folks on the farm were his responsibility. He always made sure there was plenty of year-round work for the folks who called our farm home. They paid no rent and Dad maintained the upkeep on their houses. If they were ever a little short, they could always borrow interest-free cash from the farm safe Dad kept in his and Mom's bedroom. That safe, purchased from the Sears Roebuck catalog, also held a small .38 caliber Smith & Wesson five-shot double action revolver, just in case of trouble. The loans were always paid back.

In cotton farming it was critical to plant the fragile seed in the time range of mid-May to mid-June and then to hope and pray that it would result in a good stand of cotton within three to five days. If it wasn't too wet or too dry, the seed should begin to sprout. During this time frame, farmers could be seen walking the fields, kneeling down at different points as if in prayer, picking at the seed bed, looking for signs that the planting was a success.

If the seed germinated and *if* it lived, the plant required ninety days to produce cotton. If all went well, the cotton would be open and ready for the first picking in September. If the seeds didn't germinate, a new planting was not unusual. However, the later the planting, the shorter the growing season. And, even if the late plantings produced a good stand of cotton, the yield would more than likely result in immature stalks with green bolls that partially opened, or died.

Each additional planting cost the same amount of money as the original, driving the farmer deeper and deeper into debt. Farming, simply put, was optimism turned to pessimism turned to despair turned to prayer. If the crop was bad and the seed money couldn't be repaid, the farm sale signs went up, adversely affecting the fragile agro-economy of the Bootheel.

If the seeds did sprout and the delicate plant's bowed head broke through to sunlight, a farmer could be the most contented man you ever saw. During those tension-filled days during May, June, and July when the nights were hot and sultry and it was virtually impossible to sleep, Dad and I would often sit on the porch swing and he would say to me, "Just listen...you can hear the cotton growing."

* * *

Our frame house was painted white and set up on blocks to protect it from minor flooding. A wide, inviting front porch with a double swing was shaded by two large cottonwood trees that rose from a sea of Kentucky Bluegrass. A row of multiflora roses, some ten feet high, ran along the north boundary of the yard.

After years of haggling with bureaucrats, Dad was able to get County Road #228, the one that bisected our farm, graveled. Prior to this, the graveled portion of the road had stopped just short of our farm. We could now drive our car in most every kind of weather. And to top it all off, we got modern plumbing. The two-hole privy could now take its place in history. There was still no phone service, which no one seemed to miss.

In this age of prosperity, our new propane tank held 500 gallons and sat next to the south side of the house, between the house and the driveway. We even got a luxury item, an Admiral Television console with an immense antenna on top of the house tall enough to capture signals from Memphis. Three guy wires staked into the yard supporting the antenna caused some cuts and bruises when we played tag or hide-and-seek near dark, but it was worth it.

The need for mules and muleskinners had disappeared years before. They were replaced by two new tractors, a wide front-end Ford and a bright red H-Model International Harvester with tricycle gear. A bright new Butler grain bin made of aluminum guaranteed that rodents couldn't sneak into the inner sanctum full of corn, cotton, and soybean seeds.

After years of Dad's hand-seeding, a pasture replete with knee-high alfalfa and framed by fourteen-foot-high multiflora roses was overseen by two stately cypress trees left over from the great swamp. Two or three head of beef cattle, a milk cow, an assortment of pigs, and two saddle horses, Paint and Rebel, one for Johnny and one for me, grazed and frolicked in that tranquil setting.

Dad loved horses, but I never saw him ride one. Yet, he wanted us boys to have one and to ride as much as possible. He preferred that we learn to ride bareback before using a saddle, which Johnny did. I challenged that requirement, finally causing Dad to give in and get a hand-carved saddle, which he eventually purchased in Nogales, Mexico.

On many afternoons, after the school bus dropped off our bunch, Johnny would grab a halter and place it on his horse. He'd grab a handful of mane and swing upon her back, riding bareback, as she leapt into a full gallop across the fields, jumping ditches and racing the wind with a slew of community dogs running headlong beside them. It was a wonderful sight. Dad beamed as he said, "Johnny can ride like a Comanche."

Regarding our beef cattle, Dad would have preferred to have Black Angus steers, but, for the most part, they were too expensive. We mainly had odds and ends of cattle purchased at the Kennett, Poplar Bluff, or Malden sale barns.

A collection of barn cats held down the rodent population that attempted to feed on the grains stored in the old log barn. The cats made their bed in the hay loft, and Dad, during the morning milking ritual, saw to it that they always received their fair share of fresh milk.

The only oddity was a large king snake allowed to slither around at will. The snake assisted the cats in controlling the rodent population and froze me with fear each and every time I saw it, adding fuel to my phobia. However, it never bothered the cats or the cuddly kittens that came with them.

I couldn't believe that snake could live peaceably with the cats. Yet, they must have worked something out because I never saw a mouse that wasn't running for its life. Ironically, the only thing that threatened the lives of the kittens was a tomcat.

Behind our house, a couple of dozen white leghorn chickens were kept in a big henhouse behind a well-built fence meant to keep out predators. There were always foxes trying to get a late night chicken dinner. During the day, the chickens were allowed to roam free. At night, they all came home to roost and laid grade-A large eggs, gathered each morning by Mom.

My dog and close companion was Buddy, a beautiful collie. He would occasionally take advantage of the chickens' free roaming privileges to have a spirited run through the clucking mass of hens, causing all sorts of mayhem. Amid the cackling and fluttering of feathers, the hens ran as the roosters prepared to face him down. But he'd never go any further than harassment for his own amusement.

On many occasions, I would hear Mom hollering at Buddy when he started chasing the chickens. He seemed to know from experience just how far he could go. Then, he'd prance off, looking at the hens that had lost all of their dignity, and nimbly avoid the two big Leghorn roosters' fighting stances. The claw-like scars across his face suggested he didn't want to test the roosters' grit and determination. However, if you looked real close, you might have seen a mischievous grin as he trotted away from the terrified brood.

Mom's pride and joy was her vegetable garden. On many occasions, I saw her standing at the kitchen sink, washing dishes while admiring her garden through the double windows she insisted upon having. Brightly colored curtains, sewn on her Singer treadle sewing machine, framed the view. From this horn-of-plenty, Mom used a large pressure cooker to vacuum seal a variety of vegetables in quart-size Ball Mason jars.

Mom, the former Glenda Opal Robbins, hailed from Gravel Hill, a small town in Bollinger County, Missouri, and met my dad in Flint, Michigan. Mom, at five foot four and 110 pounds, with big brown eyes and brown hair, always dressed neatly. She wore a variety of colorful aprons and could cook up a meal in a flash for anyone who arrived hungry. She would make a pallet on the floor for unexpected guests when there were not enough beds to go around. On many a morning, Mom, enjoying her propane cook stove, would be busy in the kitchen, rattling pots and pans, listening to and singing along with gospel favorites on "Old Camp Meeting Time," hosted by Mr. Ruddy on KBOA in Kennett. I must have heard Ferlin Huskey's "Wings of a Snow White Dove" hundreds of times during my years at home.

The farm labor had finally become sufficient so that Mom didn't have to work in the fields and, for the first time in her life, could devote time to what she wanted to do. She was an expert seamstress who browsed through patterns at JC Penney and purchased yards of material as most ladies did during that day. She sewed most all of our clothes and all of her own. On one morning, she even sewed me a new shirt before I caught the school bus. She was also constantly redecorating the house. She went about transforming the small home with a fresh new look by doing her own re-upholstering, painting, and wallpapering.

Mom was also a devotee of reading. Reader's Digest Condensed Books, a set of encyclopedias she earned by redeeming S&H green stamps, and a few classics: *Tom Sawyer*, *Huckleberry Finn*, and *Life on the Mississippi* were available in our small family library. Higher education and the arts, especially the piano, were all important to her.

"Time to practice the piano, young man," she'd say when I preferred to head out for the Floodways with Raymond Busby, or ride Rebel through the fields with Buddy running alongside. Mom would stop all those activities by simply pointing at our upright piano, an old converted Steinway player piano, which she had professionally tuned each year.

"Darn, Mom, do I have to?" I'd whine.

There was no need for her to speak. I knew her answer. I had to practice for those half-hour lessons my brother and I took from Miss Ring every Saturday morning in Kennett, across the street from Sheriff Raymond Scott's jail. When other kids on the farm were outside the house, they could hear me practicing. My awkward attempts to play Hungarian Rhapsody No. 2 embarrassed me to no end, especially when the kids giggled and said, "I heard you playing the piano."

I felt it very un-masculine to play the piano because I only saw women playing the piano at church and at home. As a result of that delusion, I suffered through good and bad years of piano lessons and formal recitals at the Bank of Kennett's community meeting room. I eventually became proficient at playing one of Mom's favorites, "Deep Purple," and one of Dad's favorites, "St. Louis Blues." Not until my brother and I reached 16 years of age respectively were we allowed to stop taking lessons. We did, and it broke Mom's heart.

4

The cotton patch was a reflection of the farm community and a perfect place to hear all the gossip of the day, especially on a small farm like ours. We were picking on the home forty, hemmed in by Feeder Ditch 68, First Ditch/Canal 259, and the Cotton Belt that invited a stillness from breezes, exaggerating the heat and humidity. Nine pickers made up our crew. This included the Busbys, the Robinsons, and me, age 10, the weakest link in the chain.

The early morning procession to the field by the pickers was something to behold. They wore long-sleeved shirts with wide-brimmed straw hats and deep-brimmed bonnets. Startled rabbits and an occasional quail or two sprang upward before the onslaught. Morning birds like robins and mockingbirds trumpeted our arrival.

The diminutive Mrs. Martha Robinson led her family to the field that morning like a military procession. There was strong, friendly seventeen-year-old Charles, carrying a couple of blankets over his shoulder, and his nine foot sack. He kept tabs on his sisters. Arlena, age fifteen, held the hand of Ernest Dale, "Buddy," age six. Alma Faye, age thirteen, carried Violet Louise, age four, on her right hip. Helen, age ten, and small for her age, held the baby, Bobby, age seven months, on her hip.

During the long day in the field, Helen mothered all the younger children, including seven-year-old Li'l Joe, the youngest son of Bill and Ruth Busby. She saw to it that the kids took naps on the blankets, laid out like a picnic under the cotton trailer. She played games with them and they picked small amounts of cotton to pile in the middle of their mother's row, little surprises fashioned by small hands, learning the feel of the cotton and the cotton patch.

She also kept the little ones, as they were collectively called, out of the cotton trailer. Playing in the cotton trailer, although appealing, was not allowed. Each fall, children were smothered in play tunnels they dug in the cotton. There was no doubt about it, Helen had the toughest job of all.

She regularly carried drinking water in a Mason Ball quart jar from the Igloo cooler to her mother, sisters, and brother in the field, even bringing water to me and Raymond Busby on occasion. She paid particular attention to Raymond, making small talk about the day. We enjoyed her company.

The sun was coming up to mid-morning with a fair amount of time to go till noon. With no wristwatch, I had learned to tell about what time it was by the sun's position.

Charles had already weighed-in his second sack of cotton and was beginning two more rows. He was like a world-class athlete, getting his second wind.

Everyone in the cotton field was spread out at this time, kind of like a cross-country foot race when the runners have settled into their pace. Conversations had begun to drift across the field and, if you remained quiet, you could hear voices from near a quarter-mile away.

From the direction of Arlena and Alma Faye came the following: "Did you hear about what he did?"

"Who?"

"Why, Hokey, of course. He drove that black car of his through Pascola at top speed, with folks flying all over the place trying to get out of the way."

When Hokey's name popped up, I paid attention. "Raymond, did you hear that?" I said in a whisper.

"Yeah," he responded as he continued to pick.

"Did he really do that?"

"What?"

"You know, drive his car like they said."

"I don't know," Raymond said. "Maybe."

Hokey, at twenty-one years of age, was handsome and wild, like a cowboy. He lived at home and worked at the Gideon Anderson Lumber Company. He drove one of those big yellow Ross Straddle Carriers, the kind of machine you could see at big lumber companies, moving large stacks of lumber. A skilled job that paid much more than a common laborer could make. The voices continued.

"Why would he do such a thing?" said one.

"Just for fun, I guess," said another.

"Anyway, who's he dating nowadays?"

"I heard he's sweet on some honky-tonk angel named Dorothy."

"Who else does he date?"

"Anyone he pleases," said with a giggle.

"That Hokey's something, ain't he?"

"Yeah, he's one handsome son-of-a-gun."

"Yes, and who's that good looking man he runs with?"

"Harry. That's all I know. He's cute."

* * *

Harry Leslie Shell was big. At over two hundred pounds and standing more than six feet tall with short cropped brown hair, wavy when worn long, and deep brown eyes, he stood out from the average sized-man of the day. At twenty-two years of age in 1956, he was a gentle soul, affable and strong as weathered oak. He answered to and was unoffended by the nicknames, "Fats" or "Fat Boy" even though he was simply big.

He was a close friend of the Busby family. He, like Hokey, had Hollywood good looks and loved the wild life that friendship with Hokey afforded him. He had no car and no driver's license, nor did he have access to a car other than Hokey's.

Fats' biological father was Otto Shell. His mother was Elsie Huddleston, who later married Homer Huddleston. Harry and his sister, Mildred Shell, lived in Clarkton, MO. with his mother and half-sisters: Sallie, Alice, called Allie, and Dallie Huddleston. Harry quit school in the elementary grades to work full time in the fields. When there were no jobs in the fields, he chopped and stacked firewood with his relatives in Zalma and Eminence, Missouri. He normally wore bib overalls like most men did. Yet, as mild mannered as he appeared, with his natural born strength and sculpted build, it was said that Fats finished every fight Hokey started.

* * *

At the end of the day, when everyone gathered at the trailer, a couple of visitors showed up.

"What are you two up to?" It was Hokey with a friend, a big guy with a big smile I'd seen around some. Hokey had parked his hot-rod, a black '47 Ford flat-head V8, on the gravel road and they had walked to the cotton trailer.

"Nothin, much," I said.

"Hey, Mr. Walker," said Hokey.

"Hey, Hokey," responded Dad with a grin. "When you gonna grace us with your presence in the cotton field? I could use ya, ya know."

"Well, if that load of lumber don't show up at the yard, I'll be at your beck and call."

"Okay, and bring your friend. He looks like he could pull a big sack."

"Yes, sir! I'll sure do that, if he gets up in time. He's lazy."

Dad's attention returned to double-checking the weights.

I always liked to see Hokey; he was different from the other folks I knew. Everything around him seemed exciting and I thought of what the girls had said about him racing through Pascola.

"Hey, Hokey," I said. "Nothin' much going on here, except me and Raymond are going fishing tonight."

"Well, ain't that something," he said. "Y'all gonna catch some more waterbugs to eat, are ya?"

"Them things weren't waterbugs," I said, grinning.

"Looked like bugs to me," said Hokey, as he ducked and faked a jab to my stomach. I doubled up like I had got hit and laughed.

* * *

One time, Raymond and I fished for crawdads in a pond under the old plank bridge. We got a willow stick, tied a fishing line to it, and used a piece of bread for bait. We let the bread lie in the big mud hole and those big red crawdads would grab hold of the bread and hang on as we lifted them out of the water and placed them in a jar.

We caught plenty of them tasty morsels, roasted their tails over a fire, salted them down and ate them all right there. Hokey had come to watch and had just sat there amazed at what we were doing. He never forgot and always teased us about it.

* * *

Hokey Busby stood about five feet eight inches tall and weighed around 130 pounds, sack and all, as was said in cotton country. He was smooth-shaven with a lean, muscular, frame, pale blue eyes, and dark blond hair worn in the popular rockabilly style of the day. A wide smile with even teeth completed his look. An aura of restlessness and mystery surrounded him.

He wore Levis, not any off-brand like Tuff-Nut, and this day he was wearing a white, western cut, long-sleeve shirt with the sleeves rolled up to his elbows. His outfit was completed with black high-heeled cowboy boots that made him seem near six feet tall. With the brim of his white Stetson-style cowboy hat pulled down to about an inch above his eyes, he looked his best. Hokey always looked like he was getting ready to drive his Ford to the nearest honky-tonk, because most times that was exactly where he was headed.

Hokey drove that hot rod of a car at breakneck speeds when he and Fats were on a bender, maneuvering on gravel and slick blacktop roads like a bootlegging stock car veteran. He knew every gravel road, farm lane, and path in and around the Floodways and, on occasion, gave many hard-eyed deputies the slip. It was reported that a black Ford traveling at high rates of speed was known to race through small crossroad communities, endangering life and limb before disappearing into the night.

"Didn't you have to work today, Hoke?" asked Raymond, grinning real big.

"Well, that load of lumber that was supposed to come in today didn't. So, I didn't have to work and thought I'd pick up my best friend here and we'd come over and watch everyone else work."

With everyone gathered at the cotton trailer and the shadows beginning to grow longer, Dad told them, "We got a load, and I'll be taking it to the gin tomorrow. Since tomorrow is Saturday, when I get back from the gin, I'll be paying at the house and we won't be working this weekend. It's been a good work week." This brought cheers from the Robinson girls and it meant that Raymond and I might be able to stay out fishing all night.

"Why, Arlena," Hokey said, "I didn't know you were picking today." Arlena was the oldest daughter of Ernest and Martha Robinson living at home. Good natured and pleasant, she was tall and slim with long brown hair and brown eyes.

"You would have if you'd've asked," she responded with a coy smile.

"Well, it's nice to see y'all."

"You too." She blushed and half curtseyed.

"Who's that with you?" Arlena asked.

"Oh, him?" Hokey smiled. "That's my friend. Just call him Fat Boy."

Grinning, Harry responded, "What did you call me, Hoke? Fats? I guess I could give you what-for if I wanted."

"I don't know about that," laughed Hokey, backing up slowly.

"Oh,yeah? Just watch." Fats grabbed Hokey up in a bear hug and held him off the ground. Hokey's feet kicked in mid-air and Fats laughed.

Hokey laughed a little at first, then hollered, "Now don't, goddammit"

Fats grinned while Hokey struggled. It was like a cat holding a struggling sparrow in its grasp.

"Damnit, Fats. Put me down."

"Not till you say 'Uncle'."

"Oh, shit!" hollered Hokey, his feet flailing in the air and his cowboy hat falling off his head. "Uncle, you gorilla. Now put me down!" Hokey's calm exterior changed abruptly with the color in his face turning red, and an unnatural intensity in his eyes, not seen by most.

Ruth's initial grin at the horseplay began to dissipate. She stepped forward to intervene. "You two quit that now, someone's gonna get hurt." Ruth was stout and little more than five feet tall. She had an oval face with prominent cheek bones and dark eyes as though she might have had Native American ancestry. Her hair was cropped short in a pageboy cut, practical, and never obscured her vision. She was intelligent, but uneducated, a typical circumstance in the Bootheel, the poorest region in the state, where work came before schooling.

"Yeah, me," hollered Hokey. "But I ain't the only one that's gonna get hurt."

"I gotta let you down," laughed Fats, setting Hokey down. Then, as an afterthought, he reached over and mussed up Hokey's hair, "'Cause your momma came to your aid," he said.

"Damn it, Fats," Hokey said, picking up his hat and brushing off the dirt. "Ya messed up my hat and my hair." Pulling a comb from one of his shirt's snap breast pockets, Hokey drew the comb through his thick hair and, with both hands, adjusted his hat on his head, cocked a little to one side.

"That's good for you," replied Fats, laughing as he reached over and tugged Hokey's hat brim.

"That's enough godammit!" snarled Hokey, his voice more like a growl with no measure of playfulness in it. Fats stopped and stepped back a bit. The color in his face paled and his smile changed to one of concern, almost fear.

Bending at the waist with both hands at his belt line, Hokey coughed and took a deep breath. While still bent over, He looked up at the group that had become awkwardly silent. An easy grin began to spread over his face. "Now," said Hokey, looking at the Robinson girls, "any of y'all want a ride home?"

"No," Mrs. Robinson quickly responded. "Ernest will be here in a bit to take us home. Come on, girls," she said.

"Well then, come on, Mom," Hokey said to Bill and Ruth. "Let's go."

Fats continued standing apart from Hokey, his thumbs hooked into his jeans pockets. Raymond had turned his head and quietly left when he heard Hokey curse at Fats. He was climbing up to the railroad tracks, through some wild blueberry bushes.

"Raymond!" I yelled.

He yelled at me, "I'll see you at the trestle."

I yelled back, "I gotta talk with Dad first." But Raymond didn't hear me. "Dad, I gotta talk with ya."

Dad, who was figuring the final weight of the cotton said to everyone, "I think we got just enough to make a good bale. So, y'all can call it a day and don't forget to come by the house tomorrow after dinner and get paid." Then, looking at me, Dad said, "Just what are you up to?"

"Since there ain't no pickin' tomorrow and I don't have to take a piano lesson, Raymond and I thought we'd do some fishing tonight."

"Well, where ya going?"

"Oh, just over here on First Ditch. Where we usually go."

Dad thought for a minute. "You know I don't like you being out on those Floodways overnight."

"But, we'll be here on this side of the ditch, barely off the farm."

"I know where you say you go, but where do you really go?"

"Mom said it was okay with her."

"Did she now? Tell me true. Are you sure she said it was okay?"

"Well," I said, looking down at my shoes. "She said she didn't care, if you didn't."

"Now, that's better. Okay, but don't go any farther than where you said you'd be. You never know, I might just walk down to see if everything's okay."

"Everything'll be okay. I'm gonna take the .22 rifle anyway."

"Okay, but remember the rules."

"Yes, sir. Hit what you're shootin at, right?"

"That's right," he laughed. "What else?"

I thought for a moment, drawing a blank.

"What do I always tell you?"

I thought and thought, then it came to me. "Stay away from Elmer."

"That's right, now go on. Tell your mother I'll be a little late. I'm bringing the trailer to the house."

I took off for home. As I left, I heard Hokey talking with Mr. Robinson who'd just walked up.

"I'm headed that way, Mr. Robinson," said Hokey.

"Well, I don't know," said Mr. Robinson, pulling his cap off and running his hand through his thinning hair.

"Daddy, can we go with Hokey?" asked Arlena, with Alma Faye chiming in, "Please?"

"Okay," he said, "I guess so."

"Thanks, Mr. Robinson," said Hokey, "I'll be real careful."

Mr. Robinson thought for a moment, and then said as an afterthought, "You wouldn't mind, would you, Hokey, if Martha rode along with you and the girls?"

"No, sir. Everyone's welcome."

"Ok," said Mr. Robinson, "y'all can go with Hokey and Fats as long as your mom is with you. Helen, you and the little ones come with me."

"All right, let's saddle up," said Hokey, slapping his hands together.

Hokey, Arlena, and Mrs. Robinson crowded into the front seat of Hokey's car, with Alma Faye in the back seat with Fats.

"Mom," Hokey shouted toward Ruth, "I'll be right back to get you."

The radio came on and rockabilly blared as Mrs. Robinson laughed and placed her fingers in her ears. Ruth just grinned and chuckled.

"It ain't too far to walk," Ruth said as she, Bill, and Li'l Joe began to walk down the road toward their house.

Arriving home, I threw my cotton sack in the tractor shed and began gathering up what I needed for the night. First on my list was a fishing pole and a trotline. I dug some red worms and placed them along with some dampened soil into an empty lard can. I grabbed our old JC Higgins .22 caliber bolt-action rifle with a couple of boxes of Western Auto .22 longs, and a box of matches.

Mom gave me a sack with two peanut butter sandwiches, two pieces of fried chicken, a half dozen chocolate chip cookies and a quart Mason Ball jar of water, enough for both me and Raymond. I took some 6-12 insect repellent from the house and grabbed a Pic mosquito coil out of our car. Johnny used those mosquito coils at the drive-in theater. I took a flashlight off the back porch and grabbed my old sleeping bag. Everything else I placed in an old pillow case and threw it over my shoulder. About to head out, I looked like an ol' hobo.

Mom, ever vigilant, stopped me and looked me over, placing her hands on both my shoulders. "Give me a hug," she said. "And remember, your dad and I might come down to the camp tonight if I get to missing you."

"Ah, Mom, we'll be okay." I knew Mom and Dad wouldn't be coming to the campsite. But, I kinda felt better, knowing they might.

"Where's Buddy? I sure want him with you."

"I don't know where he is, probably out hunting. He'll find me if he wants. Love ya."

"Love you more," she called out as I walked toward the Cotton Belt.

5

Raymond waited for me on the Cotton Belt tracks behind the house. He had a blanket, food, bait, the Busbys' old 10 gauge double-barrel shotgun, and a bright new red tin of King Edward crimp-cut cigarette tobacco.

As I walked west along the railroad tracks, my world felt right. The orange-colored sun was settling into the horizon, its last rays reflected from the rails that ran before us as the cicadas' screams resonated throughout the Floodways and the temperature began to cool.

As we approached First Ditch, we left the tracks heading north on a path hidden by weeds near waist high. We continued walking north along the east side of the canal to our intended campsite.

The spot was near where Feeder Ditch 68 flowed into First Ditch/Canal 259. Rattlesnake Hill, a ditch-dump mountain, was on the west side of the ditch from us. Years before, my brother had broken the stock of his new Red Ryder BB gun on an imaginary foe in the form of a stump, while leading an all-out frontal assault. The charge was patterned after John Wayne's iconic charge up Mount Suribachi in the movie *Iwo Jima*. The hill was taken and a red neckerchief tied to a willow pole was planted at the summit. There were no rattlesnakes on Rattlesnake Hill, but it sounded better than calling it Water Moccasin Hill.

The sun's rays soon began disappearing behind Rattlesnake Hill, casting our campsite in light shadows. Night was fast approaching. We had to hurry.

As we set up camp, I glanced toward the trestle, some hundred- plus yards south of us. It was as though I was seeing it for the first time. The intersecting geometric angles made from creosote-soaked beams that held the rails were framed by the barely visible full moon on the southern horizon and the sight of them caused me to stare. That majestic view of the trestles was an image I never wanted to forget.

Soon, the normally drab, brown water flowing slowly south would be transformed by moonlight into a shimmering silver stream and the giant bullfrogs would begin their deep-throated chorus. We brought with us a fifteen foot trotline, a heavy length of fishing line, called the main line, with fishing hooks beginning at the six foot mark, set at one foot intervals on ten-inch branch lines.

We baited the hooks with red worms and threw the line into the canal. The line was staked into the soft mud of the bank and anchored in the ditch by an old rusted wrench. The hooks laid on the bottom and mostly enticed bottom feeders like catfish, turtles, or mocs.

Next, we set up our bank fishing poles, a couple of eight-foot flexible cane fishing poles that had been in my family ever since I could remember. We baited the hooks and set them at about two feet deep, beneath a red-topped plastic bobber. Like all pole fishermen on the Floodways, we shoved the butt end of the pole deep into the soft bank, allowing it to stand alone out over the water.

Once we had gathered plenty of kindling and scrap wood, we started a campfire and sat on an old log that had floated up on the bank during the last flood. Raymond rolled a smoke and I opened those chocolate chip cookies Mom made for us.

Every once in a while, Raymond's keen eye would detect the tension on one of the poles tightening up before the bobber began to dance. He moved quickly and quietly to the pole, placing his fingers lightly on the shaft, like we did when touching the train rails to determine whether or not the train was coming by the intensity of the vibrations. He could feel the moment the fish touched the bait and he waited for the right moment to jerk that pole out of the water. Normally, a silvery crappie, largemouth bass, or just an old perch was caught. But, whatever it was, it was coming out.

"Look at that," he'd say. "It's a bass, darn near ten inches in length, perfect for roasting." He'd cut and gut the fish, and have it on a stick roasting over the slow fire before you'd know it.

"How'd you ever get that fast?" I once asked.

"You gotta be fast to keep the mocs from gettin' it," he grinned. And he was right. A water moccasin would strip a hook fast if you weren't careful.

It was normal for bank fishermen, like we were that night, to have their stringer of fish attacked by mocs. The thought of it made me shiver.

With our campsite set up, we settled back and talked some more after the fire began to die down.

"I wonder if Elmer's home tonight." I asked.

"I don't know, probably," Raymond said.

"As long as he don't show up here, that's all I care."

* * *

Some say Elmer had done time in an Arkansas prison and even now was hiding out from Arkansas law. He lived on the west ditch-dump of Canal #251, called Swift Ditch, which had the widest, deepest, and fastest current of all the five canals. It was the only trestle of the five that had concrete pillars on each end holding up a big iron frame with eight foot high banisters a foot wide. This kind of structure allowed an unrestricted flow of water under the structure, preventing piles of logs and trash building up against the pilings like the other four canals do when the floods come.

Elmer was just another hard case drawn to our Floodways by his brother, John, who, at one time, was Dad's top tractor driver. Elmer stood tall and skinny, with rotting teeth, thinning hair, calloused hands, and a beard that wasn't quite a beard. He walked hunched over with an awkward lunging gait and, when hunting, carried an old goose gun. He had dark beady eyes that darted about in all directions like he was always watching for someone in particular. You could smell him before you could see him and he dressed in an old shabby Sunday suit and wore a felt hat that had lost its shape years before.

His cabin looked like a pile of logs with a makeshift wooden door made up of various lengths of lumber salvaged from high water drift wood. There were always skinned critters: possums, rabbits, squirrels, and such hanging from the logs that protruded from the structure. He said, when asked, that he was drying out the critters for supper. Those critters were his food supply, kept in a similar manner as the Native American tribes that inhabited the area centuries before, except the tribes were civilized.

If Elmer was home, those critters were hung out for all to see, meaning he was still in the area somewhere. Sometimes Elmer's brother, Harrison, was there. Many times we had heard Elmer cussing Harrison and pushing him around. We'd hear him yell at Harrison on many occasions. "Damn you, Harrison. You're dumb as a sack of rocks. I'm gonna hafta kill you some day."

Elmer was an especially mean drunk and Harrison was his kind, not-so-bright older brother that we all liked. Dad also liked Harrison, but had no use for Elmer and didn't trust him around. People were always saying things that don't make sense. Regardless of Elmer's ravings, no one really believed he would kill Harrison. The Floodways gave cover to many whose pasts were unknown and their futures uncertain.

Years later, Elmer was finally run off the Floodways when the railroad found that his shack was built too close to the rails. The real truth was that they didn't want him on the Floodways. He was, simply put, an embarrassment to anyone with eyes or a sense of smell.

I got up and grabbed a piece of an old limb and threw on the fire. When the limb hit the glowing coals, a cloud of sparks sprayed into the air, causing a glow strong enough to cast shadows to the far bank. As I stood between the fire and the water, my shadow lay against the high ground on the west side of the bank and made me think of the night I saw my brother on stage at Bragg City High School. Johnny sang with a group called The Key-Noters, and he was good. I remembered him singing "The Banana Boat" song made popular by Harry Belafonte. Momentarily inspired, I burst into song right there by the fire. It was terribly out of character for me since I was pretty shy and couldn't carry a tune in a bucket.

I could see my shadow and it seemed like a stage, right there on First Ditch. Raymond laughed and I began to laugh too. The fire died down in a few moments. My shadow and my inspiration also disappeared. We continued to catch fish, some a good size, and Raymond roasted each one of them. We ate till we almost burst.

A while later, as Raymond and I began to doze off, he suddenly woke up, like he'd slept all night. He said, "Ya know something?"

Startled, I said, "What?" Raymond must have sensed something wrong. He could do that.

"I kinda like Helen."

"Helen Robinson?"

"Yeah."

"She's nice."

"Yeah," he said, "she's nice."

I never saw them together except when we all worked in the fields. That's all he said about it. Sometimes Raymond didn't talk so much.

Sharp yelps intermingled with the rich mournful sounds of what sounded like big wolves and bobcats or panthers cut short our conversation. The hair on the back of my neck rose up and my heart raced. "What the heck is that?"

Raymond, his eyes fixed upon the darkness across the ditch from which the sounds erupted, eased toward his shotgun, breaking it down and checking to see if it was loaded. It was. The sounds stopped as suddenly as they began. An unnatural silence settled upon us.

"I've been coming here for years and I've heard all kinds of things," I said. "Even a wolf or two and weird noises but nothing like that."

Raymond, his eyes wide, cradled his shotgun. "This might not have been a good idea, coming over here tonight." When Raymond became unsure, I knew there was something to be worried about.

The howls and screeches began anew, closing in on our campsite til they seemed directly across the water from us on the west bank, in the reeds and willows, no more than thirty feet away.

I suddenly realized that I hadn't heard Buddy's bark and began to worry where he might be. He hadn't come with us on this outing because he had been somewhere with Dad when we left the house, or he sensed something we didn't sense. Yet, I expected him to show up because somehow he always knew where I was on the Floodways.

There followed another terrible string of yelps and howls, sounding like a woman screaming. They could chill you to the bone. Then we both saw the dark profile of a creature beginning to cross the trestle over First Ditch, from west to east. Our side of the ditch.

From our campsite, the full form of the creature looked to be big as a man but walked on all fours with its large head held low, close to the rails. Each step was deliberate, requiring a highly developed sense of depth perception to place each paw on a railroad tie, rather than through the gaps in-between.

"That must be Buddy," I said, refusing to consider any other possibility.

"You sure?" asked Raymond. "It looks too big to be Buddy."

"It must be Buddy, don't ya think?"

At any moment, the creature would be across the trestle, on our side of the ditch where there would be no barriers between us. The closer it came, the less sure I was that it was Buddy. Just then, a long, lonely wail pierced the air and another chill shot up my spine. Raymond quickly moved toward his fishing lines, pulling them in. There were no words between us, just action.

There were many tales about the Floodways; some folks believed there were haints: ghostlike manifestations, apparitions, mythical shape-shifters, panthers and wolves the size of a man inhabiting the deepest, darkest heart of the Floodways, holdovers from olden times when the great swamp ruled the land.

Even though I didn't believe such stories, I held my rifle close. Raymond had the Busbys' old turkey gun with a barrel as long as we were tall and rather than stay for the night, we decided it was time to head home.

Our breathless retreat from the campsite with only our firearms was nothing less than a rout. We tripped and stumbled over fishing poles and lines and ran through a briar patch, leaving the smoldering campfire to burn itself out. We ran into the high leafy cotton patch where we had been picking for the last week.

My heart pounded as we heard the sound of crashing and thrashing coming from the direction of the trestle, signaling the creature's imminent arrival. It was time to stand our ground.

As we turned to face the beast, our fears, strengths and weaknesses fed on each other. I shook so hard I darn near dropped my gun. Raymond seemed cool, even though I knew he was scared. He dropped to one knee, eyes wide open, and pulled back both hammers on that old 10-gauge as we awaited the onslaught. My legs had become heavy and rubbery. My hands, although shaking, gripped the rifle so hard I felt as though they might break. My mind flashed, thinking this must be the way it would feel if I were hypnotized, frozen, unable to move, my heartbeat pounding in my ears.

Then, before the creature could crash through the heavy cotton, I heard a familiar bark. "Hold it," I heard myself shout as if my voice were coming from an unseen presence. Buddy came bounding through the cotton. Our "wolf" ran to me, no doubt curious as to our odd behavior. His tongue hung out like he'd been running a great distance; his eyes were afire and cockle burrs were buried in his white mane.

Our relief turned to immediate exhaustion. Catching my breath, I hugged Buddy and said, "Where you been, boy? I really missed you." I rubbed his great head. He panted happily and looked around, licking Raymond's face, unaware of the panic he had caused. Or had he?

Raymond sat back on the ground, wrapped his thumb around one of the cocked hammers and cautiously squeezed the trigger, easing one hammer to rest on the firing pin, then repeating the procedure for the second barrel. Taking a deep breath while wiping his forehead with his sleeve, he said with a grin, "I knew it all along, it weren't no haint."

I began laughing, like everything was funny, and said, "Me too. I was just trying to act like I was scared." Yet, before I eased the bolt into the safe position, I took one more look around. Our rout had trampled down many big stalks of cotton. Dad'll be mad as all get out when he sees this, I thought.

We both had a good laugh as we looked around in the darkness for signs of something other than Buddy. Another distant howl convinced us that the night's expedition was over. As we made our way home, we planned to collect our gear the next day and not to tell anyone of our experience under threat of death, haints or no haints. Raymond headed to his house and I to mine. It was another adventure on the Floodways that would live in our memories forever.

I woke early the next morning, not really having slept all night since hightailing it home. The events were still vivid in my mind. The "wolf" had left an indelible image in my mind that I couldn't reconcile with Buddy's profile.

Mom, on her way to the kitchen, saw my clothes strewn on the floor and looked in on me, sensing I was awake. The floor squeaked as she walked softly into my room. Realizing she was there, I turned my head toward her.

"Good morning. What're you doing home? I thought you and Raymond would be out till at least mid-day."

Mom sat down on the edge of the bed. I scanned the room briefly and looked out of my big double window facing north. The day was going to be nice. A blue sky greeted me that morning.

Without lifting my head, I looked at Mom. "Morning...well, we thought it better to not stay all night after all."

"Oh, and why not?"

What could I say, that Raymond and I were scared off by a horrific howling wolf as big as a man that turned out to be Buddy? No! This experience was a bond between me and Raymond and I'd keep it that way.

"I thought I'd like to go with Dad to take the cotton to the gin this morning."

"Well then, you better rise and shine, cause your dad's about ready to go."

"Okay, I'm up."

"Oh yes, and put that rifle up in the closet and see to it that it's not loaded."

"Yes, ma'am."

6

Dad always pulled the cotton wagon to Bragg City with the Farmall or Ford tractor because we didn't have a truck. I always thought that odd, not having a truck. On this occasion, he was going to use the Ford tractor. I sat on the tractor, leaning against the fender of one of the large rear wheels, the sun shining and the wind blowing in my hair.

After the cotton was weighed, it was sucked out of the trailer through a large metal pipe, handled by Bobby Mullenix, a friend of mine from school. Dad was in the gin office where the deal was made and he was paid in cash by one of the gin managers, Sonnie Walker.

After returning home, at about noon, Dad placed the money in the safe and waited for the pickers to show up to get their money. At about 1:00 p.m., the Robinsons came by. Their car was full, except for Arlena and the baby, Bobby. They were headed to town, usually to Kennett, where they shopped at Hamras' department store.

Mr. Robinson was paid for his family's picking, from money Dad took from the farm safe, after re-verifying the pounds of cotton picked. Dad counted out the cash. Mr. Robinson, who most always wore overalls, folded the cash and shoved the money into the front pocket of his bib overalls. Mom visited with Mrs. Robinson and asked about the baby, Bobby, while Dad and Mr. Robinson discussed the next week's work schedule.

The Busbys didn't have to come to the house to get paid because Dad always took the money to them. He enjoyed talking with Bill before Bill had a chance to get some wine. On this particular occasion, I had gone with him.

As Dad knocked on the Busby's front door, he said, "Hey Bill, are you ready to get paid?" However, Dad always gave the money to Ruth and he always talked with Bill, who made Dad laugh.

"Come in, Fred," Bill said.

"Hey Bill," I said, following Dad into the Busby's front room.

Looking at Raymond, who was cleaning the old shotgun, Dad said, "Raymond, I hear you and Harold cut the night short. What happened?"

"Yes, sir, we did. We had caught enough fish early."

"Yeah, that's what I heard," Dad said, turning and looking at me. I almost froze because that wasn't what I told Dad.

Dad always had a sixth sense about me. He could always tell when I was saying something that might not have been quite right and he didn't really believe we left the Floodways early because we caught so much fish. I began to sweat about the way the conversation was headed and said, just to change the subject, "Hey, Raymond. Whatcha doing this afternoon?"

"Don't know."

"Then let's get back to the campsite and check the trotline. I also forgot some of my things I need to get."

"Where's Hokey?" Dad asked, breaking into my conversation.

"Ahhh," Bill said, "he's over there at the Robinsons. He's over quite a bit." Chuckling, he said, "I think he's sweet on one of those girls."

"What about Fats?" Dad asked.

"He's back at Clarkton with his folks, but we'll be seeing him at some point this weekend."

"He looks like he could lift a mule. Do you think he'd like to pick some cotton?"

"I don't know, I'll ask him. He's a good man, and he'd do a good job for you, I know that. He's like a member of the family to us and he's Hokey's best friend."

"Be sure and talk to Fats for me."

"Will do."

"See y'all later."

"Gotta go now, come on Harold."

"See ya later Raymond."

Later that afternoon, when Raymond, Buddy, and I went back to the campsite, the fishing poles were pulled out of the mud and thrown into the reeds alongside the ditch. The food sacks were all torn open and tracks were everywhere. Big tracks. As we came closer, Buddy stopped, stuck his nose in the air, and began to whine. He wouldn't go a step farther.

"Those ain't Buddy's tracks," Raymond said, kneeling down and looking real close at the imprints. There was more than one set of tracks. Some appeared to be roughly shaped like a wolf's paw, but much larger. Some were much larger than the wolf prints and less clear, elongated.

"What do you think it was?" I asked Raymond.

Raymond again closely examined the strange tracks. Then, looking at me, shook his head like it hurt. "I think," he said. "We shouldn't tell anyone what we've seen here. I think these tracks are real big wolf prints and those," pointing to the larger prints, "are elephant tracks."

"What? Elephants? Do you think we should hunt that thing down?" I asked, hoping his answer would be no.

"What I think is that we need to stay out of here for a while and not tell anyone what we've seen. Folks'll think we're crazy."

"Good idea."

We never did tell anyone about those big tracks.

* * *

We had a bumper crop the year of 1956. We got a bale of cotton, five hundred pounds of cotton fiber, to the acre, and forty plus bushels of soybeans an acre, with plenty of golden ears of corn, filling the crib in the barn to the ceiling. Everyone was doing well.

New pickups were appearing on the blacktop roads, but none came back as far as we lived. They didn't want to get their new trucks muddy. Everyone seemed genuinely happy, which is hardly the normal state of affairs in cotton country.

The Robinsons were happy with their share of the crop and Bill Busby could always be counted on for a wine-enhanced songfest at the plank bridge. Bill's songs and insights into life through his Homeric tales were the highlight of every Saturday night, and Fats, who everybody liked, had become a part of the farm family.

That fall after cotton picking vacation, Alma Faye, Helen, Raymond, and I all returned to school. Alma Faye was in the seventh grade, Raymond and I were in the sixth grade, and Helen was in the fifth. Johnny was in his senior year of high school. He had his driver's license and was head over heels in love with his girlfriend, Helen, from Wardell. He was growing away from the Floodways and me.

Christmas holidays were soon upon us. It was a good Christmas and I got what I wanted, a carton of .22 long rifle bullets from Western Auto.

1957 arrived under a sheet of ice from '56. Ice storms with some snow were our winters. The old hand pump became our source of water as the supposedly well-insulated modern plumbing froze up. The Rural Electric Authority (R.E.A.) trucks were a welcome sight as the heavy ice downed electrical lines all over the Bootheel.

The storms brought on conditions that required greater awareness and care of the livestock. Alfalfa hay filled the mangers, and ears of corn harvested from the bumper crop of '56 were thrown into the barnyard.

On the Floodways, ice coated every twig, plant, and trestle, bringing out the full majesty of that realm. With a half inch of clear ice or more covering every surface, crossing the trestles became a death-defying ordeal.

During that winter, Johnny played on Bragg City High School's championship basketball team. Everyone believed they were once again on their way to state finals for super-small schools held at the University of Missouri, Columbia like in 1956. And this time, they'd bring home the prize. Sometimes, because of his activities, I got to read the Floodway gauges in his place. During that winter, I got to know most every person living on the Floodways by their first name.

Occasionally, I'd take off with Buddy, not to read the gauges or hunt, but to be on the Floodways with no other person in sight. The sweet smell of wood smoke wafting from unseen chimneys provided the only signs of life. I learned to cautiously place my feet squarely on each icy railroad tie, making sure my foot wouldn't slip, before placing my full weight on it. When in the middle of the trestle over Canal 251/ Swift Ditch, I'd stop to just look and listen. It was a mighty canal that looked like a river. The snapping, popping, and crashing of tree limbs under the weight of the ice was an awe-inspiring symphony, magnified by the natural echoing effect created by high ditch-dumps on each side of the canal. On many of those occasions, I was the sole human observer of that crystal cathedral.

Buddy, who by this time probably wished he hadn't followed me, began whining and looked at me as though I had lost my mind. "Come on, boy, let's go home," I'd say as I turned to head back. Occasionally, I'd hear the lonely howl of an alpha wolf, but I had lost my fear of the unseen inhabitants of the Floodways. The howls and yelps now reassured me that they were still present, still watching. I enjoyed the solitude and wished it could remain that way forever.

* * *

Following the ice-encased winter, I continued taking daily walks over the trestles after school. I made mental notes on what I saw and became familiar with the railroad workers who performed routine maintenance. The brakemen in the red caboose of the Cotton Belt recognized me when I waved at them, and they waved back, just like they did my brother. I was comfortable in that world, much more than in school. I didn't see any real value in going to school and my grades reflected my ambivalence.

Not long after the winter eased, the spring rains of 1957 began. Walking the railroad during violent storms was exciting, what with thunder cracking and the wind howling. I even got to where I could say, "Hey," to Elmer without having my finger on the trigger of my rifle, and holler at old Hombre who still lived on Old Floodway, and get a polite wave in response. No, the Floodways hadn't changed, but the weather had. This year was gonna be hell.

7

During the latter part of '56, Dad had rented an additional forty acres about a mile from our farm and purchased forty acres near Reaves, Missouri. Those deals enlarged the acreage Dad farmed to 210, raising the stakes of his gamble. The spring rains continued erratically throughout the planting season.

There were late night kitchen-table talks between Mom and Dad about what to do, plant again or gamble on a different crop, maybe Milo[ii], a new crop, or a very old crop, depending on one's perspective. It was touted as a last chance for a money crop of any kind, but Dad didn't take the gamble. He chose to stay with what crop he had. I lay awake several nights, as rain pounded against my window, wondering what we were going to do.

Three to five inches of rain in a two-day period could bring the water out on us. The fields filled with water that drained into the field ditches that drained into the roadside ditches that drained into the lateral feeder ditches that filled the canals. When the canals were full, the water in the feeder ditches backed up into the fields until the canals could accept the additional runoff.

When Johnny came back from reading the gauges, he said, "Dad, I haven't seen the Floodways ever rise quite as fast as they seem to be doing now. There musta been some big rains up north and the water is starting to stack up on us."

For the second time in memory, the water was again above the gauges and within six feet of the rails on those 60-foot-high trestles. The water was running a reddish brown, meaning the red earth of the Ozarks was coming down with trees and every kind of debris imaginable. Small buildings floated down the Floodways, coming apart and hanging up against the trestles, placing unimaginable stress on them and stopping the Cotton Belt train from crossing.

Dad said, "The last time this kind of flooding occurred, the water flooded the fields to such a depth that cattle and chickens drowned and folks were run out of their houses. Let's pray that doesn't happen again."

That year was 1945, the year I was born. Dad had always kidded that I was found in a hollow log floating down the canals during the floods that year, like Moses. And, in remembrance of that year of floods, he often called me "Top Water."

The floods of '57 routinely floated the 500 gallon propane tank in our yard. On many occasions, the water was within a couple of inches of getting into our house. During the days of the flood, Dad parked our car on high ground near the blacktop road by the Strothers' farm and took a tractor, or walked the Cotton Belt to and from the house, wading with hip boots from the railroad to the house.

The floods also meant a reshuffling of houses by the Busbys and the Robinsons. The Busbys had to move from their house by the plank bridge where they had been living since late 1944, where Raymond and Li'l Joe were born and where Hokey killed Ol' Tom in late 1955. The house they moved to was the unpainted house, south of our house near the railroad crossing where the school bus turned around.

The Robinson's moved from the big red house to the old Laden house that sat on higher ground. The Busbys and the Robinsons were now three-quarters of a mile from each other. The wet weather made the ditch-dump road alongside Feeder Ditch 68 impassable except on foot. These moves left the three tenant houses, situated near the plank bridge, empty.

Another aspect of the bad year was a huge economic downturn in the Bootheel that affected businessmen just as much as it did the farmers. Hokey, whose job at Gideon-Anderson was an on-call position, hadn't been called except for a few times since October of 1956. Fats didn't have a job, except what was available in the fields around Clarkton and on our farm. It boiled down to scraping up what cotton there was by pulling bolls. Fats began to spend more and more time on our farm, living with the Busbys.

At mid-year, Bill asked Dad if Hokey and Fats could batch in Big Red, just to get Hokey and Fats out of his house. Dad agreed.

So the deal was cut. Even though Hokey couldn't drive his car over the ditch-dump road, he and Fats didn't mind walking in the mud and began living in Big Red. It was as close to the Robinsons' house as they could get.

8

Despite this being a bad crop year, it became a catalyst for evolutionary change, from manual labor to mechanization and chemicals. The change was taking place, making its debut in the Bootheel as farmers sought to reduce their dependence on hand labor costs. New terms were being introduced into the farming lexicon such as "pre-emergent chemicals," "flame-cultivators," and, "mechanical cotton-pickers."

It was a strange thing, but I saw my first mechanical cotton picker in a year when there was very little cotton to be picked. It was a marvel, an ugly marvel but no less a marvel. A bright red M model International Farmall tractor had been reconfigured to run backwards. It was fitted with a large basket capable of holding a half-bale of cotton, sitting above the engine. The driver sat directly above the part of the contraption that held the mechanical fingers called spindles. Those spindles rotated and spun, pulling the cotton off the stalks but also stringing the white fibrous lint all over the place, making a mess.

The loss of cotton fiber caused by the spindles was an appalling sight to farmers, causing most to dismiss the mechanical picker as nothing more than an oddity, a joke. A good hand cotton picker left a neat row: no missed bolls of cotton, no random pieces of cotton left in the boll, known as gooselocks, no debris, and no disturbance of the green cotton bolls yet to open.

The new machine ignored these niceties, and when turning at the end of the quarter-mile rows, it destroyed about ten to fifteen feet of cotton, crushing the stalks until it could be properly lined up on the next row. Although unrefined, awkward, noisy, and susceptible to breakdowns, the mere appearance of these mechanical manifestations signaled the beginning of the end of hand labor.

The farmhands took a unique pride in what they did. A good cotton picker had status in this small community. The mechanical picker would not only take their primary means of making a living from them, it would reduce them to serving the machine by picking off the ends of the cotton rows, making it easier for the beast to do its job and robbing them of money and dignity. There were reports of barbed wire or baling wire being strung in the cotton rows to wrap around the spindles and disable the machine, resulting in costly damages.

Some have said that this dramatic change in the economy with the bad year and the coming industrialization of the cotton patch may have contributed to the demons dancing in Hokey's head. Hokey seemed to have days, like me, when he just wanted to be on the Floodways, to look at them with no other objective in mind.

On many of those lazy days in the fall of '57, when the sun seemed to stand still and water was at a normal stage, I would head out for the Floodways, once again, going fishing with Raymond. On one occasion Raymond and I, along with Buddy, settled in at a prime fishing spot about midway of Bay Ditch trestle, sitting on steel rails still warm from the day's sun and the recent passing of the Cotton Belt freight train. Once Buddy was sure I was settled, he trotted off the trestle into the deep woods and underbrush, chasing rabbits and squirrels, while occasionally checking in on me.

Our hooks were in the water at just the right depth, determined by where we set the bright red bobber. The bait can full of wiggly red worms, contemplating their dire circumstance, was set within easy reach. I sat back, taking in the scene, hoping I would always remember it that way.

Raymond, as was his usual practice, rolled himself a cigarette to replace the one in his mouth. He took a cigarette paper from his pocket and added smooth-cut smoking tobacco from the ever-present tin of Prince Albert tobacco he kept in his shirt pocket. He licked the edges of the paper, then sealed and smoothed the cigarette between his thumb and forefinger. Pulling the Zippo lighter out of his pocket, he opened the lid with the upward flick of his thumb, making that unique metallic *click*, then flicked the small wheel with a downward plunge of his thumb, producing an orangish yellow spark and a small flame on the wick. Cupping the Zippo and the cigarette with both hands, he pulled a couple of drags, producing a small cloud of the sweet-smelling smoke that encircled his head.

He then took a couple more deep drags, filling his lungs, and tilted his head back a little, allowing the aroma to slowly boil from his nose and mouth, looking as content as anyone I ever saw. I always thought I'd like to smoke like everyone else, but was stopped by nagging allergy-induced asthma. Even more importantly, Mom strictly prohibited me and my brother from having anything to do with tobacco in any form.

Sitting on that trestle, we settled into a trance-like state common to pole fishermen. In this condition, we studied everything about the water, instinctively watching for the tiniest of ripples moving in concentric circles away from the bobber. Bass, brim, catfish, carp, or crappie could be nibbling on the ill-fated red worm twisting and turning on the hook, enticing the possible catch. When the bait was taken, the bobber plunged underwater, as the quarry ran with its prize. Raymond's reflexive flick of his wrist, like slapping a mosquito, set the hook. Then the catch was reeled in and kept for supper or thrown back if it was too small.

The fish that day were not yet biting, and Raymond and I began talking about the day's events in the field. We laughed while recalling Raymond's playing a trick on his mom. He pulled up on her cotton sack while it was being weighed, making it look like there was much less cotton in the sack than the eye would suggest. She caught on real quick and chased him around the cotton trailer with a cotton stalk, cut for such an occasion. She stopped after a little bit and, out of breath, began laughing at which time we all started laughing.

After work, the Floodways, as usual, were the main attraction. They were beautiful, even that year, as the monsoon-like rains of the spring had fueled a lush landscape. Various shades of greenery were woven together, both inviting and foreboding and interspersed with random splashes of color created by songbirds emitting exotic sounds.

The prime time for fishing was always between dusk and evening, a time when great-winged dragonflies hovered low over the slow-moving streams, feasting on droves of mosquitos and water bugs. Their luminescent wings revealed prisms of color not seen in our everyday existence.

Soft and hard-shell turtles lounged on waterlogged tree limbs that slowly bobbed up and down in sync with nature and the slow moving current. Full-throated bullfrogs bellowed as the high pitched scream of cicadas echoed against the Floodway trestles.

The cooler temperatures in the early evening also brought out the meanest mosquitos that flexed their wings in squadron strength. Their thirst for blood brought them upon us in the form of shifting shadows. I always seemed to be the sole target of their attention. I winced at their bites and randomly slapped at them as they buzzed my ears. My efforts amused Raymond. He looked at me, grinned and took a long drag off his roll-your-own, exhaling the smoke into a billowing cloud surrounding his head. "It keeps the skeeters away, don't ya know," he'd say with a smile and chuckle. At that moment, the smoke smelled so good, and with the added benefit that it'd keep the pesky bloodsuckers away, I began to have second thoughts about not smoking and thought of how I might approach Mom about my becoming a smoker.

After a bit, with the shadows getting longer, Hokey happened along and sat down at the east end of the trestle. I didn't mind his presence, and he didn't seem interested in fishing. He sat back and stared into the languid waters for minutes at a time, spontaneously beginning a conversation or joining in on some topic without regard to the topic or person who may have been talking at that moment.

Normally the conversation was about the Floodways and the people who lived in this outback culture. Juggling a couple of rocks in his hand, he occasionally tossed one into the water without any apparent awareness or regard for the fact that we were trying to lure the fish to our lines. The ripples caused by the rocks he tossed moved across the surface, ending at the water's edge.

Hokey carried his favorite weapon, a sixteen-inch sawed-off, bolt-action, single-shot .22-caliber rifle, with a crudely fashioned pistol grip wrapped in black electrical tape. It was tucked inside a makeshift leather holster tied to his right leg. Hokey always carried a gun, which was not unusual by Floodway standards, if for no other reason than to protect oneself from snakes—maybe humans, too.

I had seen the short rifle on many occasions and witnessed Hokey's normal firing stance. He pointed his left boot directly toward the target with his right foot back a bit, and the toe of his boot at about a thirty-degree angle to the right, to lend support and stability. The weapon was normally fired from his waist with both hands, his right hand holding the pistol grip with his forefinger on the trigger and his left hand cradling the forearm of the sawed-off. Hokey, like everyone else, routinely fired at tin cans, turtles, and snakes. He was not the best shot.

I thought he went to an awful lot of trouble making that gun when, in my opinion, a shotgun would have been much more effective and easier to hold. Still, I wouldn't say any such thing to him, not when he was so proud of that thing. I wondered why Hokey was here instead of at one of his usual haunts.

Some of those places were tough joints like the B&B Club, known locally as the Bloody Bucket, a little south of Gobbler, where a big country store was located. It was a favorite watering hole of airmen out of the Blytheville Air Force Base. Two upstarts, Elvis Presley from Memphis, and Narvel Felts from Bernie, Missouri, played to packed crowds there. Hokey's other favorite haunts included the Chez Parée Club in Malden, near the Air Force Training Base; the El Morocco in Gideon that catered to Gideon-Anderson lumberyard employees; the 25 Club, north of Kennett, where heads were busted on a nightly basis; and the Midway Inn on 25 Highway at Holcomb, with an occasional excursion to the far off Club Zanza just outside the eastern boundary of Hayti on 84 highway.

Hokey lit up an unfiltered Camel, his favorite, and leaned back on his elbows, just looking.

After a bit, he said, "Ya'll see Elmer lately?"

"Not lately," I said, being closest to Hokey.

Hokey responded with a grimace. "Well, he must be around someplace, just look at that pile of logs where he lives with all those rats hanging on it. Who eats that shit anyway?" Continuing in a near whisper as if talking to himself, he added, "I haven't seen him in a while and thought I might join him in some coon hunting."

I never much cared for coon hunting, which was done at night with flashlights and dogs. A gang of hunters with rifles, shotguns, and whiskey would wade through the underbrush like skirmishers in front of General Lee's army. They always had a variety of mongrel hunting dogs they called bloodhounds with not one blooded dog among them.

They'd loose them ol' dogs and they'd begin yelping and carrying on until they treed a coon. Then they'd shine their lanterns up into the tree. The desperate critter's eyes reflected the light, revealing its position. Then, they'd all cut loose with their cannons. It was hardly a fair fight.

"Well," I said to Hokey, "I wouldn't know where he is." Turning my head toward Raymond, I added, "How about you, Raymond?"

"Nope, and I don't care to see him," said Raymond.

"Why? What's wrong with Elmer?" asked Hokey.

"He's just a mean ol' son-of-a-bitch, that's all."

"You just don't know him well enough. He's okay."

"Nope," Raymond responded, "he's not."

At that very moment, with my attention diverted to Hokey, something grabbed my line and nearly pulled the rod and reel out of my hands and me along with it. Everyone's attention focused on me. Raymond quickly jumped up, moving farther away from me to make sure our lines wouldn't be entangled, yelling, "Bring it in!" Hokey straightened and, with a slight grin, looked on in amusement.

Nervous and a little scared, I held onto my rod and reel with both hands as the reel screamed. There had not been any indication that anything was interested in the bait on my hook. No nibbling, no nothing. Then, all of a sudden, the red-topped bobber plunged underwater several feet before I could react. When the line loosened, I began reeling it in as fast as I could, but the line went taut again. It seemed like I had hooked a big turtle, or maybe a huge catfish that had first run, then doubled back on me. However, the strength and speed of the hooked creature ruled out a turtle as the thirty-pound test line seemed ready to snap.

After a few moments, the line went limp again. I thought I had lost the catch. All of a sudden the undulating body of a serpent-like creature shot five feet or so straight up through the surface of the water. It looked like it was coming straight for me. At the height of its flight, it crashed back into the depths, twisting and flopping in a frenzied attempt to free itself from the hook. A primal fear gripped me. I could only think of one thing, that I had hooked a powerful, large moc, that terrible, deadly water snake that plied southern waters. Hokey, sensing my fear, began casually walking toward me across the trestle. Raymond, seeing my terror, belly-laughed at my predicament.

The creature would probably have weighed no more than twelve to fifteen pounds but it seemed much larger. It wasn't a moc. It was a gar, an alligator gar, a much-feared mega-fish with a crocodile-like head and rows of razor-sharp teeth. They lived and flourished in slow-moving southern waterways like our floodways and seemed to be taking over from the regular fish. All my bad dreams had a gar in them. No one ever eats a gar, except maybe Elmer. They're usually used as target practice from the safety of the high trestles and killed, by bludgeoning, when caught on a fishing line. I wished my line had broken.

I continued reeling the beast up out of the water as it flopped around. After a long struggle, I finally hauled it up onto the trestle. Buddy heard the commotion and came running out of the underbrush, as he had done since he was old enough to run faster than me. His feet were moving fast, landing precisely on each railroad tie like a great pianist, never missing a note. As we were some sixty feet above the water, a miss could have been his last. Seeing the gar flopping around, Buddy stopped cold and began barking, inching forward toward the gar, only to jump backwards when the snapping mouth turned toward him, causing him, for the first time I ever saw, to miss a tie with one foot.

I couldn't take my eyes off the revolting creature. Yet, unexpectedly, I felt the utmost respect for the way it fought for its life against all odds, against creatures it must have seen just as hideous. There was total pandemonium, what with me cringing and prancing about to stay away from the gar while keeping my feet on the ties in order not to fall, with Buddy barking and Raymond laughing. One person came straight ahead with no obvious fear or hesitation—Hokey.

He grabbed the fishing line about two feet from the mouth of the beast, pulled a big knife from his belt and, in one smooth motion, cut the line. Wrapping the line around his palm to secure it, he turned and walked back to the end of the trestle, dragging the beast to solid ground. The beast's elongated tail drug all the way with blood tracing their route. My relief was quickly replaced with a dread of what was going to happen next.

Hokey laid the beast down on the ground beside the railroad tracks and stepped back a couple of feet. He appeared to think for a moment, then pulled his firearm from its holster, cocked it, and studied the distance. He stepped forward to the gar whose eyes seemed fixed on him. Placing the barrel of the gun within an inch or so from the beast's head, he couldn't miss. *Crack!* A bullet entered the head of the gar near its left eye with blood-splatter reaching Hokey's boot.

As he turned to walk away from the gar, it feebly tried to swim away from this assault. Hokey reloaded, turned, *Crack!* Another bullet ripped into the head of the monster. More blood splattered, this time onto Hokey's Levis. The dying gar, bloodied from all it had endured, finally lay still. Hokey holstered his gun and approached the beast, tentatively nudging it with the toe of his boot. It jerked, a death spasm. Hokey recoiled.

"Goddammit, you son-of-a-bitch!" he shouted, showing a rage that came from nowhere. His perpetual good-natured smile evaporated, replaced by an unexpected anger. Raymond turned his head away like he'd seen things like this before. I stood transfixed.

Hokey withdrew that Bowie-like knife again from his belt, and dragged the gar back over to the railroad tracks, placing its head onto one of the steel rails. He placed his left boot on the body of the gar, some two or three inches behind the monster's gills. Then, with the precision of a surgeon, placed the razor sharp blade of that knife directly against the leathery hide next to his boot and, in one swift motion, drew the blade across the gar, cleanly slicing off the beast's head.

"Take that, you bastard," he said. "You're dead now, ain't ya? Ha!"

Grinning, Hokey looked at us. He grabbed hold of the fishing line that still protruded from the beast's mouth and carried the beast's head, like a trophy, back to the center of the trestle, where he tossed it into the ditch. Raymond and I remained silent. The headless body of the gar remained on the railroad tracks where the killing had taken place, to rot in the sun.

"Thanks," I said. "That thang sure scared the heck out of me."

"It ain't gonna scare nobody no more, is it?" Hokey grinned. Then, as an afterthought, he paused and said, "Guess it'll make a good supper for the turtles and mocs, and the rest of it can rot right up here on the tracks. Maybe Elmer'll eat it."

It was getting dark. I'd had enough for this day and was getting sick to my stomach. Gathering my fishing gear, I yelled for Buddy and gave what remained of my red worms to Raymond. I bid goodbye to Raymond and Hokey as Buddy and I headed home, giving a wide berth to the body of the gar already gathering flies in the heat and humidity.

We walked the railroad back to where waist-high weeds marked the narrow path leading to my house. Buddy, ever my protector, went first in the tall weeds, watching for any transient moccasin that might be lying in wait.

9

Hokey's emerging reputation was based on much more than having killed a cat or an alligator gar. The growing and picking season of 1957 was poor, and both Hokey and Fats were living close to the edge. Dad had let them live in the house called Big Red, and they worked the fields with the others, picking what cotton was available. In the winter they pulled bolls. The traveling carnivals were not as prolific as in past years and the overflow of migrants was a thing of the past.

Each town still had a constable and a few part-time deputies whose duties were not unlike those legendary lawmen of Abilene and Dodge City when the large herds and Texas cowboys hit town. The small town city jails in the Bootheel took many forms. Typically, a primitive concrete-block building with barred doors and windows and an outside privy greeted the drunk and disorderly before the local municipal judge slammed his gavel.

Tent revivals were more prevalent. This was a time to pray for redemption and better days, the constant prayers of the farmer. Traveling preachers were in full swing, serving up hellfire and brimstone inside old army tents, giving the more God- fearing folks someplace to go.

When Hokey got tight (drinking),and Fats was with him, he drove his car at high speeds through these towns, mostly just crossroads, like Bragg City, Pascola, Braggadocia, Peach Orchard, and Wardell. His barnstorming and hurrahing of the town, like cowboys of yesteryear, routinely resulted in a chase from one town to the other or from one county to the other. These chases invariably led to the law looking for Hokey.

When I worked in the fields, chopping cotton with the Busbys during the summer of 1957, Bill Busby once spoke of a chilling incident that occurred during the previous year, when Hokey was working at the lumber yard in Gideon. He said that one day Hokey came home after having waded and swam the Floodways, crossing all five canals without setting foot on the railroad trestles.

Bill laughed nervously before telling this tale, not like it was funny, but like it was something he couldn't shake out of his mind and it just seeped out without anyone asking. He began by saying, "Hokey came into the house about midnight, looking like hell, and smelt like it too."

Hearing Bill, I stopped in the middle of chopping down an old red vine that had wrapped itself around what little cotton there was. Bill leaned on his hoe like it was a long walking stick, and wiped his brow with an old neckerchief. Ruth also stopped work and looked at Bill with a questioning look on her face.

"He was wet from head to toe," said Bill, "all scratched up, and had a pretty bad cut on his arm. He looked like he had rolled around in a briar patch or got caught in some barbed wire during a rainstorm, but that weren't what happened."

"You shouldn't be bringing that up." said Ruth. Bill ignored her, something that I hadn't seen before.

Bill said, "I couldn't imagine what might have happened. He was hungry, real hungry, and Ruth rustled up some biscuits and gravy. I asked him what had happened and where he'd been for the past week."

Raymond stood nearby, stone-faced. Bill continued. "He said, 'Hell, Dad, I been in jail! Where'd you think I was. I got the hell outa jail too, Goddamned cops! That'll teach 'em to leave the door open. I'll tell you something, they come after me? I'll not be taken alive! I got throwed in jail at Gideon for being a little tight and they said I was disturbing the peace. Hell, other guys do that shit and nothing happens to 'em. Then, I have a beer, just one beer mind you, and they toss me in jail like I was just another drunk cotton picker from Arkansas. God damn them!"

Bill stopped speaking and, after a few strokes at some weeds with his hoe, he stopped again. He pulled a blue handkerchief from his back pocket and wiped his forehead. In a weakened voice he said, "I just don't know what to expect next."

I looked at Raymond and said, "Wow, where's Hokey today?"

"Anywhere he wants to be," Raymond snapped.

Later that fall, I was present when Fats told the story of the time when a state trooper, named Jeff Hickman, came to the big red house where he and Hokey were baching[iii].

Fats said that as the trooper's car started toward the house on the field road, Hokey began cussing and pacing back and forth. He headed to the back door, but stopped, realizing that he could be seen by the trooper if he attempted to run across the field. So Hokey stayed in the house. He said over and over, "They'll never take me alive. They'll never take me alive." Hokey picked up Fats' 16-gauge single-shot shotgun, loaded it, pulled the hammer back, and stepped behind the front door. Hokey told Fats, "If he comes in, I'm gonna kill him."

Fats, telling the story, stopped talking and looked around at who was listening. It was me and Raymond and a couple of the Robinsons nearby. Fats took a deep breath and said with a nervous chuckle, "When that trooper knocked on the door, I darn near fainted."

Fats didn't know what was going to happen. When Fats opened the door, Hokey was directly behind it, with that shotgun ready to fire. Fats said he didn't want to, but he had to open the door. He couldn't believe the trooper didn't know Hokey was in there so Fats tried to act normal.

"I put a big smile on my face," he said, "and I opened that door."

Fats thought his heart was going to jump out of his chest and that the trooper must have been able to hear his heart beating hard and fast. Trooper Hickman said, looking at Fats, "You Donald Busby?"

"No sir, I'm Harry Shell."

"You got any identification?"

"I ain't got no driver's license or nothing if that's what you mean."

"Where's Donald?"

"Why, I don't know."

"You do know Donald, don't you?"

"Yes sir, I do. He lives here too, sometimes."

"Okay, where is he now?"

Fats was getting scared. He just knew that, at any time, Hokey'd let go that shotgun right through the door and kill him and the trooper.

The trooper stepped back from the door, looked around the yard and said, "When you see Donald, tell him Trooper Hickman outta Caruthersville is looking for him. He's been doing some real fancy driving around here lately and I need to talk to him."

Fats said he was so relieved that the trooper didn't force his way in that he got weak in the knees and had to steady himself against the doorjamb.

Fats' strong voice trailed off to a whisper. His face paled, he coughed, and turned his head away, then straightened to his full height. With a forced chuckle and a slight stammer, he said, "I was scared to death knowing that Hokey had that shotgun behind the door. I'm sure glad that trooper left the porch and didn't ask to come in the house, 'cause Hokey would've sure enough killed him right then and there."

10

My brother Johnny and Hokey were friends, but not as close as Raymond and I. When Johnny was home from college in late fall of '57, Hokey asked him if he would sell his black motorcycle jacket, which Johnny did. He sold that jacket to Hokey for five dollars.

I had become the new gauge reader when Johnny headed off to college that summer at Cape Girardeau. The pay was raised to ten dollars a month and, with my new job, I began spending even more time on the Floodways. Buddy remained my closest friend outside of Raymond and, anytime I wasn't on the Floodways, I was with my horse, Rebel.

On Halloween night that year, at age 10, I went to Bragg City to trick or treat with some of my school friends. The drizzly night chilled my skin, yet the idea of trick-or-treating at a store appealed to me. What better place was there to get candy? Danny, Bobby, Don, and I hit every store, getting candy and sodas.

It seemed like every kid in school trick-or-treated in Bragg City that night. About 9:00 p.m., a forty-something black Ford came flying through town east to west over State Highway K, the main street. Kids scattered and adults cussed as the car blew by.

Two men could be seen hunkering down in the car, their eyes peering over the dash. The clientele at Red's 5%, a pool hall and beer joint, the brown bag drinkers inside the stockade at Snake's package store, and those eating hamburgers in Edith's café, emptied into the street.

After a while, when everyone felt it was safe to be back in the street, the headlights of the black car came fast from the east. Its heavy engine roared. "Here it comes again!" someone yelled, as the lights bore down on the town. The car thundered past the old livery barn at the east edge of town as parents grabbed their kids and men picked up bottles and bricks.

Someone standing near the deserted hotel threw a bottle that missed its mark and crashed into the sidewalk near Curtis' general store, sending shards of glass across the legs of some trick-or-treaters. This act of defiance bore fruit. Another bottle flew through the air, tossed by a man named Dixie. It crashed into the right front fender of the car as hoots, hollers, and curses filled the air.

Finally, from somewhere in the darkness, *Boom,* a load of buckshot was introduced into the fray. The car accelerated, its taillights dimming in the distance as a couple of local toughs clambered into their cars and gave chase. They all disappeared into the dark Halloween night.

Later, the chase cars, defeated, returned. Their drivers said the black car seemed to disappear some four miles north of town on State Highway A. Many said they'd recognize the car should they see it again and swore that should they find it, revenge would be exacted. Some, well-supplied with bricks and bottles, took up positions in windows and alleyways. Waiting.

11

Saturday, December 7, 1957. The sixteenth anniversary of the Japanese attack on Pearl Harbor. It was our family tradition for Mom to retell the story of Dad's nephew Harold, my namesake, who served aboard one of the battleships attacked at Pearl Harbor and lived to tell about it. He was our hero and my brother and I never tired hearing of his courage under fire.

That evening, if the signal captured by the TV antenna mounted on the roof of our house was strong enough, and if there were no electrical storms between us and Memphis, some one hundred miles south, we might be able to see the full episode of *Gunsmoke* without interruption. We were in luck this evening. The light drizzle and chill in the air didn't seem to disturb the signal. It was almost perfect. It's safe to say that a large portion of television owners all over America were settling in to watch the next weekly episode of this much-beloved western drama.

The show had just begun. Two combatants approached each other in the middle of the street, an Old West dueling ground. The intensity of the moment was magnified by each camera angle and the heart-pounding score of the orchestra. Each week, my family anticipated this opening scene and my dad and I commented on it with little variation from week to week.

On this Saturday night, we could momentarily forget the desperation caused by this year's failed crop as the smell of freshly popped popcorn filled the room.

Mom made the popcorn by covering the bottom of a cooking pot with cooking oil and garden-grown sweet corn kernels, then placing it upon the blue propane flame. As the treat began to pop and spew forth that sweet aroma, Mom pushed, pulled, and shook the pot to ensure every kernel was popped just right. Once the corn popped into delicious mouthwatering kernels, she scooped the delicacy into individual serving bowls. Now it was time to pour the Safeway Cragmont Cola over ice cubes. The soda fizzed and the ice crackled, heralding the beginning of the evening's main event. It just couldn't be better: fresh popped popcorn, Cragmont, and *Gunsmoke*.

Mom, Dad and I settled in. Even Dad seemed to relax. We never tired of watching Matt Dillon, Chester, Miss Kitty, and Doc confront another frontier bad man. Johnny was home from college for the weekend but had the family car and was out with his girlfriend that evening.

Mom sat with us rather than going about her business of preparing to attend services the following morning at the First Southern Baptist Church in Wardell. Tomorrow, we would again pray the prayers of farmers for better weather and the strength to endure, a recurring theme in farming even though the growing season of 1957 had come to a dismal end.

However, no matter what amount of preparation Mom might have gone through, on Sunday morning, without fail, she would complain that she had nothing to wear as Dad nervously fidgeted with his car keys while reviewing the week's Bible lesson. Dad's job as Sunday School Superintendent and Deacon consumed him as Mom fluttered about.

It seemed to me that all the church going and praying hadn't amounted to much this year. I figured God had pretty much forgotten about us. Many family farmers would be unable to repay their bank loans. Those overdue and unpaid loans by many small family farmers caused farm sales and bank repossessions to soar, threatening this simple way of life. Dad was one of a few small farmers who were able to avert terminal financial trouble with the banks or Production Credit Association. By always being frugal and not risking the deed to the farm by signing it over as collateral, we made it through. However, this year broke Dad's spirit. I saw it and it broke my heart.

Dad, who had farmed most all of his life and lived to the age of eighty-two, once confided to my brother, "I have been near broke on many occasions but I never recovered from 1957."

For now, during this special 30-minute block of time, all of this could be forgotten. It was time to become lost in this beloved weekly television event.

A rapid knocking at the door shattered the moment. A muffled voice shouted, "Mr. Walker...Mr. Walker!"

It wasn't unusual for people to come to see Dad at odd hours, their arrival normally heralded by Buddy's barking and carrying on. But, on this occasion, Buddy wasn't barking. Apparently he sensed no danger from this visitor, or perhaps the nasty weather kept him holed up in his custom-made doghouse. "Mr. Walker... Mr. Walker!"

The knocking at the door could have been any one of the folks we knew and trusted. However, there was always an outside chance the visitor was an outlaw, desperate and dangerous. This was not an area where you could carelessly leave your doors unlocked and your defenses down.

If visitors pulled into our driveway at night, the headlights of their car would provide more than adequate evidence of their presence well before a knock at the door. This time, however, there were no revealing headlights. The uninvited visitor could have been someone whose car had broken down, who had walked to our house in need of help. It wasn't a common occurrence, but it did occasionally happen. He could have been one of the permanent tenants needing a gallon or two of gasoline or a loan of a few dollars against future earnings, also not an uncommon occurrence. It could, however, be a bandit who had left his car somewhere down the road so as not to raise suspicion before knocking on the door. This was not a common or a very successful occurrence because most farm houses had a good dog like Buddy and a shotgun waiting for just such an occasion. The most common concern most farmers had was the daylight theft of gasoline from bulk storage tanks when the tractors and workers were in fields and dogs like Buddy weren't home.

All of these possibilities must have whipped through Dad's head as he leaned forward in his chair. He paused for a moment, ran his hand through his thinning hair and, with a furrowed brow, glanced at Mom before rising from his easy chair.

I tried to stay in touch with what Marshall Dillon was doing. As Dad made his way to the front door, he conducted his routine security maneuver. He peered through the Venetian blinds by pulling one of the metal slats upward just enough to see outside without being noticed. He saw nothing. The Venetian blinds covered the large set of double windows providing a southerly view from the house. The view from this window took in the graveled horseshoe-shaped driveway running from the main road back past the house, then arching past the tractor sheds and barn before returning to the main road, providing entry and exit from two points.

During the daylight hours, or at night when there was a full moon, the window provided a view to what was going on near the house. With no moon, Buddy was the primary alarm on a nasty night like this. He always watched from his well-built and insulated doghouse that provided a panoramic view of the premises. He could see directly out his door to the bulk gasoline tank, tractors, and barn, and was a formidable deterrent to any would-be troublemaker, having proven his mettle in battles with both wild dogs and foxes.

Dad walked to the front door, pausing for a moment to lower the TV's volume, flip on the porch light, and peer through the small set of Venetian blinds covering the door's upper windows. The light bulb in the ceiling of the porch fully illuminated the area, including a large portion of the front yard. A moment's glance and Dad's natural defensiveness changed to relaxed recognition.

"It's Bird," he said, using the nickname Raymond's family gave to him when a baby. Dad's smile relieved any concerns I might have had. I diverted my eyes from the travails of *Gunsmoke*, a little irritated at the intrusion, but happy to see Raymond, and curious about what was happening.

"Come on in." Dad said. "Get in here out of the cold and warm yourself." As Raymond stepped into the room, Dad looked past Raymond into the yard, always vigilant. "Buddy!" Dad called out. "Where are you, boy?" Hearing Dad, Buddy showed himself. Wagging his tail, he moved from the darkness into the area of the yard illuminated by the porch light. "I wondered why you weren't barking. Now I know." Buddy didn't view Raymond as a threat or a stranger.

Raymond removed his rain-soaked cap, holding it with both hands near his waist and nodded with a polite "Thank you" as he stepped into the house. Raymond stood unusually tentative after such a grand entrance. He briefly acknowledged me with his eyes as he looked past Dad, toward Mom. He appeared pale, as pale as anyone I ever saw.

"Hi, Mrs. Walker," he said.

"Hi, Raymond," Mom replied in a soft, questioning tone.

Raymond glanced at me and I said, "Hey, Raymond...what're you up to?" He acknowledged me with another nod, but didn't otherwise respond to me. He had the same terrified look on his face as the night we saw the creature.

On this cold and dreary night Raymond was scared, but it was not about any haint or werewolf. This time, Raymond's mannerisms were quite different. He referred to Dad as "Mr. Walker," not "Fred" as he usually did. Likewise, I always referred to Raymond's dad as "Bill," not "Mr. Busby." His strange formality brought forth my full attention.

Mom got up from her chair and moved closer to Dad and Raymond. "Can I get you anything? Popcorn or Cragmont Cola?" she asked.

"No, ma'am," Raymond said. Mom, sensing a problem, deferred to Dad.

Dad said, "Now, Bird. What in the world's the matter?"

Raymond's eyes darted about as he seemed to gather in the strength to speak. His hesitation was unusual. Instinctively, I knew something serious had happened, or was about to happen, and I could tell by my father's manner that he was far ahead of my observations. This was adult talk, and Raymond, for all practical purposes, was an adult. I was the only child there.

Raymond, staring directly at my dad, spat out the words as if he couldn't hold them in a moment longer.

12

"Hokey's gone to kill Fats."

Mom, who was standing, slowly moved toward Dad, wringing her hands in a way I had never seen before. Raymond's words hung in the air as the images and sounds of *Gunsmoke* faded from my consciousness.

"Hokey has gone to kill Fats?" Dad asked. His words forced their way into my world, barging into the room like an unexpected evil, stunning us all. All eyes now fixed on Raymond, awaiting his reply. When no response was forthcoming, Dad pressed on.

"Where is Hokey? Where is Fats?" The staccato questioning came from a lifetime of experience dealing with people and their problems. I had never heard my dad so exacting, so deliberate. Not mad. Not angry, simply dealing with it.

Raymond stood mute and eyed the door as if desperate to leave after dumping this news in the middle of the room. Dad continued to ask questions. "Tell me what happened."

Raymond looked away, as though his mind were elsewhere.

"How long has Hokey been gone?" Dad asked, being more direct.

Raymond broke his silence, saying quietly, "It's been a while, more than an hour or so ago. He went to get Fats' shotgun." He began inching his way toward the front door.

"How did he leave? Was he walking or driving?"

"He drove his car."

"Which direction did he go?"

"North," Raymond paused, his hands stuffed in his pants pockets. "He went north, to the plank bridge."

"Why did this happen, what caused the blowup?"

"He's drunk," Raymond added, "and Fats is at the Robinsons'." He remained mum about specifics leading up to Hokey's decision to kill Fats. Dad took a couple of steps back from Raymond, then turned and looked at Mom for a moment, his eyes lost in thought.

Dad pivoted toward Raymond, looked him squarely in the eye while placing his left hand on Raymond's shoulder and in a sincere and compelling manner, said, "Raymond, listen very carefully." Raymond slightly bowed his head, avoiding eye contact, softly clenching and un-clenching his fists and shifting his weight back and forth from one foot to the other.

"If there is to be any chance of stopping Hokey, you've got to cut across the field to the Robinsons' as fast as you can. You've got to get there before Hokey. You're his little brother, he might listen to you but, if someone else was to approach him, he might just let loose with that shotgun." Raymond lifted his head and, as his eyes met Dad's, the meaning of the message became clear. Raymond's delivery of this message to Dad was not unlike the principles by which military couriers are bound. Protect the message. Get the message to the intended person. Mission accomplished. Now, however, Raymond knew, that contrary to this principle, he would be leaving with the same burden he had intended to leave with Dad.

In coming to our house this evening to speak to Dad, Raymond was, without doubt, responding to the demands of his mother, who ran the Busby household. Raymond's dad was most likely full of wine that Saturday night. Ruth would have assumed that Dad would handle Hokey. As it turned out, that would not be the case.

As Dad and Raymond faced each other, my eyes moved from Dad to Raymond and back again. A sense of helplessness came upon us. I could feel Raymond's anxiety, but I didn't know what to say or do, or what Raymond would do. Would he go on the mission across the wet cold field to find and stop Hokey as Dad suggested? Or would he go home, having delivered his message?

Breaking the silence, Raymond said, "Well, I'd better be going now."

"Right," Dad said. "But be careful and make sure Hokey knows it's you before you get too close."

Mom began to say something but the words didn't come out. Instead, taking a step toward Raymond, she reached out, touching his sleeve saying, "Please be careful."

Raymond, his lips slightly pursed, nodded and moved toward the door. Dad, still following his routine, flipped on the porch light, peered briefly through the blinds, and then unlocked and opened the door, allowing the cool damp air to rush into the warm house. As Dad stepped back, Raymond quickly eased by him and onto the porch. Brushing by my parents, I followed Raymond. Mom and Dad remained in the house. Wanting to say something, not knowing what or how to say it, I remained silent.

At the edge of the porch, Raymond hesitated, quickly glancing about, surveying the darkness surrounding us, before bounding down the steps into the yard. He glanced back at me. No words could relieve the serious nature of the moment. Wearing an old hunting cap pulled down over his head, his eyes barely visible, his jacket zipped up to his neck, his collar up and his hands shoved deep into the jacket's pockets, Raymond began making his way back. Depending on his choice, he would either go northeast to the Robinson house or due south to his house.

Buddy trotted out from under the front porch, yelping and wagging his tail like a puppy. Since it was Raymond, his defenses were down. He followed Raymond and both were swallowed up by the night. I yelled, "Here, Buddy! You stay here."

"Go on back, Buddy," Raymond said.

Moments later, Buddy re-entered the yellowish glow from the porch light. He turned his head slightly sideways, making that "what's-going-on?" dog whimper before turning and looking back in toward the direction Raymond had taken. Buddy had an innate ability to sense trouble, and he suddenly went on full alert, ears fully extended, eyes flashing in preparation to perform his duties as the first line of defense for our family.

I stood on the porch, thinking of what had happened. A chill came over me as I realized I was all alone under the glare of the porch light. I looked north toward plank bridge, slowly panning east along the ditch-dump road. It was the only route Hokey could take to the Robinsons. It'd be a hard walk through the merciless mud with that shotgun, and with murder his intent.

I tried with all my might to see something that would give me a clue, something that could shed light on events now taking place but hidden by darkness. There were no lights, no clues, and the only sounds other than the beating of my heart, were the rustling of the few leaves left on the old cottonwoods and the rhythmic sound of rainwater dripping from the eaves of the house. Mom's and Dad's voices, speaking in low tones, were too muffled to understand. Suddenly, Dad interrupted this moment frozen in time.

"Harold, get in here and shut the door!"

"Huh?" I muttered as though waking from a trance

"Harold Gene Walker get in here this minute and lock the door!" Mom shouted.

The meaning of Mom's demand, coupled with the use of my middle name was inescapable.

"Yes Ma'am." I closed the door, giving it that extra tug to ensure it was securely seated in its wooden frame. The slight squeaking noise made by turning the old key gave further assurance that the tumbler had fallen securely into place.

I looked at the clock. 9:15 p.m.

"Always lock the door" was a house rule here in this place so far from the beaten path, in this wild corner of Pemiscot County we called home. The Sheriff's Department rarely patrolled this part of the county and the only real police available to us were the Missouri State Highway Patrol, occasionally seen notifying next of kin, chasing hot-rodders, or searching for outlaws. There was no telephone service, so most "real" justice was handed out on an ad hoc basis, by those involved.

Now, with the door securely shut and locked and Buddy on full alert, I entered the living room. Mom and Dad still spoke in hushed tones.

"Fred, what are we going to do?"

"I expect we'll know something before long," Dad said, "In the meantime, we have to be ready should things get worse."

13

There would be no going to sleep that night, and I suspected we wouldn't attend church in the morning, a benefit as far as I was concerned. Racing to my bedroom directly off the living room, I moved quickly to the double window with a northern exposure. I left the light off on purpose, as the glare would seriously restrict what I could see outside. During the day from this vantage point, I could easily see the ground Hokey would have to cover to get to the Robinsons. I pressed my face against the glass with my hands on either side shielding my eyes.

The cold, damp night air against the single pane made the tip of my nose cold. I saw nothing. However, seeing something didn't really matter because this was my post and I meant to remain on post throughout the night. Also, I could easily overhear Mom and Dad's conversation in the living room.

"Fred, do you think you should get one of the tractors and go to the Robinsons." A tractor was the only way to get across the muddy field. Johnny had the family car.

"Look, Glenda," Dad said, his voice slightly rising. "If the worst happens and Hokey comes by here for money or gas, you would have only Buddy and Harold between you and no telling what, and I won't take that chance." By mentioning my name, Dad acknowledged that I, at least, had a role in the defense of our home. That slight mention emboldened me; it was time for me to get my hands on our old shotgun. I had handled firearms throughout my young life and now that Dad had officially identified me as being in the line of defense, albeit after Buddy, I vowed not to let him down.

The time was approximately 9:20 p.m. My thoughts turned to the 410-gauge single-shot shotgun that was in my closet along with a half-full box of Western Auto birdshot shells on a nearby shelf. Knowing I could get to the gun in a hurry comforted me. Now, only time and daylight would bring answers.

Dad's decision not to dart off into the night to find Hokey stemmed from experience. Hokey didn't scare Dad. He'd dealt with hard cases all his life. What was unacceptable to Dad was not being home to greet Hokey, should he come our way.

Dad continued, "Hokey knows about the safe and he might decide to make a try at it. If, as Raymond says, Hokey's drunk, I have no reason not to believe him. And, if he carries through with his threat to kill Fats, he'll be desperate and he'll probably need both money and gasoline, both of which are available here."

* * *

On some occasions, Dad loaned money to individuals known to him but who were not working for him. He would then hold something of value offered by the borrower as collateral. A regular borrower, I only knew as James, a black man, always brought Dad a small snub-nosed Smith & Wesson .38 Cal. Lemon Squeezer pistol for collateral. The farm's daily journal, the pistol, and a small amount of operating cash were stored in Dad's safe. Eventually, James didn't return for his pistol. Dad kept the gun. He never handled the gun in a conspicuous manner and no one outside our family knew that Dad sometimes carried the pistol for personal safety.

* * *

After more speculation, Dad said, "There's still a chance nothing will come of all this."

Mom said, "We can only hope that will be the case."

If Hokey was walking the ditch-dump to the Robinsons' house from the bridge, as suspected, his task would be formidable.

That night, anyone trying to negotiate the ditch-dump road, no more than a path, would have to do so in pitch darkness while contending with a chilling drizzle and the Mississippi-like mud that comes with it.

A few days before, while Hokey and Fats were pulling bolls, Hokey had done just that. He left his boots in the mud during the morning and continued to work the remainder of the day barefoot, pulling that nine-foot cotton sack weighed down with mud and water through those quarter-mile long rows. If

Hokey walked from the bridge to the Robinsons, it might require much more time and effort to achieve his immediate goal of reaching the Robinsons' house, especially while drunk. But his past efforts in the cotton fields showed he had the tenacity to do it.

Raymond's information was that Hokey had left their house within the past hour, so that would be between 8:00 and 9:00 p.m. Whatever was going to happen might have already taken place, but without knowing for sure, we would have to be vigilant. Mom voiced concern about Johnny being unaware of any of the goings on that night, and the possibility that Johnny might pick up Hokey haunted Mom. Dad was unresponsive to Mom's concern about Johnny, which meant to me that Dad didn't expect such a danger. I didn't give it much thought either, because I couldn't conceive of Hokey harming Johnny.

At 9:30 p.m., an eerie wail invaded our senses, a bizarre and frightening sound heightening our sense of vulnerability.

Shaking her head and placing her hand up to her mouth, Mom said, "What now?" to nobody in particular.

Grimacing, Dad, with furrowed brow, looked at Mom and said, "It's a car horn Glenda."

"A car horn?" Mom questioned as she shrunk back into her chair, weary from the weight of the evening's intrigues. "What's next?"

"I don't know." Dad said, "But stay away from the windows and turn off the lights. Harold! Go ahead and turn off all the lights in the house. We don't want to be targets. Do it now."

"Yes, sir."

Sprinting from my room, I almost ran into Mom. I pivoted at the last possible moment, like a basketball player making his way around an opponent. Mom cringed and braced herself for the impact. "Goodness, watch where you're going. Let's not start running into each other."

"Sorry," I said as I turned off the kitchen light. In another couple of strides, I was at the enclosed back porch, pulling the string attached to the small-wattage light bulb in the center of the ceiling. Darkness now enveloped the house, except for the small table lamp in the front room.

Overruling Dad's request, Mom said, "Don't turn off all the lights. Leave the table lamp on."

"Yes, ma'am."

The table lamp bathed the front room in an eerie yellowish glow, similar to what an old coal oil lamp would produce. The unwavering sound of that horn continued.

"That sound is awful, it's driving me crazy," Mom said, placing her hands over her ears. Dad sat in his chair within the soft glow of the lamp, unresponsive.

Dad's lack of response to Mom's comment caught my attention. I had seen this before when he was deep in thought, staring into nothingness with a slight furrowing of his brow. He placed his left hand against his face, his chin resting in the palm of his hand, with his elbow braced on one arm of the chair and his right forearm relaxed on the other arm. His right hand held a small bright ring of miscellaneous farm keys. He slowly flipped through each key over and over and over, a clear indicator he was preparing himself for action. I had seen Dad on many occasions flip those keys when he was deep in thought. It was apparent to me that he was thinking through our circumstances and deciding on a course of action should it come to that.

Mom noticed Dad's silence and didn't address the maddening blare of the horn again. She began to pace back and forth in the front room, her fingers interlocked under her chin in a prayer-like manner. I had never seen this before. The air seemed to thicken with each breath. It was clear to me that we all believed the sound of that horn was a warning: He's coming, Hokey's coming.

How long would it take for the car battery to run down, and why had the sound never varied in intensity? The intensity of the sound should waver as the battery weakened, but it didn't. The sound came from the direction Raymond had told us Hokey had intended to go, to the plank bridge.

When the ditch-dump was too muddy to drive a car to the big red house where Hokey and Fats were batching, Hokey would leave his car at the log cabin. We suspected he did the same thing that night.

Just come on, get it over with, I thought. Even Buddy began to howl. Dad stood from his chair and made the trip once again to the window in their bedroom, looking north into the darkness.

Without any wavering, the horn fell silent.

"It stopped," I said, and cringed at having stated the obvious. Racing to my window, I imagined Hokey crashing through the front door at any moment, his eyes glowing red and his hair on fire.

"What now?" Mom said. I strained to see something, anything, out my window. The night revealed only the blackness of the land.

14

Maybe Hokey didn't kill anybody. Maybe he was so drunk he passed out in his car, accidentally pushing the driver's seat into the steering wheel causing the horn to sound. Then, maybe, he came to and pulled the seat to its normal position. Yeah, that was it. That could explain everything.

Yet the worry lingered. Dad wouldn't be satisfied until he knew Hokey wasn't headed for our house. I had begun to dismiss the whole affair, what with my suspicion that Hokey was simply sleeping off a drunk. But, what if Hokey comes to the door. I thought, what then? The questions were circular, coming and going, swirling in my mind.

Dad had the .38 S&W revolver in his pocket didn't he? And Buddy would give the alarm and attack Hokey if he considered him a threat, wouldn't he? *Would Hokey shoot Buddy? Would he shoot Dad? Would he kill us all?* It was time to make sure the shotgun was ready. Closing my bedroom door, I retrieved the .410-shotgun and shells from my closet. I sat down on the edge of my bed and pulled a blanket on top of the shotgun. Reaching under the blanket, I held my breath and slowly opened the breach. The slight metallic sound that escaped the blanket was almost imperceptible. Certain I had not yet been discovered, I retrieved a .410 long shotgun shell from the ammo box that held a critter-load of shot and slid the shell into the bore. Still hardly breathing, I clinched my teeth, closed my eyes and slowly closed the breech with as little sound as possible escaping from under the blanket. Breathing easier, I opened my eyes and pulled back the blanket. I gently laid the gun down on the floor in the small space between the side of my bed and the window. Mom and Dad could not easily see it even if they came into my room.

The shotgun gave me a sense of security. Even though I was only twelve, I was a good shot, especially with a scatter gun. I had no doubt Dad could take Hokey in a fair fight, but I also knew of "fair fights" that turned brutally unfair. A migrant hill person and a local tough got into a fight in Bragg City, near Edith's cafe, over some long-forgotten dispute. The hill person had knocked the local down a few times and tried to walk away only to have the local drive a screwdriver into his back, plumb up to the handle. The hill person's friends wasted no time getting the man into their truck and off they went, slinging gravel all over the front of Edith's Café. He was never heard from again. The local who stabbed him, had garnered a reputation for foul play that followed him like a bad dream. He walked away from the fight bloodied but unbowed. There was never an inquiry by the Sheriff's Office even though the incident was reported by some patrons at Edith's cafe. In Pemiscot County in the '50s, nothing much ever came from reporting a fight.

I knew Hokey was a dangerous person. In the past year or so...his actions and the rumors about him had caused me to believe he would not hesitate to do the same as the Bragg City tough—stab a person in the back. If that happened, I would not hesitate to use the shotgun to protect my family.

Nobody yet knew it, but Johnny had already used his gun to protect our family. A trespasser had driven his car over our cotton field to the Cotton Belt Railroad trestles, an unpardonable sin and one that Dad zealously enforced. Anyone who would drive his car or walk over someone's cotton crop, or any crop for that matter, must have had serious mental problems. Dad always dealt with these trespassers in the same manner. He disabled the trespasser's car by taking the distributor cap and left a note telling them to come to the house to pick it up, forcing the trespasser to see Dad in person.

Johnny knew the trespasser by reputation. He was the same tough who stabbed the hill person. While Dad was making his way to the trespasser's car to get the distributor cap, Johnny grabbed his .22-caliber lever-action Marlin and made his way through thick brush to within range of the inevitable confrontation, without being noticed by Dad or the trespasser. As Dad arrived at the car, the tough, carrying a shotgun, returned.

From a distance, Johnny could see that Dad was making his position clear. No trespassing! Johnny watched, hidden in the brush, with the bead of his rifle trained on the unsuspecting trespasser. Had the shotgun been raised toward Dad, Johnny was prepared to drop him on the spot.

It didn't happen. No one ever knew about Johnny and his gun. Not Dad. Not the trespasser, who apologized for driving across the crop. Not Mom. Not me. Nobody knew, until many years later when Johnny told me.

Johnny said he had no fear for Dad in a one-on-one fight with anyone, but he wouldn't allow a weapon to be used against him. Both my brother and I would have done whatever was necessary to protect our dad, just as we knew he would have done whatever was necessary to protect us.

More time passed with nothing but darkness and drizzle. At 9:50 p.m., after what seemed like forever, a car zoomed past our house, moving so fast it threw mud and water into our front yard. Buddy barked and I ran to the front room, looking south through the double windows. I thought it must be Hokey heading south, fleeing the area, but there were no visible taillights. I hurried back to the windows in my bedroom, brushing past Mom and Dad, and again pressed my face against the window, looking north. This time, I could make out dim taillights.

"Did you see that?" Dad asked, with as much emotion as I had ever heard from him.

"Yes, sir, I sure did, but I can barely see it now. It stopped at the bridge. It seems to be trying to turn around. I can't be sure." As I could see much better than Mom or Dad, I became their eyes.

My parents came into my bedroom and they waited for my description of what was happening. I feared they might spot the shotgun lying on the floor, but the bedroom light remained off and they didn't see the gun. Squinting, I tried desperately to see into the deep darkness. The car was maneuvering with its headlights shining across the field, illuminating the log cabin, revealing a car parked by the cabin.

Was it Hokey's car? It had to be. A brighter light, maybe, a search light danced back and forth across the blackened ditch-bank west of the log cabin. After what seemed to be no more than a few minutes, a pale interior light from inside the car became vaguely visible, flickering on and off as shadowy figures seemed to pass between the light and me. Like calling a ball game, I repeated everything to my parents as I observed it.

Becoming excited, I turned to Dad and said, "Let's go to the bridge!" I was no longer sleepy.

"No," Dad said with startling force.

"Absolutely not," Mom added.

Mom left my room and sat in the front room, resting her left elbow on the arm of the couch with her hand over her mouth. She looked tired and scared as tears welled up in her eyes. She realized this was bad, really bad, but she stiffened, determined to see this through.

Seconds seemed like minutes and the lights of the mysterious car once again began to move. As the car backed into the road, the headlights briefly illuminated the field sweeping from west to south before it settled into the center of the gravel road.

The car headed back south from the direction it came, picking up speed. Its headlights swerved slightly, held steady, and swerved again. I couldn't help but admire the obvious skill of the driver, as navigating muddy gravel roads at any speed was extremely dangerous.

Realizing I had to move fast to get to the front door if I wanted a closer look at this mysterious car, I cried out to Mom and Dad: "Here it comes!"

Within the time it took me to get from my bedroom window to the front door, about five or six strides, the car flew south past our house. The engine screamed and mud and water again flew from the tires into our yard, as Buddy howled. The time was 10:00 p.m.

Dad, after a few moments, said, "I think it must all be over. We'll know in the morning how good or bad it is."

"I'm going to check on Buddy, just to make sure he's okay," I said, a ploy to get out of the house and see what there was to see.

"Oh, no you're not," ordered Dad. "Buddy's okay. No one leaves the house tonight."

"What about Johnny?" I said.

Mom agreed. "I'm worried about Johnny coming home and driving into something that could be bad."

"Johnny'll be okay," Dad said. "He won't be coming home for hours."

Still unable to sleep, we waited. Mom and Dad eventually went to bed and we all said our good nights. After getting into bed, I reached down and picked up the .410, pulling the shotgun under the covers. I double-checked, reassuring myself the shotgun was loaded and ready to go. Once again, I eased the shotgun out from under the cover and laid it on the floor within easy reach in the space between my bed and the outside wall. Unable to fall asleep, I found myself standing at the window, flinching at every sound, real or imagined. Reluctantly, I fell back upon the bed, exhausted. Somehow, exhaustion turned to sleep.

15

Sunday Morning, December 8, 1957. Sundays were normally filled with church activities, but not today. I woke with one eye partially opened. Soft daylight bathed the room. It must be eight or maybe nine I thought, and tried to make sense of both time and place. Then I remembered everything.

Sitting upright in the same blue jeans I wore the night before, I brushed the hair out of my eyes and forced myself through the fog of sleep to stand. I made my way to the bedroom window where I had stood most of the night and the day presented itself as a typical December day: gunmetal gray, not threatening rain, but still chilly. A car was still parked at the log cabin near the plank bridge. In the light of day, it looked like Hokey's car.

I staggered to the front room. The wall clock next to the picture of the blue-eyed, blonde-haired Jesus showed it was almost 9:00 a.m., well past the get-up hour on the farm, especially for a Sunday. There was something wrong—too much silence. Suddenly I remembered I had placed the loaded shotgun within reach from my bed. I returned to my room, fell headlong across the bed, and reached for the shotgun. Thankfully, it was undiscovered and still there.

If Mom had seen this, she would have been mad as a hornet. She didn't much approve of guns, but tolerated the fact they were sometimes necessary. I picked up the shotgun and slowly walked into the living room. Still, there was silence. Where's Mom and Dad? Where's Johnny?

Looking outside, I saw our family car, a green 1955 Chevy sitting in the driveway by the propane tank. Moving on, I opened Johnny's bedroom door, almost afraid to look. Seeing his rumpled head above the blankets, I backed out of his doorway, closing the door. He's okay.

Turning my attention to the whereabouts of Mom and Dad, I heard the back door open, then close. Small talk, familiar voices. Mom and Dad.

Thank goodness. Moving fast, and without their noticing, I made it back to my bedroom, and returned the shotgun to its spot in the rear of my closet. As they were making their way into the kitchen, removing their jackets, I walked out of my bedroom as if I had just jumped out of bed. Then, I remembered, the shotgun was still loaded. I'd have to unload it later. At this moment, I couldn't risk them hearing the metallic sound of the shotgun being broken down.

Quickly hugging Mom and Dad, I hurried past them. Opening the back door, I saw Buddy trotting down the driveway. An immense weight instantly lifted from me. The people and dog I cared about were all alive. Everything was okay. The rains of the previous day and night left behind a drenched landscape: muddy roads, puddles on the graveled driveway, and water standing in the fields.

Closing the back door, I made my way to the kitchen. "Where've ya'll been? I was scared near to death when I woke up and everyone was gone."

Mom's eyes reflected an enormous sadness. Reaching out to hug me, she said matter-of-factly, "The absolute worst thing has happened. Hokey and Fats are both dead."

I looked at Dad for some response as Mom hugged me. He simply nodded, removed his jacket, and hung up his hat. He accepted Mom's statement with the same hard stoicism he always exhibited.

While my life thus far on the farm had been a fairy tale of saddle horses, Floodway adventures, and piano lessons, I understood, or thought I understood death. Death was no stranger to farmers, but this had a different feel to it than when a calf died shortly after being birthed, or a pet got taken by a hungry fox, or a too-shy-to-hunt half-beagle, half-basset hound huddled down in fear was cut to pieces by the Cotton Belt freight train.

My grandmother had passed away in our home following a long bout with cancer, under the gentle care of my mother. It was terribly sad, but not unexpected. Butchering livestock and the birth of a beautiful long-legged colt happened side by side here. I was raised on stories of outlaws and walked the railroad trestles over the Floodways with men who thought no more of killing a man than a rabbit. Again, this was different, much different.

I took a deep breath, and my eyes met Dad's.

"Tell me everything."

16

While I slept late that Sunday morning, Dad had begun his own investigation after enduring a night of sleepless vigilance. This was his farm and it was his responsibility to know what had happened. Raymond's message, coupled with the eerie wail of the car horn followed by the speeding car, all pointed to something horrific.

With Buddy running ahead, Dad walked up the gravel road in the dim dawn of that gray, rain-soaked landscape to the plank bridge where the car still sat, and then to the house where Hokey and Fats batched, and finally to the Robinsons' house. Dad normally walked everywhere on the farm. He understood the condition of the roads and he knew walking the route was the only way to really learn what had happened the night before.

He inspected the mysterious black car, confirming it was Hokey's '47 Ford Coupe. He followed a blood trail from the car to a spot he later described as looking like a bloody hog wallow.

After inspecting the bloody scene at the car, Dad and Buddy made their way east from the county road. They followed an established walking path on the ditch-dump to the big red house where Hokey and Fats batched.

Dad's inspection of the house revealed a few 16-gauge shotgun shells strewn about the floor among scattered debris. It appeared as though the house had been ransacked. Following his examination of the premises, Dad headed for the Robinsons', about a half mile farther east along the ditch-dump on which there was no field road, only a path grown high with weeds now turned brown and prickly.

Arriving at the Robinsons' house, he met with Mr. Robinson and his son, Charles. Mr. Robinson looked as worn and tired as Dad had ever seen him. He confirmed that Hokey had killed Fats and that the Sheriff's department had sent out some deputies from Caruthersville.

After returning home, Dad accompanied Mom to the Busbys' where the rage had begun, leaving me and Johnny sleeping. Since Mom was with Dad, he drove our car to the Busbys' where they remained for about an hour. After talking with the Busbys, Mom and Dad returned home exhausted. As they opened the door, I met them. That was the moment I learned both Hokey and Fats were dead.

"I'll fix some breakfast," Mom said.

Dad responded, "Glenda, there's no need to cook anything and I can't eat anyway. Coffee'll do just fine."

"Well," she said, "I need to do something to steady my nerves. I'd feel better if I fixed something."

The smell and sound of fresh coffee bubbling up into the small glass dome of our much-used percolator, in concert with the melodic sounds of "The Old Rugged Cross" coming from the radio, brought a small measure of normality to this Sunday morning.

Dad, seated at the head of the kitchen table, looked much older and worn out. I paced back and forth between the living room and kitchen, reading the moment, keeping my mouth shut, trying to overhear anything said, when Mom removed her apron and announced, "Breakfast is ready."

Taking our seats, we bowed our heads for the obligatory "Thanks." Dad mumbled his "hurry-up" version of grace: "Dear Lord, thank thee for these blessings, Amen." Then we ate. Mom and Dad sat quietly, extra quiet, not what I had expected from their early morning travels.

Unable to control myself any longer, I blurted out, "What'd ya'll find out?" Dad, took a sip of his coffee, wiped his mouth with a soft cotton napkin, cleared his throat and glanced at Mom.

"Well," Dad said, "Hokey did kill Fats last night and Hokey's also dead. And, this afternoon, you and I are going to take Bill and Ruth to the Gideon Funeral Home."

"What about the car? Ain't that Hokey's?"

"Yes, it is."

"Well, what all happened?"

"I'll tell you what, I'm exhausted. I really don't want to talk about it now. I gotta get some rest. Then you're going with me to take Ruth and Bill to the funeral home. We'll talk later about what all happened." Dad moved away from the table, having eaten little, to sit in his favorite chair in the front room as Mom and I finished our breakfast.

Moments later, Johnny stumbled out of his bedroom into the kitchen. "What are y'all talking about? I could hear some of it. What about Hokey?" Johnny ran his hand over his head, trying to wake up.

"What are we talking about?" I said, and then blurted out without waiting for his response: "Why, Hokey killed Fats last night and Hokey's dead too." I was extra excited. I got to tell Johnny something he didn't know. I suddenly felt like I was much older than twelve.

"What?" he said, trying to take in the meaning of this news.

"Johnny," Mom said, "you just go ahead into the bathroom and clean up. You can catch up later." Then, looking at me, Mom said, "Now, Harold, Don't you go running off anywhere with Buddy. Stay close, cause when Dad wakes up, you gotta go with him to the funeral home."

The reality of what had happened the night before overwhelmed me with curiosity. I ran to my bedroom window to look at the car once more. I couldn't wait any longer; I had to see the car for myself.

17

Following a late breakfast, Mom left the dishes on the table and sat with Dad in the living room, just the two of them, leaving me behind in the kitchen. Stunned that Mom left me when I had so many questions to ask, I gulped down my food and joined them, listening, making no attempt to enter into their discussion. The air was filled with "What ifs?" "Whys?" and "What nows?"

"What if the Busbys had acted earlier to warn Fats without having come by to see Dad?" "What if it had not been rainy that Saturday?" "What if Fats had just gone back to his home, to his family for the weekend, wherever that might be." And, the biggest question: "Why?"

If the Busbys had reacted immediately to Hokey's threat to kill Fats, maybe the killing could have been avoided. If there had been no rain, they'd probably have been pulling bolls someplace, maybe up on the Earl's place. Hokey wouldn't have had an opportunity to drink wine all day, getting him to that point. Fats would have most likely been working with Hokey rather than being at the Robinsons' all day. Furthermore, Fats was a wanderer and he could have just as easily decided to go to his mother's house in Clarkton rather than to the Robinsons'.

"Well, what now?" Dad said, while running his right hand through his thinning and graying hair. Mom, staring off into inner space, didn't immediately respond. After a few moments of silence, Dad said, "Glenda, I think I should go to the Sheriff's Office about all this. What do you think?" Mom remained in thought, pondering the prevailing philosophy in our area that justice on the Floodways was normally dispensed by those involved.

"Fred," Mom said, her voice deliberate and clear. "Sheriff Clyde Orton probably knows as much about this killing as he wants to, and if he needs to talk with us, he'll let us know. As for right now, the Busbys need us here. And what about the Robinsons? What did Ernest say about his family?"

Mom knew Dad had spoken to Ernest Robinson near daybreak. The Robinsons were proud, strong, and independent folk who seldom needed or sought support from anyone outside their large family, which was evident when Mr. Robinson hadn't come to Dad about the killing. He just handled it.

"When I was there this morning," Dad said, "Fats' body was gone. Ernest said that Fats had been moved last night by Jimmy Osburn and a helper." Dad stopped to sip some coffee.

"Goodness," Mom said quietly with reddened eyes and a single tear making its way down her cheek.

Dad shook his head, "Osburn told Ernest that they'd be taking Fats to his funeral home in Wardell." Osburn owned his own funeral home. Like most any coroner of any county in the Bootheel, he would conduct his examination of the body, determine if there was going to be an autopsy and/or an inquest, and prepare a death certificate.

"Ernest said it took four men, the coroner and his helper along with him and Charles, to get Fats up on the gurney." Dad stopped for a moment. "Fats' body was wedged into the doorjamb between the kitchen and front room. There was lots of blood. But, it didn't compare to the bloody mess up there at the bridge."

"What about Martha and the kids?" Mom asked.

"Ernest said he'd taken Martha and the rest of his family to Joe's over at Tatum." Dad paused. His eyes teared a bit. "That bloody mess at the bridge on the ditch-dump and at the Robinsons made me think of that time when I found that gambler when I was a boy. This brought it all back to me."

* * *

When Dad was twelve years old, he was cultivating cotton with a matched team of mules just north of Yarbro, Arkansas near a ditch called the Belle Fountain. A shot rang out from behind the levee running alongside the Belle. A man had been killed in a crap game, shot in the head, and was lying in the grass. A bright new dime was lying on a gambling blanket, used by crap shooters. He thought of that man on occasion and always wondered if his killer was ever caught.

* * *

"Are the Robinson kids coming back today?" Mom asked.

"Oh yeah, I almost forgot. Ernest said they'd be back in school tomorrow. He insisted that they weren't going to miss any more school than necessary over this."

"Well then, it's settled," Mom said. "Our first responsibility is clear, it's to help Bill and Ruth. There'll be funeral arrangements to make and I'll fix some food to take 'em. I know they haven't had anything to eat during all this. Taking Ruth to the funeral home today is the first thing we do."

Dad nodded, "I told Harold I'm taking him with me. But first, I need to take a short nap. By the way, how's Johnny getting back to school?"

"He's catching a ride back to school with some friends this afternoon," Mom said. "We don't have to drive him back." Mom finally addressed me. "Don't forget you're going to Gideon with Dad later to let Ruth and Bill tend to funeral business. Don't go and get lost."

"Yes, ma'am, I know," I said, though I really didn't know why I had to go with Dad to Gideon. But it would be okay because I'd get to hear more about what happened. "What about Hokey's car?"

"What about the car?" Dad called out, having heard me from the bedroom where he had gone to lie down.

I stuck my head in the door to the bedroom and said, "Well, sir, I was wondering how long it's gonna sit up there."

"I don't know. Maybe the sheriff might want to keep it there for a while, to investigate."

"They're not going to investigate anything!" Mom hollered out to Dad. "No one outside of this farm even cares. It's over. Now," she said, looking at me while closing the door to where Dad was lying down, "let your Dad sleep, he's worn out."

Johnny made his way into the kitchen after washing and getting dressed. He could stay out all night, sleep a couple of hours and it would be like he'd never went out the night before. "Now, let's start over. What's going on?" he asked, speaking louder than usual.

"We're in the living room!" Mom responded.

Johnny came into the front room flopped down into Dad's chair and, as he sat, he asked, his hands palm up, "No one's going to church today?"

"No," Mom said. "We kinda had a rough night. Glad you weren't here."

"Okay," he said, his voice taking on a somber tone. "What's all of this about Hokey killing Fats? That can't be."

"What time did you get home?" Mom asked.

"I don't know for sure," Johnny said, dodging the question. "Anyway, on my way home, I saw Hoke's car up there at the bridge. I thought it kinda unusual 'cause Hokey's car isn't normally parked at the log cabin. But, I thought, that's just Hokey. Who knows? What did he do?"

"He killed Fats!" I hollered. "And Hokey's dead too."

Johnny glared at me, unable to speak. Mom said to me, "That's enough." I knew I'd made my point and it was time to shut up.

"Hokey and Fats are both dead? Who killed 'em? What in the world happened?"

What with all these questions flying through the air, and with Mom getting set to tell Johnny what I already knew, I saw my opportunity.

I eased out of the room, like I was just going to the bathroom. While Mom and Johnny talked, I took off. Not that they really cared, because I most always did what I wanted anyway. That is, except when Mom or Dad really didn't want me doing something; then I had to take that into consideration.

Maybe I'd go down to see Raymond. Then, thinking better of it, I figured this was the absolute best time for me to get to the bridge and see the car for myself, before the sheriff roped it off or took it away. I wished Raymond was with me. He could tell me everything about why Hokey went to kill Fats. But I couldn't take the time to go to his house. Anyway, who knew where he might be.

18

Moving as fast as I could without bringing attention to myself, I picked up my cap and jacket that were hanging from the hooks inside the back door. Easing the door open, I stepped out into the wintry day of gray clouds and the sour smell of water-soaked ground. Buddy trotted toward me as I carefully closed the door. His tail was wagging and he made that high-pitched whiney sound he did when first greeting me. Kneeling down, I gave my pal a hug.

"Mornin' boy," I said. Buddy licked my face and offered his paw, a trick I taught him only once and he never forgot. "Let's go."

Off we went on our quarter-mile trek north to the car. Buddy trotted alongside me, making our way along the soaked gravel road, my shoes scrunching a wet sponge covered with grit. Instead of leading several feet ahead of me, as usual, Buddy remained by my side, almost touching me. He wasn't usually so possessive unless he sensed imminent danger. He had already been to the bridge with Dad at daybreak. He knew more than I did about what we would find, but I dismissed his behavior.

I covered the distance lost in thought and the big black car was suddenly right in front of me. It seemed much larger and blacker than I recalled. An uncommon chill embraced me and the hair on the back of my neck stood up. I found myself standing no more than ten feet from the car. It held a macabre appeal for me, similar to Bonnie & Clyde's death car Dad had once taken me to see on display at Tommie's Drive-In Theater in Kennett. No longer was Hokey's car an image in my mind without substance. Its presence was foreboding, an ominous monument, a specter standing in stark relief against a panorama of gray clouds on a rain-soaked landscape.

I forced myself forward against a natural aversion to what seemed an overpowering evil. I was taken aback upon catching a glimpse of my reflection in the car door's window. It seemed I had somehow become part of the very object I wanted to see, yet deeply feared. I struggled to overcome an intense feeling similar to being in a dream state and trying to face down my inner demons. Reaching out, I placed my hand on the door handle, steadied myself, then gripped the handle tighter. Twisting it downward, I found the door unlocked. Buddy whined, gaining my attention. "It's okay, boy," I said. But what I said didn't seem to matter to him. He backed up several feet before turning and skulking away, his tail tucked.

I took a deep breath and pulled. As I did, a squeaking noise was the only sound in the entire landscape. There were no birds chirping, no dogs howling, no distant tractors humming. Even the slight breeze that had accompanied us to the car seemed suddenly stilled. Opening the door brought forth movie images of violating an ancient crypt.

My first sense, oddly enough, was the lesser of two smells, the smell of an old car: musty, moldy, trash-laden, the ashtray running over with Camel cigarette butts, Hokey's favorite. An empty bottle of Mogen David Concord lay on the floorboard with a few drops remaining. The overpowering smell in the car was thick and sweet, sickeningly so. The palm-size horn ring in the center of the steering wheel captured my immediate attention. Pressure on that horn had created the eerie sound we heard last night.

My eyes were drawn to something on the front floorboard: a dark glob of meaty material the size of a small pie plate and, next to it, another. Blood. Big clots of coagulated blood, gelatin-like, dark and angry. As my eyes adjusted to the darkened interior, the outline of another pool of drying blood came into focus, and yet another, soaked into the fabric of the front seat.

I slowly pulled the back of the driver's seat forward toward the steering wheel. More thick, nauseating blood revealed itself on the rear bench seat, mixed with mud and spread all over and on both sides. Most notable was a bloody boot print on the back of the driver's seat, the potential answer as to where the pressure came from to keep that horn blaring the night before. The aura of violent death was raw and powerful, causing me to reel away as my stomach churned.

I stumbled a few feet away from the car and my stomach revolted against breakfast. That distinctive chill once again passed over me. Steeling myself,

I straightened, making sure my jacket was zipped up to my chin. Then, overcoming a powerful urge to leave, I moved back to the car. Taking hold of the door handle, I looked inside one last time before closing the door.

I called out, "Buddy, where are you boy?"

Buddy whined, alerting me to his whereabouts. He was in a spot on the ditch-dump, some twenty-five feet from the car along a well-worn narrow path. That path led west, alongside Feeder Ditch 68 to Canal 259, First Ditch. It was used by anyone wanting to get to the Floodways without walking over the cotton crop. Stiff brown weeds stood about waist high. Numerous shoe and boot prints had been pressed into the soft earth, proof that others had come before me, including Dad and the people who took Hokey. The weeds had been trampled along the path, like a sack full of something heavy and bloody had been dragged along the ground. As I made my way toward Buddy, I came to a beaten down area. I wasn't fully prepared for what I was about to see.

An area about six to seven feet in diameter had the look of a hog wallow, like Dad said. The mud was discolored, pinkish, with varying depths of color from the blood. The smell was not as overwhelming as it was inside the car, but the fact that it was blood was inescapable. A muddy, bloodstained flannel blanket, dull pink with pale white stripes, lay in the wallow. It appeared to have been loosely rolled up when dropped. One corner of the blanket had been pulled away from the rest as if it had been stepped on while being carried.

Even at my age, I had some experience in this area. The agony of death favors no species, and the aftermath of death throes by man or animal appears no different. I could envision the kicking, the screaming, the blood, and also the quiet dying. I wondered if Hokey cried out for his mother.

Kneeling down, my elbows on my knees and my hands clasped, I closed my eyes, trying to imagine the moment. I could see the darkness and the drizzling cold rain as Hokey, desperate and armed with that shotgun, tried to make his getaway. He trudged along this very path to this spot, trying, without success, to make it to the cover of the Floodways. I couldn't see Hokey being scared. Scared and Hokey didn't go together.

My suspicion was that before returning to his car after killing Fats, Hokey stopped at big red, the house where he and Fats had been baching. There he picked up a bedroll. Or, did he have the bedroll in his car? Why didn't he just take the car and leave? Because, the car wouldn't start. If it wouldn't start, I wonder if he thought of going to our house. For whatever reason, he didn't. Then, he would definitely be headed for the Floodways, possibly to cross over the trestles heading west, then north to Gideon, where he had friends. Or, maybe he intended to hide out in the deepest recesses of the Floodways. He could have hid out for a few days then walked all the way to Gideon, miles away, into New Madrid County, out of reach of Pemiscot County but not out of reach of the Highway Patrol. I wondered.

How did he manage to shoot himself? Why would he shoot himself? To my twelve-year-old mind, he wouldn't have shot himself. Would anyone else have had the nerve to follow Hokey from the Robinsons' house and ambush him? No, that wouldn't have happened. The Robinsons were not hurt, and they would have been more protective of their home and family than out to avenge Fats. My mind whirled. I had to go back to the car. I didn't know why, but I felt I must.

My stomach stopped churning and I cautiously followed the path back the way I had come, back toward the car, my head down, my eyes on the path. I concentrated on the blood clots that looked like globs of mud, lying in a random broken pattern, leading back to the car from the bloody wallow. It appeared to me that Hokey had probably crawled back to the car. The pain from a wound or wounds gushing that much blood must have been horrendous. I forgot about time, engrossed in the puzzle. Buddy's barking brought me back to the moment. The family car was approaching.

Dad eased the Chevy to a stop directly behind Hokey's car. He rolled the window down. "I wondered where you ran off to. Shoulda known you'd come here."

Making my way past Hokey's car, I stopped, thought for a moment, and then asked, "Dad, were you the first person here this morning?"

"Only Buddy and me were here. I didn't see anybody else, but it's possible someone was here before us."

"Do you know for sure if Hokey was found in the car or the mud hole?"

"I couldn't say which came first, the bloody hole where the blanket is or the inside of the car. But it sure looks to me like someone butchered a hog in both places."

"Yes sir, it does. Where do you think the shotgun is?"

"I don't know, but you're asking a lot of questions I can't answer. Tell you what, Bill and Ruth might remember more than what they said to your mom and me this morning. We'll ask them on the way to Gideon. Now, get in."

"Yes, sir."

19

I crawled into the front seat alongside Dad, feeling a little skittish for having slipped away from the house. Instead of driving on, Dad turned the ignition key off and stared into nothingness across the landscape of withered cotton stalks, the lost crop, the manifestation of broken dreams, without saying a word.

Maybe he was thinking about what he wanted to say to me. Never a person who talked too much, he especially didn't allow anyone to know what was on his mind. On this occasion, I didn't try to figure him out. I believe we both were thinking about the same thing. How did all of this happen on our small farm?

I sat there staring out the passenger side window, not imposing myself on his moment of silence. Buddy was half sitting and half lying down on a nearby grassy area, scratching his chin with his hind paw, at peace with the world but ready for us to go so he could get on with his day.

As Dad sat behind the steering wheel, he shifted his weight, straightened up a bit, stretched, and pushed up the bill of his cap. The cap, tilted slightly to the back of his head, exposed his graying hairline and the distinct outline of his leathery tanned face against his pale upper forehead, a look common to those who earn their living working outside. He looked plain weary. He leaned slightly forward and with a furrowed brow and half grimace, looking at me. His forearms rested on the steering wheel with the fingers of his left hand wrapped around his right wrist; his worn wedding ring and the gold watch I so much admired were easily visible. I had seen this position so many times before, especially during long periods as he sat behind the steering wheel when we were traveling west over two-lane blacktop roads on our way to visit my sister and her husband in Tucson. But this time he wasn't driving; it was fatigue caused by his coming to terms with what had happened. I couldn't readily understand so I continued staring out the window, saying nothing.

He broke the silence with a question. "Well, what do you think?"

Slightly bewildered that Dad asked my opinion, I didn't know how to respond, so I just said, "I don't know."

Looking into the distance, he said softly, almost to himself, "When you grow up and have a family, you have a job to do."

"Yes sir. I guess." I hoped this would be about something not involving me.

"Well, last night my job was to make sure you and your mom were safe."

"Yes, sir." Now my interest piqued because he was talking about something on which I had an opinion. Our safety.

"And that's what I did." Dad was working it out in his mind, aloud. He kept us safe from a danger so close that at any moment it could have spilled on us. That's why he had said, "Nobody leaves the house." He had to protect his home and family against all outside threats. I understood that, and he would also be prepared if the threat came our way. I got it.

Dad asked, "Why do you think Hokey killed Fats?"

I remained quiet, looking at him.

Dad responded to his own question. "I doubt anyone knows why. I heard some talk this morning that there might've been some jealousy involved."

"About what?"

"Arlena."

"That don't make no sense. Arlena wasn't Hokey's girlfriend." I tried to sound confident, as if I knew anything about what was going on between Hokey and Fats and Arlena.

"She didn't have to be," Dad reasoned.

"But that don't make no sense either."

"Harold, listen to what I'm saying. It doesn't have to make sense. Most things like this don't make sense. People kill each other all the time for no reason at all. We'll never know for sure what was floating around in Hokey's head. He was different, but not that different. I've seen his kind before: friendly, moody, unpredictable, and deadly. There was a smoldering anger in Hokey that never seemed to go away. He was able to mask the anger from those who didn't know him well, but every once in a while, it boiled over. You do remember the cat don't you?"

"Yes, sir. I sure do."

Dad continued. "It's a terrible thing that Fats was there when Hokey exploded. But better him than anyone in our family. That's a hard way of looking at it, but that's the way you have to look at it. It's just that simple. Throughout your life, you're going to run into people like Hokey and you've got to be able to recognize the good from the bad. You've got to know the difference. You're lucky. You've had an opportunity to see the difference, the good side and the mean side. Now learn from this. And never make it easy for someone like Hokey to kill you."

Pausing, Dad looked away, cleared his throat, and continued. "Fats was killed over nothing. That's just the simple truth of it." Tears welled up in his eyes as he gritted his teeth, showing his gold tooth. These were not tears of sorrow but tears of anger, or maybe remembrance of his rough-and-tumble beginnings. Placing his right hand on my shoulder, and following a momentary pause, he said firmly, "Look at me."

I turned my gaze from looking out the window to looking directly into his eyes. He said, "Promise me right now you will always look out for yourself. Don't be so trusting of people. It can get you killed. Do you understand?" He finished his talk with, "Hit first, hit hard, and never let the other man up." It was a creed for survival he'd learned as a small child in Meridian, Mississippi, at the tender age of six, selling newspapers.

A little frightened at Dad's intensity, I quickly said, "Yes sir, I promise. I really do, I promise."

Dad turned the ignition key and the powerful V-8 roared to life with its heavy, thunderous rumbling sound of mechanical muscle. As Dad turned the car around, Buddy stood up and began trotting toward the Floodways on his own adventure for the day.

As for me, another troubling question popped out of my mouth, seeing as this was Sunday. "Do you think Hokey's in Hell and Fats is in Heaven?"

Dad, his eyes on the road, hesitated. Then, without taking his eyes off the road, he said, "I just don't know. I've been going to church all my life and, to tell you the truth, I just don't know. I would hope that Hokey and Fats are in different places so that Fats can rest in peace. As for Hokey, there should be no rest and no peace for him." The car was now straightened out into the soaked ruts on the gravel road, headed south at a slow speed.

"Do you believe in ghosts?" I asked.

Pressing in the clutch and stepping on the brake, Dad brought the car to a complete stop. He turned his head toward me. "What?"

Turning my head to face him again, I repeated the question, "Ghosts. Do you believe in 'em? I think I do. I think I saw a ghost on the Floodways once."

Dad thought for a moment, then said, "There are many things we don't know. I've seen questionable things in my life. Some were nothing more than a gust of wind on a calm day or an unexpected chill on a warm day, or an unexplained fog drifting across a field. Most, if not all, can be explained if people would take the time to think on it. But most believe what they want to believe." He paused momentarily. "That's enough questions for now, we have to be going."

"Yes, sir."

Easing out on the clutch while adding just enough pressure on the accelerator to keep the tires from spinning, Dad once again headed us down the road. "I want you to stay in the front seat here with me," he said. "Bill and Ruth will be getting into the back seat. And, listen good. You be polite. Don't ask any more questions, ya hear?"

"Yes, sir. But is Raymond coming too?"

"Probably not," Dad said as he pulled the bill of his cap down to mid-forehead. We left Buddy to make his way home.

20

On our way to the Busbys' house, Dad was careful not to pull too far out of the ruts in the road. The saying was, in wet weather, "Never get out of the ruts."

A road ditch, little more than knee deep and overgrown with knee high twisted brown weeds, ran alongside both sides of the road. A makeshift walkway directly in front of the Busby house, constructed with a two-by-twelve-inch cypress plank, provided access to and from the road.

Pemiscot County's road-grader, operated by Fatty Mac Water from Bragg City, worked on all the gravel roads. Throughout the year, Dad would request that Fatty use the big blade on his rig to clear the roadside ditches of weeds and debris. But that hadn't been done since early fall and it would be spring before the road ditches would again be cleared. Whenever the grading was about to happen, Dad would tell Bill, who would take down the makeshift plank footbridge, saving it from destruction, and replace it afterwards.

The Busbys, due to the floods that year, moved into the house that was normally reserved for the migrant families during picking season. It was a two-room unpainted house that sat upon high concrete blocks. A waist high plank porch ran across the front of the house.

I routinely rode my orange and black Western Auto bicycle, with those wide balloon tires, up to the Busbys' porch. The bike was at the exact height that allowed me to simply lean against the porch without having to get off. I'd plant my elbow squarely on the porch and rest my cheekbone against my open palm and listen to Bill tell stories of the old days. If he'd been drinking wine, he'd grab his old guitar and strum a few tunes of church music. He was a great storyteller and could lose himself in vivid descriptions of "the way things used to be." Bill had once been a master muleskinner. Mules, as opposed to horses, had a reputation for being extra stubborn, independent, and just plain ornery. Mule-handling was a much-valued skill in the early development of America but time had passed in favor of the tractor. This porch was my favorite destination after school or on weekends and a portal through which I could see yesteryear between adventures on the Floodways.

Shortly after we arrived, Ruth walked out of the house and onto the porch. She looked up for a moment, reassuring herself we were there, before grabbing hold of a post near the steps. Lowering her head, she carefully watched every step she took. She dressed in her everyday clothes: a plain brown print dress, paired with a cream-colored, well-worn knitted sweater, and a beige headscarf with a pink floral design tied in a knot under her chin, framing her chubby face. Her hair was cropped short in a pageboy cut, practical so as her vision was never obscured. Ruth, though uneducated, was not unintelligent, a common condition in the Bootheel, the poorest region in the state, where work came before schooling.

She had a remarkable memory, like many who depended solely upon their recall to survive. She could recite the birthdays and dates of marriages and deaths for everyone in my family, and anyone else with whom she felt close and she took great pride in her ability to do so. When she received letters from her eldest child, Betty Sue, she would bring them to my mom or Mrs. McMahan, a close neighbor who lived across the road from the Busbys on the Gill Farm. They would read Betty's letters to her and write back for her. Betty was a beautiful girl who had married a few years before and moved to Oregon. Mom carefully read the letters to Ruth, sometimes over and over. The letters were heartfelt, each containing a plea from Betty for the rest of the Busby family to pack up and come to California where there was year-round field work picking fruits and vegetables. It was a dream Ruth never forgot and one that had yet to come true.

Occasionally, after working in the fields all day, Ruth would gaze into the western sky. She'd give her little laugh as she picked up her hoe or nine-foot sack and say, "I wonder if the sun's going down in California." Then she would turn and trudge back to their modest home with Bill and the boys. She was the matriarch and ran the Busby household, handled all the money, and managed any and all family business. Her frugality and the family's hard work kept them in food throughout the winter. Her strategy for surviving the winter months was built around flour and navy beans. She supplemented the basics with food from her garden and all the fresh meat Raymond could bring home from hunting and fishing. Bill wasn't much help on that front.

Making her way to our car, Ruth was careful not to step off the planks or into any mud. Intuitively, I jumped out of the car to help her, holding the car door open. She climbed into the front seat where I had been sitting. Dad looked at me with that what-did-I-tell-you look. I simply thought it would be nice for her to ride up front with Dad. I shut the door for her and climbed into the back seat. I didn't say anything.

"Is Bill coming?" Dad asked.

"No, he's sick."

With calloused hands, she clutched her purse while holding onto a small white handkerchief. She handled this like she handled all the hard breaks in her life, with dignity. Of all the tough times she and her family had suffered over the years, this was the worst. Once settled into the seat, she said nothing.

Dad eased the car back onto the muddy road and into the ruts that were now beginning to dry a little, and we were off. Sitting in the back seat, I twisted around so I could see out the back window. I wondered if Raymond was home and why he hadn't come to the door with his mom. No one had come to the door to see her off.

* * *

It was about a half hour drive to Gideon, approximately fifteen miles north. Gideon was one of the old sawmill towns originally built to harvest the trees: cypress, oak, hickory, and gum from the great swamp that made up the Bootheel of Missouri. Employing at its height approximately two hundred people, the Gideon-Anderson Lumber Company, or The Box Company as some called it, manufactured all sorts of wooden boxes, shipping throughout the United States and to other countries. The Busch Brewery in St. Louis was one of its customers.

The Busbys once lived in the Clarkton/Gideon area for a few years. Hokey worked on and off for the Gideon-Anderson box company, learning to operate a Ross straddle-carrier, unloading and stacking lumber taken off the Cotton Belt. Fats did manual labor on local farms during the year and when the harvest was finished, he chopped firewood around Zalma, MO. It was in Clarkton where Hokey and Fats' friendship, at a young age, was cemented. The Busbys and Fats' family (mother Elsie, stepfather Homer Huddleston, and his sisters and half-sisters) were friends and neighbors of the Busbys.

* * *

Ruth said little. I said nothing. Dad drove. Ruth looked out the side window as she was barely able to see over the dashboard. She seemed disconnected from what was going on. Maybe it was her way of coping.

"Fats was like a member of the family," she finally said in a whisper, stopping short of saying anything as to why Hokey had killed him. It wasn't as if Ruth was trying not to say anything. I think she simply didn't feel there was more to say.

Dad said quietly, "Glenda and I are going to help with expenses."

"I've kept up the burial insurance," she said.

Burial insurance? I had never heard of such a thing. Car insurance? Yes. But, what was burial insurance?

"Fred," she said in an abrupt manner, as though she remembered something important. "Can we get Hokey's car brought back to our house?"

"I don't see why not, as long as the sheriff has no objections."

After a moment, she said, "Fred, I really appreciate you and Glenda coming down to the house this morning."

Dad, still thinking of the car, said, "Maybe we should just bring Hokey's car to our house and park it out by the tractor shed away from the road. That'll keep unwanted visitors away from it."

"Okay," said Ruth. "But Raymond said he wants the car. I just don't know if I do."

The death car, as I began referring to it, was coming to our house. I really didn't know what to think about all this, whether or not I wanted that car at our house. It gave me a creepy feeling and I didn't understand why Raymond would want it, what with his brother's blood all over its insides.

We approached Gideon from the south. The funeral home was quiet this time of day on Sunday. A couple of cars were parked in its graveled parking lot. I supposed they belonged to the funeral workers.

Getting out of the car, Dad stretched a bit and then walked the path to the door. I got out, opened Ruth's door and she followed Dad. I followed them both.

When we entered the funeral home, it was eerily quiet and reeked unnaturally of overwhelming perfume or a forest of flowers. A large door immediately opened off the small entry area into a room the size of our house, but longer than it was wide. The wall on the far end of the room consisted entirely of heavy off-green. Two large floor lamps about eight feet apart framed an area devoid of furniture. Off this room was another room, longer and much wider, with rows of folding chairs, similar to a church. The smell and the low lighting gave me chills, sickening me. The odor from inside the death car and the smell of the funeral home had all intermingled; the combined scent haunts me to this day.

Ruth and I sat in a small entry area while Dad went into the funeral director's office. After what seemed like hours, I heard a few mumbled words between Dad and a voice I didn't recognize. Dad reappeared with a man who identified himself as the funeral director. He greeted Ruth like a long-lost relative whom he had known all of his life. I found this odd because I had never seen him before this day, and never heard of a funeral director visiting the Busbys or anyone else.

"I'm so sorry for your loss, ma'am," the funeral director said in a smooth southern drawl. Ruth appeared wary, unaccustomed to such genteel consideration, yet hopeful. Maybe it was because her burden might be eased by this caring person. Dad, his hat in hand, stepped aside in deference to the director. Instinctively, I rose to my feet in awkward silence, feeling like I was in some kind of church. There must be some rule requiring others to stand in the presence of a man who lives in both worlds—the living and the dead.

I heard Ruth say in a barely audible whisper to no one in particular, "This is so hard. I don't know why he did it. Fats never did him no harm."

"I know, ma'am," The director took her hand in his. "Please, step into my office, won't you?"

Dad's earlier jitters seemed to have calmed. I couldn't hear him fondling his keys, a dead giveaway as to his level of anxiety. His breathing eased and the full color in his tanned face began to slowly return.

I, on the other hand, was becoming more and more curious. Dad gave me "the look," and motioned for me to sit back down, which I did, even though it didn't seem right.

While Dad was looking at me, I noticed Ruth had ceased any movement toward the office. Standing steady, she looked away from the director toward Dad. The director picked up on her hesitancy and said, "Fred, you come in, too. I'll get us all some coffee. And for you," he added, looking at me, "I bet I can find a cold Coke."

Now there would be no stopping me from getting into that meeting. Dad stood still with no indication he was willing to return to the office. Recognizing he had been out-flanked, Dad shrugged and said to Ruth, "Okay, but only if you want us in there." Ruth simply nodded her head. I heard a slight jingle of keys once again.

The office was furnished with a polished wooden desk, a rich-looking wooden bookshelf and cushioned leather chairs. However, that overpowering sweet floral smell was also there, though it seemed to bother no one but me. Framed pastoral scenes and a couple of diplomas hung on the wall. Ruth sat in the chair closest to the desk, more relaxed in our presence. Dad and I sat farther back near a bookcase. I could see the director's and Ruth's faces from where I sat.

Dad and Ruth refused the coffee and, for some reason, I felt Dad and the director also expected me to refuse the soda. But, I fully expected to receive my small cold bottle of Coca Cola. That was the deal. You don't break the deal, a rule Raymond and I lived by on the Floodways. Seeming a little put out with me, the director pardoned himself for a few moments and left the office. When he returned, he handed me that cold bottle of Coke. "Thank you, sir," I said, being as polite as I could manage.

"You're welcome," the director snapped, with what appeared to be either a grimace or a grin. However, I was now quite comfortable and prepared to hear it all.

The business at hand dealt with burial insurance and whether or not the Busbys' insurance was in effect.

Ruth opened her purse and gently retrieved a folded envelope. It looked like a letter that had been mailed to her. She retrieved an aged paper from the envelope and held it out to the director.

"Thank you," he said, accepting the document. He then retrieved a pair of gold wire-rimmed reading glasses from his shirt pocket, using both hands to place the thin arm-pieces over and behind each ear. He scoured the document for a few moments while mumbling to himself. Then, placing the document aside, he took care in removing a yellowing document from a manila file that lay on his desk.

He held the document with both hands, like he was reading a book, his pale blue eyes visible just above the top edge of the document. His head remained steady as his eyes moved back and forth, which was quite entertaining. The office was so quiet that I could hear the ticking of a small clock sitting on a shelf behind the director. Each swallow I took from the Coke seemed to draw a furrowed glance from the director and an occasional exasperated look from Dad.

It became apparent that Ruth had indeed planned ahead for what she intended to be her or Bill's funeral, not their son's. The director, removing his glasses, announced that the policy was a family policy and that Ruth had met her obligation of paying five dollars each month for however long the policy had been in effect, without missing a payment or being late. There was no way to get around it. The director announced the insurance was in full effect.

The hard words then began in earnest. "Ruth, we picked up Donald's and Harry's remains from the coroner at Wardell this morning. Those costs are not totally covered due to the distance involved, but we'll work that out later." Ruth never budged nor did she express any feelings whatsoever. She just dealt with it.

The insurance coverage, according to the director, took care of the basics: embalming, a hearse, a casket, a concrete vault required by state law, and the burying party, along with a canopy over the grave and fake grass upon which family seating would be provided. Ruth listened to the director's comments regarding Hokey's body and made a practical decision. Hokey's body would remain at the funeral home. "I can't allow Donald to be brought back home," she said. "We don't have enough room." A viewing would be held at the funeral home on Monday, December 9th and the funeral would be held on Tuesday, the 10th, the particulars were yet to be determined.

Ruth spoke up, advising that her personal choice was to have Hokey's funeral performed by Herbert Junior Crane at the Tatum Chapel. It was a small country church southwest of Peach Orchard, a tiny crossroads community that never had a peach orchard. I wondered if we were going to get to see Hokey, since the director said they had him. However, the possibility that we might see him was not discussed, and I was quite certain it wasn't my place to ask. The conversation was not that interesting until the director got to the point where he was going to show Ruth the caskets. Dad looked down at the floor, placing his forearms on the chair arms and holding his hat with both hands, saying nothing. I hopped up, ready to go forward on an adventure.

As the director moved through the office door with Ruth following closely behind, I looked at Dad. He had resigned himself to what was happening and stood. Seeing Dad get up, I felt it was okay for me to also get in line. I moved quickly through the door behind Ruth. Dad followed me. In a few moments, we were all moving through the funeral home in an odd line, like tourists, as the director spoke to Ruth in soothing tones.

The director took Ruth into a room to see the display of coffins, with Dad and me following along. Three coffins were on display, lined up like used cars on a lot with all the hoods open for inspection.

The director's gentle tone continued, speaking in the most caring manner, as he stressed that the high-end caskets offered eternal watertight integrity. The mentioning of the word eternal caused me to feel a twinge of stomach sickness. Thinking of a leaky vessel was the image that came to my mind. I'd seen muskrats that had been trapped in underwater catfish traps and not found for several days. It made me sick to think of Hokey or Fats looking like those muskrats.

The director said, "For a little more money than is covered by the policy," a phrase he repeated more than once, "this or that casket will keep your loved one dry for eternity."

The caskets, exhibited from left to right, began with the insurance-covered casket, followed by the moderately priced coffin, and last, the "Cadillac" model. For a small additional charge, something looking like a mosquito net could be purchased. This, according to the director, would keep the flies away should there be any in attendance at the viewing or funeral. The fact that it was winter didn't deter the director.

Ruth remained unresponsive to the director's comments as she took two or three small steps away from us. She was drawn to the casket on the far left, the insurance-covered model. It had a bronzy finish and bright chrome handles. In a trancelike state, Ruth gazed at its pillow and cream-colored lining. A moment passed until she raised her right hand and, with calloused fingers, began to lightly touch the metallic surface. I sensed this moment was special. The director and Dad must have, too, as we all stood in silence and watched.

Ruth had embarked on her own journey through time, gently brushing the casket's surface as though consoling a troubled child afraid of the dark, as if saying, "It's okay. Mother is here." With a hint of tears on her cheeks, she spoke in little more than a whisper. "This will do fine." The room heavy with silence, the director nodded, satisfied she had made her choice. Ruth gathered herself. Dad again fidgeted with his car keys. I was wide-eyed at having seen something wonderful in this frightening world of the dead, a mother's unconditional love.

Moving to another section of the display room, the director asked Ruth if there was any clothing of Hokey's she wanted to provide for the burial. Ruth thought for a moment, then looked directly at the director and said, "No, Donald didn't have no suit."

I had never seen Hokey in anything other than jeans, a cowboy-type shirt, boots, and, lately, the black motorcycle jacket he bought from my brother.

"In that case," said the director, "since there will be a public viewing, may I suggest you look at a variety of burial suits we have available?"

I couldn't believe they had burial suits. What was this all about? Situated on a long shelf in the room with the coffins were cardboard display boxes of suits. The outfits looked like the Sunday suits I saw at church. A white shirt and tie were also included in the price. But where were the pants and shoes? The director pulled down two boxes, one containing a dark suit and coat, one with a lighter gray suit coat. He removed one of the suit coats from the display box and then I knew why it was a burial suit. The back of the suit jacket was missing and the shirt was simply the front portion. The tie was only one small piece of material giving the appearance of a full tie. The whole thing was fake, made to be viewed once and then closed for eternity.

I was ready to get out of this place and so was Dad. This experience brought back all kinds of memories for Dad. He and Mom grieved terribly about the deaths of their second and third babies. They lived only a few days following birth, and were buried in the family plot of the old Blytheville, Arkansas Cemetery. I knew Dad kept two small metal plates, one from each of their tiny infant caskets in his special drawer. I sometimes saw him holding them when he thought he was alone. This walk through the funeral home brought those memories back to him and I sensed his deep sorrow.

I noticed another door the director didn't open; it was marked "Private". The wall was heavily-curtained with a portion opened, revealing the double doorway. The hardwood floor in this room was covered with an ornate carpet to within about a foot of the wall. The sweep of the two heavy doors opening and closing revealed indelible arcs in the carpet. Wear resembling wheeled carts particularly evident on the hardwood, disappeared beneath the closed doors.

The doors that could be easily hidden from view when the curtains were drawn tight seemed strange and out of place, like a garage door opening into a living room. Once again, an unexpected chill swept over me. I could feel it, the same feeling I had at the car. Hokey and Fats were here; I knew they were only footsteps away from me. I pulled on Dad's sleeve.

"What?"

"Dad, let's get out of here."

"Go ahead, wait in the car. We won't be much longer."

It was longer, though, about half an hour longer. Sitting on the front seat of the car on the passenger side, thinking about all that was transpiring, I dozed off a little.

"Wake up!" Dad said.

"Yes, sir," I blurted out, not knowing exactly where I was for a moment. The doors were open and Ruth was in the back seat behind me.

"We're going home," Dad said.

Ruth had done all that could be expected of her and more, and did it without any help from Bill, as usual. It was near mid-afternoon and I wanted to go home. I needed to reassure myself all was well. I needed to see Mom, to see her and be near her. I wanted to be away from that funeral home, that house of the dead.

21

As Dad pulled the car alongside the farm's bulk gasoline storage tank, I couldn't wait any longer. I jumped out before the car came to a complete halt and stumbled. I regained my balance and then broke into a full run toward the house. I had to see Mom as soon as possible. Ruth had already been let out of the car at her house and I was more anxious than ever to get home. Dad called out, "Whoa there, slow down!" as he walked to the rear of the car to remove the fuel cap.

"Yes sir," I yelled over my shoulder, but I didn't slow down. I couldn't.

The ever-vigilant Buddy, his great snout lying in the doorway of his doghouse, raised his head. When he saw me, he yawned, rolled to his side and allowed me to pass without a chase. Approaching the rear of the house at full stride, I gauged the distance to the concrete stoop. I knew, from experience and bruised knees, the precise point from which I could, with one leap, land squarely on top of the stoop next to the back door. By avoiding the four concrete steps leading up to the stoop, I could save a second or two.

Mom was busy in the kitchen. She'd seen Dad and me arrive and probably thought I was with Dad at the gas tank. Surprised to hear the back door slam, she turned from the kitchen sink at the same moment I entered the kitchen. I couldn't wait to give her a big hug. I was happy to be home and emotionally exhausted. She returned the hug, saying, "What's all this?"

"I don't know. I just missed you," I said, feeling glad I had a mother to hug. It was the first time I remember feeling that way—nothing in my life was for certain. I needed reassurance all was right in my world despite the new truth.

Dad, after about ten minutes, followed me into the house. Hanging up his jacket and washing his hands, he splashed water onto his face, dealing with fatigue. Making his way into the kitchen, he held a towel, drying his face and hands. Mom looked at me and said, "Go wash up. Dinner is now supper." In Cotton Country, in the Bootheel, breakfast was breakfast, lunch was dinner, and dinner was supper.

As I left the room, Dad took a deep breath and sat at the kitchen table. Mom placed a glass of his favorite drink, ice water, in front of him. He had been up all the previous night, then out at dawn this morning, and looked awfully tired and much older to me than he did yesterday. It had been less than twenty-four hours since the killing, but it seemed like ages ago. Obeying Mom, I hustled to the bathroom, splashing water on my hands and face. The cool water was refreshing but I hurried to get back into the kitchen to hear what happened when Dad was in the office with the funeral director without me.

Mom said to me, "That was quick. You sure you washed up?"

"Yes, ma'am, I'm getting quicker."

"You sure are," Mom said, rolling her eyes. Pulling out a chair from the table across from Dad, Mom sat down and asked, "How'd it go?"

"Okay, I think," Dad said.

"How was Ruth?"

"Tired, quiet. Handling it, like you'd expect."

"Poor thing." Mom looked down at her hands, clasped tightly together, her face drained of color. I'd seen that look many times before in this awful crop year when the rains wouldn't quit and we were surrounded by water only a few inches from being in the house.

Taking another sip of water, Dad began to tell the story. "When we got there, I had a talk with the funeral director, a real nice fella. But he knew the Busbys by name only."

"Did you tell Ruth we'd help out?"

"Yes, and guess what else she told me? I never would have believed it, but Ruth has burial insurance with that funeral home. Seems she purchased it years back when they lived in Gideon, when Hokey and Fats worked at the box company."

Mom nodded. "I wondered where Hokey and Fats met and became such good pals. Funny though, calling them pals after all this."

"Friends, I believe is the word," Dad said. "Pals don't kill each other." Dad always made a point of differentiating between the terms "friend" and "pal." When he was a boy in Mississippi, the terms were not synonymous. A friend was an acquaintance. A pal was someone with whom you could literally trust your life.

Dad continued, leaning back into the worn, straight-back cane-bottom chair. "Once I knew she had burial insurance, I felt better. When we got there, I spoke to the director in his office before Ruth met him. He was real glad I brought Ruth. He said he'd have to go looking for 'em if I hadn't and he didn't know where they lived. Rural Route Two, Bragg City, didn't mean anything to him. Anyway, I told him that anything necessary, not covered by their insurance, we'd make good."

"Good," Mom said, nodding her head.

"Ruth's a proud woman," Dad said, "and I wouldn't offend her, saying something like that in front of her. I figured I'd introduce myself privately and talk a bit before introducing Ruth. But it was me that learned something. Fats was twenty-three years old. His mother's name is Elsie Huddleston. Fats' mom and dad, split up some time ago and she re-married a Homer Huddleston who lives in Clarkton."

"Clarkton, hmmm," Mom said. "I wonder if Maxine knows the family." Maxine was Mom's second cousin who lived in Clarkton. "I'll ask her, next time I see her,"

"They're both at the Gideon Funeral Home. The funeral director told me Fats was struck directly in the heart, killing him instantly, like I was told by Ernest. 'Dead before his knees buckled,' is what Mr. Robinson said."

"Goodness." Mom said. "Makes me feel like it's happening all over again."

"The Gideon Funeral Home picked them both up this morning at Jimmy Osburn's Funeral Home in Wardell, because Jimmy's the county coroner. They rode side by side in the back of that hearse to Gideon. The director said it was a real odd feeling with the both of them in there, knowing one had killed the other only hours before, and they were supposed to have been real good friends."

"How much more awful can this be?" Mom said under her breath, more to herself than to anyone else.

"Nothing much more on Hokey. Shot in the chest and breathed his last in the emergency room at Hayti. The director said he basically bled to death. Damnedest thing he ever saw, he said."

"Has anything been scheduled yet?"

"No. He said he'd be talking with Fats' mother later this afternoon. Oh yes, one thing. Hokey's wake, or viewing, or whatever they call it, will be tomorrow night. Ruth said she didn't believe she could bear to have Hokey back in their house like this. Said it'd break her heart and might just kill her. The funeral service will probably be held on Tuesday." Dad sighed. "It was real hard watching her go through this."

Interrupting, I said, "I was with Dad all the time."

"Goodness," Mom said.

"Well, not all the time," Dad said. "You do remember you went to the car before we were done."

"Yes, sir, but I was there for almost all the time."

Dad ignored my comment and went on to say, "Ruth mentioned she wanted Hokey's car brought back to their house. But I convinced her it would be better, at least for now, to keep it here with the tractors. That way there would likely be a lot less gawking. I gotta see to it before the sun goes down. I don't want that car up there one more night. No telling what might happen to it. Has there been any word from the sheriff?"

"No, and there won't be. The killer's dead. What else is there to do? Did the funeral director say anything more about Hokey?"

"Only that it looked like the doctors had been digging around in his chest, trying to get at the buckshot when he died. He just lost all his blood and probably wouldn't have survived the night even if they had stopped all the leaks. By the looks of things at the bridge, he left most of his blood on the ditch-dump and in the back seat of the car. The county coroner should have a report out in a coupla weeks."

"God, but this is awful." Mom sighed.

"Have you seen Bill, Raymond, or anyone since this morning?" Dad asked.

"It was so sad. I saw Raymond walking up the road toward the bridge, but he didn't stop by here. Buddy ran along beside him for a while, but returned after a little ways. I believe Buddy could actually sense Raymond's sadness and despair. I know I could."

"Was Bill with him?"

"No, wasn't Bill with Ruth?"

"No." Dad shrugged. "Ruth said he was sick."

"I'll be," Mom said, showing her disgust with Bill's drinking.

"Has there been much traffic up at the bridge?" Dad asked.

"Some maybe. I guess. I haven't been keeping an eye on it."

"Well, I'm gonna see if Ernest is back home. I'll get him to help me get that car down here."

Hearing this I said, "I can help."

"No, you stay here with your Mom."

"Yes, sir." I was relieved. I didn't want to go to the car again today anyway. I also knew a little more about what happened, but not enough. Exactly how did Hokey die, by accident or what? Going to my room, I couldn't help it. I had to look out my window. The car still sat there, an eerie presence haunting me.

22

After supper, I went to bed early with images in my head of the death car, the murder of Fats by Hokey, Hokey's death, and the funeral home. I couldn't sleep and after a while I heard Mom and Dad in the front room, speaking in quiet tones.

"It's been an awful day," Mom said. "Let's sit for a while."

"Okay," Dad said. "I need to wind down a bit before turning in or I won't be able to sleep."

"What's happening tomorrow?"

"I don't know," Dad sighed. "I'd like to see if there're any legal issues and check on the Robinsons. The viewing is tomorrow night and, since the Busbys have no other means of transportation, we'll be taking 'em."

"It all seems like a horrible dream," Mom said. After a few moments of silence, Dad began to bring up his findings. He spoke in detail, like he was actually seeing things transpire in his mind. I found myself listening to every word.

"The truth is that Hokey killed Fats with Fats' own shotgun. Ain't that something? He killed him right there inside the Robinsons' kitchen in front of the whole family."

"Goodness," Mom continued. "It was near nine when Raymond came up here, wasn't it?"

"Yeah, *Gunsmoke* had just come on." Dad said.

"So, Hokey killed Fats at around six and took off toward his car at the log cabin. Then Raymond came here at about nine, and the car horn started after 9:30. Where was Hokey between six and 9:30?

Dad responded, "He was running for his car at the log cabin. And when his car wouldn't start, he took off for the Floodways. Then he shot himself or whatever. What with the amount of blood up there in the car and on the ditch-dump, I just don't know how he lived as long as he did. Ruth said he died at ten-thirty at Hayti. Bill, Ruth, Raymond, and Li'l Joe were all there. A highway patrol car took them to the hospital. They were there for the end."

Hearing Dad's comments, I slid out of bed in my pajamas and eased to the door, which stood partially open. Seeing me standing in the shadows of my room, Mom motioned to me. "Come on in," she said. "You may as well hear all of this, too."

Dad began. "The best I can make of it is that it all started yesterday, 'bout noon, when Hokey took Bill to Snake's Package Store in Bragg City. They purchased two or three gallons of wine and some beer, bringing it back home to suck on all day."

"Isn't that always the case," Mom said.

During Hokey's drinking spree that day, Ernest Robinson was taking it easy. He and Martha's large family, seven children still living at home, were content. On that December day, there were two visitors, Hokey and Fats.

* * *

In December the day fades fast in the Bootheel, slipping silently into sunset by 5:00 P.M. The full moon was totally obscured by clouds and a continuing drizzle, bringing darkness even sooner. The whole day seemed like twilight and was colder than it should have been, with the day's high temperature settling in at forty seven degrees and beginning to fall toward mid-afternoon. The nasty weather kept even the boll-pullers out of the fields and in the cozy confines of their homes.

The Busbys, Robinsons, and Fats had been working in the half-mile rows of the Earls' forty off County Road 285 the past week. It had been a brutal slog through mud and water for the few remaining scraps of cotton. A nine-foot cotton sack weighing three pounds and used by Helen Robinson, weighed in at sixteen pounds, due to the absorbed mud and water, bringing extreme fatigue to the most hardy of individuals. It was during that week that the mud of Pemiscot County sucked the boots right off Hokey's feet. He finished the day barefooted, his boots a memorial to the effort.

After being paid for a week of boll-pulling, a tank full of gas and a belly full of hooch kept Hokey and Fats going through a night of drinking and honky-tonkin'. They slept late, in the big red house, each rolled up in a quilt donated by their family. Waking, with no heat, little food, and a hangover, Hokey and Fats made it to the Busbys' house.

The Busby family was also cozied up in their house. Raymond was at work cleaning the family's old 10-gauge shotgun. Bill had received his money from Ruth which would find its way to Snake Howren's package store at Bragg City.

Hokey and Fats came into the house hungry. "Mom, got anything to eat?" asked Hokey.

"Don't you two have any food up there?" asked Ruth.

"Not much," said Hokey as he was checking to see if there was any coffee in the pot.

"Harry!"

"Yes, Ma'am?"

"Don't you cook for Hokey?" Ruth asked Fats with a grin.

"He don't like my cooking," said Fats.

"Mom, I don't call warming up beans 'cooking!'

"Okay, y'all wash up and I'll cook up some coffee and biscuits and gravy for ya."

"Thanks Mom," said Hokey

"Yes Ma'am, thanks a lot," said Fats.

Hokey and Fats went into the front room of the two-room house where Bill was still in bed. Raymond was cleaning the shotgun and Li'l Joe was playing with a knife.

There were two beds in the front room, with a chest-of-drawers between the two beds. Bill and Ruth slept in one bed and Raymond and Joe slept in the other. A coal stove sat in the middle of the room with a rocking chair and two straight-back chairs. In a corner of the room was a closet with a pole for hanging clothes and three shelves. A 10-gauge shotgun, an old turkey gun that had been in the Busby family for generations, normally stood in the corner of that closet.

The kitchen had a propane cook stove, a big round table, a dry sink to prepare food, and an old Kelvinator refrigerator. On the back lean-to porch, a hand pump supplied the water.

After breakfast, Hokey said to Fats, "Let's go."

"Where ya going?" asked Bill.

"We're headed to Snake's, wanna go?"

"Hell yes," chuckled Bill. "I need my medicine."

"Well, let's go."

"Ruth, give me some money for my medicine," Bill pleaded.

Ruth, her eyes wide and questioning, walked into the front room and, looking at Bill, said, "Are you gonna start that again?"

"Yeah, Mom," said Hokey, teasing Ruth. "Give him some money, Mom. You know you will."

"You know this has been a bad year for drankin' money and who knows when we'll have more work."

"Don't be like that," said Bill. "Fred always has work to do."

"Don't be so sure, It's been a bad year all way round, even for Mr. Walker."

During this conversation, Raymond was talking with Fats in the front room. "So, you're thinking about leaving?"

"Yep, the work has done gone and there won't be much boll pulling after we finish up with the forty. I can get wood cutting work up in Zalma and make good money."

"Who do you know up in Zalma?"

"Some kin folks, a step-brother."

"I didn't know you had a step-brother?"

"Yeah. He lives in Zalma, north of Puxico. I can get work up there but I ain't leaving today. I'd kinda like to see Alma Faye again. We went to the drive-in at Holcomb a while ago,"

"Yeah?"

"Yeah. Hokey and Arlena and me and Alma Faye. I call her Nanny Goo-Goo."

"Why would you call her that?"

"Well, when she holds her baby brother, she always says 'goo goo' to him, just like a doting nanny. So, I just started calling her Nanny Goo-Goo."

"That's funny."

"Fats!" Hokey yelled. "Let's go."

"Where we going?"

"Goddamnit, to the big city. Dad's going with us."

Grinning, Fats said to Raymond, "Well, the boss said we gotta get drunk." Then, with a big full laugh, he said, "I sure do dread it," and laughed out loud. "Let's go!"

"Now, y'all be careful," called Ruth as she followed the trio out on the porch.

"I will, I will," hollered Hokey.

"Mom," Raymond said, "did you know that Fats is thinking about leaving for work somewhere else?"

"No, I didn't. But, if I was him, I'd sure leave." Ruth turned and went back into the kitchen.

"Mom," called Raymond, "we got any shotgun shells left somewhere? I think I'll go hunting."

"In this bad weather?"

"Yeah, I'd like to go to the Floodways."

"No, we don't have any more shells."

"Ok. Guess I'll just go anyway."

"Okay, be careful."

* * *

Snake's package store was a small, white, stand-alone frame building with a stockade-like structure attached to the back. It stood on the west side of South Main Street in Bragg City, apart from the other merchants on the short street. It was a prime location for those serious drinkers who preferred their liquor straight from the bottle, discreetly wrapped in a brown paper bag.

Bill, Hokey, and Fats bought up a few gallons of wine, some Stag beer, and Camel non-filter cigarettes, one of Hokey's favorite brands.

Hokey, as soon as he got into the car, hollered out "Yippee, here I come again!" Fats laughed and Bill spilled some wine he was drinking on his overalls when Hokey floored the big V8 engine.

"Hey Hoke, take a look at your gas gauge. Does it work... or are we outta gas?"

Hokey glanced down at the gauge bouncing on empty. "Don't worry. I've drove this car halfway 'cross Missouri on less than that."

"Okay," said Fats. "If we run outta gas, who's gonna do the walking to get more?"

"Why, you of course. Ha!" laughed Hokey.

After letting Bill and his wine off at the Busby house, Hokey asked Fats, "You got anywhere you gotta go today?"

"Why, no. What you got in mind?"

"We could head down to Gobler, the B&B, where they party all weekend, or we could spend some time at the Robinsons."

"That seals it, let's go to the Robinsons'," Fats said with a full laugh. He drained the last of his beer, wiped his mouth with his sleeve and hurled the bottle out the window. It crashed onto the gravel road.

Due to the wet and muddy conditions, no car could make it over the half-mile ditch-dump road that ran alongside Feeder Ditch 68 from County Road 228 to the Robinsons' house, a small, red brick-siding shotgun style house. This caused them to make a three-mile loop when normally the trip would have taken a few minutes.

Hokey told Fats, "Now, let's just keep this booze here in the car and don't let on you're drinking. Mr. Robinson won't put up with it."

"Yeah, I know. But we hadn't had but a couple of beers."

"I know, but if you want a drink, just make an excuse and come to the car and get one."

"You bet," Fats said.

Inside the Robinson house, the roar of Hokey's car was unmistakable. "I think Hokey just drove up," Arlena cried without looking outside.

The remainder of the day saw Hokey as the only one making excuses about going to his car, between games of checkers and managing to spend some time with Arlena. He sucked down wine rather than beer because he believed wine didn't smell as bad on his breath.

Donald Ray "Hokey" Busby, 18 years old and sister, Betty Sue (By permission of Betty Busby Robinson)

Bill and Ruth Busby early 1970s

Billy Joe "Li'l Joe" Busby, 8 years old at time of murder.

Harry Leslie "Fats" Shell & Dog (By Permission of Huddleston Family)

File photo of 1947 Ford Coupe with Flat Head V8, model driven by Donald "Hokey" Busby

Elsie Shell-Huddleston, Mother of Harry (by Permission of Huddleston Family)

Harry / "Fats" and Elsie in Front Of Their Home in Clarkton (By Permission of Huddleston Family)

Harry Leslie "Fats" Shell and Mildred, his sister and half-sisters Sallie, Alice and Dallie Huddleston. Photo was taken outside of their home in Clarkton, MO. The same house in which Harry's wake would later be held. (By Permission of Huddleston Family)

Robinson Group Picture, 1956 First Row (L to R): Martha holding Bobby, Helen Violet Louise, Ernest "Buddy" – Second row (L to R): Arlena, Alma Faye, Ernest (father) – Third Row (L to R): Charles, Johnny, Marie, Joe (By Permission of the Robinson Family)

Fred & Glenda Walker - Christmas, 1957 (By Permission of the Walker Family)

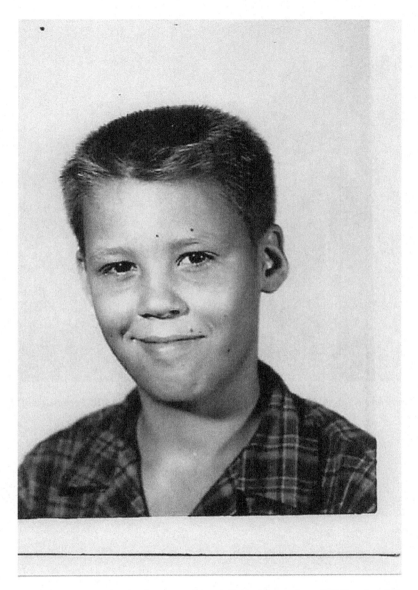

Harold G. Walker (Author) Age Twelve, 1957 (By Permission of Walker Family)

Johnny on His Horse, Paint, and Harold holding the reins of Rebel (By Permission of the Walker Family)

Buddy, my dog who was with me throughout all of my adventures on the Floodways,is seen here traversing Swift Ditch / Canal 251 from west to east. His head is held low to the railroad ties, assuring sure footing as one of our barn cats, in the foreground, faces him.

Arlena   Hokey

Ernest
Robinson

Fats   Charles   Helen   Alma Faye

December 7, 1957

DEATH SCENE

Illustration by Cal Chambers

My brother stands where the Bloody Wallow was located, alongside Feeder Ditch 68, looking west, with the floodways running north-south in the background.

Cotton ready to pick, with Floodways in far background.

Swift Ditch / Canal 251, May 1961, during Flood Season

Canal 1 / Old Floodway

Canal 258 / Bay Ditch

Clarkton Baptist Church: Where the double funeral Took Place

Pastor Wayne Wood, First Baptist Church, Clarkton, Missouri (By Permission of Maria Wood Chamberlain)

Reverend Herbert Junior Crane , Tatum Chapel (By Permission of Crane Family)

Author Standing at Hokey's Grave – Sumach Public Cemetery, Holcomb, Missouri. Note Catalpa Tree with Intertwined cypress Tree.

Rusted Pipe and Iron Fence Post marks The Grave of Donald "Hokey" Busby.

Harry Leslie "Fats" Shell Lying in Wake at the Shell – Huddleson Home in Clarkton – December 9, 1957. (By Permission of Huddleston Family)

Harry "Fats" Shell's unmarked grave is near this white shed in Stanfield Public Cemetery as told to Harry's half-sister, Alice "Allie" Huddleston-Pratt, by Elsie Huddleston, her mother.

"Harold writing down notes while getting his book ready. Raymond is taking it all in with a diet Dr. Pepper in his hand. Harold is like a long lost brother that just came home." - Helen Busby

23

The front room of the Robinson house was furnished with a sofa, a chair, a bed, a television set covered with a bed-sheet, and a rocking chair, all situated around a pot-belly coal stove. The front door had been sealed for the winter, to keep the cold north wind out of the house. The only entrance into the house was through the back door that opened directly into the kitchen.

Ladder-back chairs stood around the kitchen table in the center of the room, taking up most of the space. A propane cook stove was next to the kitchen cabinets and the kitchen sink where dishes were washed. A refrigerator hummed in a far corner of the room.

The drizzly day continued as the temperature began to drop. Checkers and popcorn had been the entertainment and everyone was jovial. The baby, Bobby, at one-and-a-half years old, was the center of attention as he was watched over by his four sisters, including Violet who was five years old, and his brother Buddy who was seven. Mrs. Robinson, Martha, had not been feeling well and was in bed resting for much of the day.

A taste of wine churned inside Hokey like a bolt of lightning from a clear blue sky. His eyes began to glass over and a peculiar glow appeared as from an internal flame. His words became slower. With the night coming quickly, Hokey was ready to leave the serenity of the Robinsons' house and begin a wild rout as his blood turned mean.

Fats, who had abstained from drinking since arriving, was alert and jovial and prepared to spend his evening with the Robinsons. The Robinsons might even go visit their neighbor's house, Archie and Lois Kilburn, who lived on a nearby farm, to watch television, especially to see *Gunsmoke* at nine o'clock.

About four o'clock, Hokey said to Fats, "I think we oughta be going."

Mr. Robinson, hearing this, said, "Why don't y'all stay for supper?"

"Thank you," Hokey said, "but I think we've taken up too much of your time today."

"Don't be silly, we love having you boys here."

Arlena said, "We're having macaroni with commodity cheese (processed cheese for use in domestic programs), pork chops, and tea at about five. It's real good."

Twelve year old Helen added, "I made a cake, too."

Alma Faye, who was almost fourteen asked Fats, "Why don't ya stay?"

"Hokey's got the car, and if I stay, I'm gonna have to walk through the mud to our place in the dark."

"Daddy, can you take Fats home if he stays for supper?"

"Sure," said Mr. Robinson. "I can or Charles can."

"Yeah, I can do that," responded Charles.

Hokey said, "I can see I'm gonna be outflanked on this. But, all the same, we gotta go."

"Hoke, I don't know," Fats said. "Having a good supper sounds pretty good to me."

Hokey, beginning to get red around his neck and face, said in a coarse whisper to Fats, "You're coming with me. We got things to do."

"Hokey, I think I'll just stay here for a while. I'll get back to the house okay."

Hokey walked to the back door through the kitchen as Fats followed behind him. Hokey said one more time, "Goddammit, I told you what we're doing, we got some honky-tonkin' to do."

"Naw, Hoke, I'm staying. I don't need no trouble tonight. Don't worry, I'll be okay here."

"Okay, goddammit, I'm done here." Then, stopping for a moment, Hokey looked directly in Fats' eyes with as cold a look as any had ever seen and said, "You sure all you want here is supper?"

"Now, Hokey, don't go thinking that. I like Alma Faye and you know that."

Hokey said nothing more. He turned his back on Fats and walked out the back door. The day was fading fast as the clouds hung low and drizzle seemed like it'd go on all night. The Ford roared to life and spun its way back to 285 and to Hokey's parents' house.

Hokey made no secret of his drinking at home. Bill was near passed out on one of the beds in the front room. Raymond sat in the kitchen, whittling on a stick, and Li'l Joe played with a toy car.

Ruth could tell the moment Hokey arrived that he was upset and becoming more and more agitated. He drank more wine, asking Raymond if he would drink with him. Raymond had seen this scenario played out over and over and he expected what might happen next. Ever since Hokey shot Ol' Tom, he knew. Nothing good was coming.

At about 5:00 p.m., Hokey began to babble, speaking in a strange manner that made no sense. Ruth heard it. Raymond heard it and, with Bill passed out and dreaming, it was Ruth who tried to defuse the situation.

It was as though demons injected evil into his very being. He began to mutter, questioning non-existent entities. "Why? Why was it that Fats stayed at the Robinsons?" Most peculiar to Ruth and Raymond was Hokey's heightened concern that Arlena was the object of Fats' desire, and that it was Fats' plan to be with her.

He spoke of the betrayal he was suffering, and that there was only one way to deal with it. To kill Fats.

Hokey's anger distorted his face into a twisted grimace, and his eyes narrowed. He glowed from within, a phenomenon Ruth had seen before.

Bill, too drunk to notice or care about any such change, would rather sleep. Raymond, however, took note. With Ruth's eyes giving him permission, he left the house with Lil' Joe to sit on the porch in the cold. He hoped Hokey would simply leave and return to the house where he and Fats were batching, to sleep it off, just as he had done many times before. Yet this time seemed oddly similar to the last few minutes of Ol' Tom's and the gar's life.

Hokey stared into nothingness. His mind sank deeper into the abyss. His mental image of Fats and Arlena being together became real to him. The imagined betrayal by Fats overwhelmed him. To be made to look like a fool by trusting Fats, his best friend, was more than he could stand.

"I'm gonna kill Fats," shouted Hokey.

Her worst fears being realized, Ruth knew this was no idle threat. Hokey didn't make idle threats. Ruth looked to Bill, who was stretched out on the bed in a semi-conscious state.

Outweighing Bill by fifty pounds, Ruth grabbed him by the shoulders, pulled him up off the bed, and led him into the kitchen, away from Hokey. Bill stumbled into the kitchen table causing the salt and pepper shakers and the forks and spoons, to tumble onto the floor. Trying not to be overheard by Hokey, she whispered as loud as she dared into Bill's ear, "Listen."

"What do you want? Go away," he slurred while trying to pull away from Ruth's grip.

"No, you old drunk. Be quiet and you listen good. Hokey just said he's gonna kill Fats."

Bill staggered backward, losing his balance, stumbling as he tried to focus with a puzzled look on his red swollen face, "What're you talking about? Fats ain't here."

"I told you to be quiet. Hokey said he's gonna kill Fats and he means it."

With his mouth slightly open, gulping air, Bill opened and closed his eyes while running his fingers through his graying hair. As Ruth's words sank into his brain, he cried out, "Oh no."

"Shut up, he'll hear you! We have to do something."

Bill held his stomach and began to feel sick. He found it too hard to think. Ruth overheard Hokey muttering something about getting a shotgun and realized it was up to her to handle this by herself. Returning to the front room, she saw Hokey retrieving the 10-gauge from the closet.

"Donald, leave the shotgun alone."

"Shut up! Where're the shells?"

"We ain't got none."

"The hell we don't, we always have shells."

Raymond yelled from the front porch, "We ain't lately had the money to buy anymore shells."

Hokey continued running his hands deep into each drawer of the chest-of-drawers, pushing and pulling on clothing, and looking and feeling into every nook and cranny. He soon stopped searching, stood silent, then announced, "I know where I can get a shotgun and shells," and headed for the door.

"Donald," Ruth cried as she tried to block his way, "Don't go."

"Get outta my way, goddammit! I'll do as I please and I got good reason. I'm gonna get him."

"I'll not let you kill Fats for any reason."

Seeing this plea didn't work, she tried another appeal. "Donald, just don't go. The weather is awful. Stay here and everything will be okay in the morning. Anyway, you'll probably get your car stuck if you try to drive tonight."

"I won't get stuck. I can drive anywhere I want, when I want."

Ruth cringed as Hokey brushed past her toward the door. This was the last thing she wanted to happen, again recalling the day he killed Ol' Tom. That day he was also outraged for no good reason; he just killed without warning, without waiting. This time was different, though. There was warning. She thought if she could keep him home, he'd go to sleep and it would be all right when he woke.

The time was 5:30 p.m., the sun had set and the night was becoming ink-like. Ruth followed Hokey out the house. She grabbed hold of his motorcycle jacket but he pulled away. The drizzle turned into a shower of half-frozen rain, pelting her face as she made her way down the steps of the porch. She stepped into the blue-black darkness, begging Hokey not to go, hoping and praying his car wouldn't start.

"Don't go, Hokey, don't go, I love you, please don't go." She stood in the rain, her shoulders stooped; tears and droplets of rain mixed, running down her face. Her last gasp was, "Why? What did he do to you? He's your friend! God help us!"

"Shut up," he hollered, his blood running cold, "I'm gonna kill that son-of-a-bitch," resonated in the rain.

There was no more response from Hokey. He jumped into his car, slammed the door shut, turned the ignition key, flipped on the headlights and began backing out into the road. Ruth, still in the yard, placed her hand on the edge of the open porch to steady herself.

Raymond rushed to her side, pleading to his mother, "Come on Mom. We can't stop him." Raymond helped Ruth back up on the porch. "Maybe nothing will happen. Maybe he's just shooting off his mouth and when he gets to where he and Fats are staying, he'll just lay down and go to sleep."

Ruth, wiping tears from her eyes, said in halting speech, "I pray you're right."

Hokey, skilled from years of driving on muddy back roads while drunk or sober, backed the big black coupe onto the road, taking particular care not to back too far and end up in the ditch on the opposite side. Handling the stick shift like a pro, he skillfully pulled forward, heading north. Once the sixteen-inch balloon tires settled into the ruts, he lightly gunned the engine. The car began to weave a little. By instinct, he eased up on the accelerator a bit to maintain control of the car and headed to the bridge.

Gathering her wits about her, Ruth, with Raymond's help, re-entered the house where Bill had collapsed on the bed. She grabbed him by the shoulders, shook him and cried out, "Wake up! Wake up!" Bill moaned while managing to slightly open his bleary, reddened eyes.

"We have to do something," She yelled.

Bill tried to focus on what Ruth was saying, but it proved too much for him, and he simply slipped back into a deep sleep.

Raymond saw his dad passed out on the bed, empty wine jugs on the floor, and his mother wiping tears from her swollen eyes. He asked, "What are we going to do?"

"Wait," she whispered as she looked out the north-facing window and watched the glow of the red tail lights on Hokey's car grow smaller. "Just wait."

* * *

Hokey, eyes ablaze, handled his car like a master. Drive easy, he counseled himself. Shift easy through the three speeds, he thought. No, stay in second gear, keep the rpm steady; stay in the ruts; never get out of the ruts.

At the cars steady speed of 15–20 mph, the windshield wipers worked perfectly, marking time. Don't do anything to draw attention, he thought. Glide by the Walker house, don't accelerate, let the engine purr, not rumble.

With his left hand on the steering wheel, he managed to pull a pack of cigarettes out of the side pocket of the black motorcycle jacket he wore, the one he bought from Johnny. As he shook the pack of Camels, an unfiltered cigarette popped up. He placed the cigarette pack to his mouth and pulled the pack away, returning it to his jacket pocket. He reached forward, pushed in the car's cigarette lighter and, in moments, it popped back out. He pulled the lighter out of the dash and pushed the glowing end of the lighter coil onto the cigarette's tip. The orange glow transferred from the lighter to the cigarette. He took a deep drag while putting the lighter back into the dash. The cigarette dangled from the edge of his mouth brightening each time he drew smoke deep into his lungs, holding the smoke a bit, letting it flow out through his nostrils, reassuring him, empowering him.

Both his hands rested on the steering wheel. He felt for and found a half-full bottle of wine on the passenger's side. He needed another drink. His thoughts were dulled but focused. His driving skills undiminished, his rage sustained. He thought to himself, that shotgun is somewhere in that big red house.

24

Arriving at the plank bridge, Hokey was careful to back the car into a small graveled parking area on the ditch-dump just west of the road next to the abandoned log cabin. Good, he thought. When his bloody work was done, he'd not have to back out into the darkness; he could drive forward and see where he was going.

Where would he run to? He'd think about that later. He could let nothing distract him from what he had to do. Shutting the engine off, he held the key in the palm of his hand, then pushed it deep into his jean's pocket.

Looking in all directions, he saw nothing that would make him suspect anyone was near. He could see the soft lights at our house down the road. Everyone was inside and their car was gone. There was no one to see him or stop him. He began making his way some 200 feet east along a muddy footpath on the rutted ditch-dump, to the house where he and Fats were baching.

Following a hard day's work in the fields, Hokey and Fats would often sit and talk with Mr. Robinson, Charles, and Arlena, if she were available. On many occasions, Hokey and Fats would sit in the Robinsons' kitchen, laughing and gossiping with Arlena and her sisters.

Hokey occasionally visited with Arlena alone when the Robinson family had gone to town. Arlena would remain home to do chores and take care of the baby. The rendezvous were known and facilitated by confidants who never betrayed their trust. In the unique parlance of the Bootheel, Hokey was "staunch on Arlena."

It was near 5:30 and, being December, it had been dark for more than an hour. The Robinsons and Fats were finishing their supper. Fats was content as he and Mr. and Mrs. Robinson and Charles retired from the kitchen into the living room. Charles stoked the fire in the potbellied stove and the warmth wrapped around them like a cozy blanket. Arlena, Alma Faye, and Helen were laughing and playing as they cleared the table, getting ready to wash the dishes. Mrs. Robinson, who had been in bed, held the baby, then sat him on the floor. The almost two-year-old Bobby made his toddling way to Fats who was sitting in a rocker near the doorway that opened into the kitchen. Fats reached for the toddler who held his arms high. Fats picked him up and sat him in his lap. The talk was about the looming new year coming year and the past bad year. Money was short and boll-pulling wouldn't last all winter.

"I think I'll see if I can get some work cutting up firewood," Fats said. "This boll-pulling in them half mile rows, in mud and water, is the toughest work I ever done for little to no money. Last week, Helen weighed her cotton, and after it was emptied into the trailer, the sack itself weighed sixteen pounds. Twelve pounds of mud and water and three pounds of cotton sack. I ain't never seen nothin' like that before."

"That's right," chimed in Charles. "That mud's nasty. Made you feel like your feet were glued in place. I don't care if we can't get back into the fields."

While listening to both Fats and Charles, Mr. Robinson had taken time to light his pipe. Sucking on the stem, getting the tobacco burning, he took the pipe from his mouth and while not looking at anyone in particular, he began. "I don't blame ya' for looking for better work." Now looking at Fats. "This year's been an all-round bust. I think Mr. Walker has gone the distance on this one too. Four plantings with little more than stalk to show for it." Mr. Robinson paused to work his pipe and continued. "I know I've gone the distance. It's time to hole up and wait till next planting time."

"Ya think Hokey's gonna stay on?" asked Mrs. Robinson of Fats.

Fats replied, "Ya just never know about Hoke. He can be going one way real strong and the slightest breeze will blow him in a whole new direction you never thought of."

* * *

Hokey knew where the weapon would be in the big red house where he and Fats bached. He picked up Fats' 16-gauge, single-barrel, break-open shotgun, the same one he'd hunted with on many occasions, the same one he had held behind the door when Trooper Hickman came for him. Hokey loaded it with .004 buckshot, placed several shells in his coat pocket, and dropped some on the floor. He had a half mile yet to walk, to sober up, to re-think what he was doing, but the rage could only be extinguished by blood. Walking onto the porch, he looked east. He could see soft lights in the distance, the Robinson house, as he began his walk through the ditch-dump's muck and mud.

At approximately 5:45, Hokey approached the small house. The soft lights flickered. He stood by the west window of the kitchen, looking in through the rain. He stood at that window for maybe a half hour, as proven by the number of Camel cigarette butts found below the sill and the cowboy boot prints leading to and from the window. He listened to the voices, easily distinguishing Fats' and Arlena's voices as the cold, wet drizzle pelted his face. His rage, rather than easing, was stoked by the conversations inside, increasing the deep rage he felt in his belly.

Quietly, he walked to the rear door. Twisting the doorknob, he found it unlocked. Gripping his shotgun, he stepped back, cocked the hammer and took a deep breath.

Soaked with mud and drizzle, he pushed the door open with the barrel of the gun. Hokey walked into the Robinsons' kitchen with the shotgun leveled and his finger on the trigger.

He took short, steady strides, holding the shotgun at his waist, the business end of the barrel pointing directly into the house.

Alma Faye and Helen saw him first, then Arlena. Their initial smiles faded into a trance-like state of terror. The rest of the family and Fats were in the front room. The immediate silence in the kitchen and the cold air rushing into the cozy rooms alerted Fats and the rest of the family.

It was between six and six-thirty

Where Arlena, Helen, and Alma Faye were working, the direct path into the living room was blocked. Hokey had to move to his left to pass between the kitchen table and the west wall, past the window he had been looking through from the outside just a few moments before. He could see into the front room where Fats sat in a rocking chair holding Bobby. He called for Fats through clinched teeth: "I've come for you, Harry!"

Feeling the rush of cold air, and hearing the gasps of Helen and Alma Faye, Ernest Robinson sensed something was very wrong. He went to the doorway between the front room and kitchen at the same moment Hokey called for Fats. Ernest began to talk to Hokey, moving to his right around the kitchen table in the center of the room, to block Hokey's progress. To protect his family, Ernest tried to get close enough to Hokey to push up the gun barrel so that if the trigger was pulled, the shotgun would discharge into the ceiling. "Hokey, put the shotgun down, there's no need for this," he said soothingly as he moved slowly toward Hokey. Mr. Robinson knew Hokey wouldn't be able to reload before they'd be on him if the gun discharged into the ceiling.

Hokey recognized what was happening and turned the shotgun toward Mr. Robinson. He said, with no inflection, "Don't come any closer, Mr. Robinson." The words cold, unyielding.

Mr. Robinson stopped but appealed to Hokey, "Hokey, you don't want to do this. Fats is your friend and if you do this, they'll hang you sure."

Fats sat Bobby down on the floor and rose from the rocker to his full height. Mrs. Robinson grabbed Bobby and hurried into a back bedroom with Violet and Bobby following her. Fats moved cautiously into the kitchen doorway. Charles followed close behind, his eyes peering over Fats' left shoulder.

Seeing Fats, Hokey's face contorted in hate. Hokey held the shotgun at his waist, pointed directly at Fats who seemed in complete control of himself, showing no fear or nervousness. The hammer was cocked and ready. The slightest pressure would now loose a deadly spray of lead.

Hokey and Fats stood face to face, across the kitchen table from each other, with six feet of space between them. The bare light bulb shadowed their bodies against the walls. Fats looked directly into Hokey's face, his hands palms up and out to his sides in an innocent gesture. "Hokey, what have I ever done to you?"

Hokey's eyes flashed. The only sounds were the nervous shuffling of feet, sobs of terror, and the rain pelting the tin roof. The moment seemed frozen in time as Arlena moved from the kitchen sink around the table, begging Hokey not to shoot. She tenderly placed her right hand on his right shoulder and begged Hokey to put the gun down. Fats appeared to take a deep breath, maybe to say something in defense of his life as Hokey's trigger finger tightened.

The gun exploded with a thunderous roar.

The full charge crashed into Fats' left shirt pocket, striking a Zippo lighter, pushing it some three inches into and through his heart. The sound ricocheted throughout the small house, causing a temporary loss of hearing coupled with a ringing in the ears as the smell of gunsmoke filled the room. The children wailed and the adults stood in stunned silence.

The impact of the load was akin to the impact of a cannon. The ounce of steel pellets had no opportunity to spread out as it came at Fats at nearly 1,200 feet per second like a fist of steel. The charge momentarily lifted Fats off the floor even as his knees buckled. A reflexive kick by his feet pushed him back into Charles as he fell on his back.

The impact of more than 200 pounds of dead weight slamming onto the plank floor caused the small frame house to shudder. Fats' only movement was the post-mortem twitching of his left leg and the fingers on his right hand. A dark stain began to saturate his shirt, then the floor, as blood poured out of him. His eyes hollowed, staring into nothingness.

They all stood, unable to move, frozen in terror as the moment took root. The strong smell of gunsmoke hung in the room and the ringing in their ears refused to subside.

In some, the ringing lasted for months. In others, it lasted longer. Charles, who stood directly behind Fats, looking over Fats' shoulder, was temporarily deafened by the concussion, causing him not to be able to hear the blast. Blood seeped from his nose for weeks.

Hokey, not saying a word, backed out of the house. "He was gone, like a puff of wind," recalled Helen. The yellowish light from the small wattage bulb in the kitchen followed him to the edge of darkness where he dissolved into the night, an evil entity returning from whence he came, a murderer on the run.

Hokey's tracks told the tale. He ran west through the cotton field, avoiding the ditch-dump but not the mud. With each step, he left deep imprints, revealing long strides.

25

Mr. Robinson gathered his dazed family into the family car and drove to Archie and Lois Kilbourne's house on a nearby farm, leaving Fats' body where he fell. After ensuring the safety of his family, Mr. Robinson and Charles, accompanied by Archie, drove the five miles to Bragg City where he reported the murder by telephone to the Sheriff's office in Caruthersville.

Convincing the Sheriff's communications officer that there was a shotgun killing on a remote far-west farm on the Floodways was not an easy proposition. The population of Pemiscot County in 1957 was near 50,000. Clyde Orton was the Sheriff and there were only two patrolling deputies for the entire county.

As with most Saturday nights, the deputies were extremely busy on the southeasterly side of the county that included Caruthersville, Hayti, and Steele. The deputies didn't like to stray into the remote western area of the county near the Floodways, preferring the Missouri State Highway Patrol assist them in that area, which they most often did. Mr. Robinson vehemently denied his call was in any way a hoax finally convincing them. The communications officer accepted the report and promised to send out a deputy as soon as one became available.

Mr. Robinson gave directions to his house and was told that the coroner, Jimmy Osburn, would be notified to go to the site of the murder and that he, Mr. Robinson, should return to his house.

Chief Deputy Sheriff Charles Albert Faris, called "Charles Albert," in keeping with the southern tradition of using both the first and middle name or simply by his initials, "C.F." was a hardened, no-nonsense deputy and well-known lawman in that rugged county. He was notified by the sheriff's radio operator to go to the murder site, using the directions provided by Mr. Robinson.

Deputy Junior Upchurch, a radio operator, not a patrol officer, volunteered to go with deputy Faris, just in case. However, due to communication and coordination difficulties, it was an hour or so before Faris and Upchurch got underway. Once both deputies were in the patrol car, they sped across the county from the Mississippi River at Caruthersville to the Robinson house.

Before the deputies arrived at the murder scene, the coroner, Jimmy Osburn, arrived at the Robinson house with his helper, Harry Fields. It was nearly 8:00 p.m. The cold drizzle continued as the hearse, sinking down into the soft gravel of the ditch-dump road, made its slow way to the Robinson house. Mr. Robinson and Charles were there to meet them.

"Have the Sheriff's deputies already been here?" asked Osburn.

"Why no," Mr. Robinson said. "You're the first to get here."

"What? You mean the killer is still loose and around here somewhere?"

"That would be Donald Busby, but he ain't in the house if that's what you mean. I don't know where he went, probably long gone from here by now."

"Let's hurry up and get out of here. Tell the deputies I'll have this one at Wardell if they need to see him." Osburn's hands shook uncontrollably.

It required all four men: the coroner, his assistant, Ernest and Charles to lift Fats' body and get it on the gurney. A heavy layer of blood on the linoleum outlined the upper portion of Fats' body. The blood had begun to congeal and turn color from bright red to a dark brown.

The four men strained under the weight of the gurney with Fats on it, their feet sinking deep into the mud. The sheet covering Fats' face slipped off, revealing the stark stare of his last breath.

* * *

At 8:30 p.m., Ruth said to Raymond, "It's been too long. Bird, go now and tell Fred. Tell him everything. Tell him Hokey's gone to kill Fats. He'll know what to do. Now go."

Raymond hesitated, making sure he heard correctly, "What exactly do you want me to tell Fred?"

Looking at Bill, shaking her head back and forth, she said, "Just tell him Hokey has gone to kill Fats!"

Raymond pulled on his jacket and hunting cap, hugged his mom and told Li'l Joe to stay in the house. Then he left to walk the quarter-mile to our house.

At about this same time, Deputies Faris and Upchurch arrived at the Robinson house. The deputies questioned Mr. Robinson and Charles. They used flashlights to follow Hokey's footprints into the cotton field, heading west toward the house where he and Fats had been batching.

Deputy Faris had a reputation for being a tenacious man-hunter. In later years, Faris said that upon seeing the murder scene and getting the story from Mr. Robinson and Charles, he had the feeling that it was going to be an old fashioned manhunt with dogs, long days and longer nights before they would be able to drag Hokey out of the Floodways dead or alive.

He put out a radio call to the Sheriff's Office in Caruthersville, confirming the killing, identifying the location, and naming the killer of Harry Leslie "Fats" Shell as Donald Ray "Hokey" Busby.

While Deputies Faris and Upchurch were at the Robinson house, at a little past 9:00 p.m., Raymond was walking up to our house. "Hi, Buddy," he said as he hurried up the steps and walked across the porch to the door. He paused briefly, looked toward the bridge, then back to the door, and knocked. When Raymond finished talking to Dad, he returned home.

The Busbys also heard the car horn from the direction of the plank bridge.

"Mom," said Raymond, "that's Hokey's car at the bridge. I recognize the sound of that horn, I gotta go up there, I gotta help him."

"No! You're not going anywhere. I'm not going to risk losing you. Hokey's drunk and we don't know what's happened. You're staying here and that's my last word on it."

"That ain't right," Raymond said as he ran out on the front porch and stared into the darkness toward the bridge. Hearing a speeding car coming from the south, Raymond ran back into the house.

Within moments after the horn stopped, Deputy Faris, driving as fast as conditions allowed, slid to a stop in front of the Busby house. Leaving his headlights on, he used his automobile search light to scan the area. He saw there was no car in the small driveway and went directly to the front door with his flashlight in one hand and his revolver in the other.

Deputy Upchurch circled around to the back of the house all the while shining his flashlight around and under the house, looking for any movement—any eyes that might reflect the light. Satisfied there was no one hiding in the yard or in the privy, Upchurch followed the path from the privy to the Cotton Belt tracks just behind the house. He saw nothing, no fresh tracks in the mud. He made his way back to the rear of the house and steadied his light on the back door.

Meanwhile, Ruth opened the front door for Deputy Faris, her eyes wide and searching. "Yes, sir," she haltingly said.

"Mrs. Busby?" Faris asked.

"Yes, sir," Ruth said, opening the door farther. "Come in." Faris, his weapon drawn, his finger on the trigger stepped inside the house. All of Ruth's fears rained down on her and she felt herself go numb.

"Mom," said Raymond, stepping back from the door to the center of the room.

"Who are you?" came the pointed question from Deputy Faris to Raymond. Faris had no idea what Hokey looked like.

"I'm not Donald, I'm Raymond. Verlan Raymond Busby, Donald's brother." Raymond's eyes widened, his face now covered with sweat, and he felt his heart beating against his chest.

"You sure you're not Donald?" Faris questioned with his handgun leveled.

"That's my boy, Raymond." Ruth cried.

"Who's that in the bed?"

"That's my husband, Bill."

"Get 'em up and get those covers off him...Y'all got any guns in here?"

"Yes, sir," Ruth said. "We got an old shotgun."

"Where is it?"

Ruth began walking to the closet where the shotgun was kept. "Ma'am, don't go to the gun, point to it."

Ruth stopped and pointed weakly toward the closet where the gun was leaning.

There was a knock at the back door. "Charles Albert," a voice yelled out.

"Yo," Faris responded.

"It's me, Junior."

"Come on in," Faris yelled, "all's clear."

"The door's locked!"

"Raymond, let him in," Ruth said.

"No!" Faris shouted. "Mrs. Busby, you let him in."

Lying in the other bed, Li'l Joe, his eyes wide and darting were visible just above the top quilt on the bed.

Bill woke, rolled over, and, upon seeing the deputy Faris, his mouth gaped open. "Oh no," he cried as he managed to sit upright on the side of the bed, his feet on the floor, his hair in affray, his head in his hands.

When Deputy Upchurch entered the front room, Faris directed him to, "Check that closet for a shotgun."

Junior moved cautiously to the closet, as Ruth pointed.

"It's here," Upchurch said, reaching into the hanging clothes and picking up the old 10-gauge. He broke open the breech, smelled for fresh cordite and said, "Damn, how old is this gun?"

"It's real old," Raymond said, having recovered from his initial fright. "But it still works. I rabbit hunt with it all the time."

"Got any shells for this gun?" Upchurch asked as he broke down the shotgun and smelled the breach.

"No. We're out of shells."

Deputy Faris, holstered his pistol, placed is hands on his hips and squared his jaw. Where's Hokey?

"Why?" Raymond said.

"Raymond," snapped Ruth, "just answer the question."

"Why?" Deputy Faris said. "Cause he blew a hole in a fellow named Harry Shell. Killed him dead as hell."

Ruth went limp and sat down. Tears flooded her face, rolling down her cheeks. Bill openly sobbed, reaching for Li'l Joe and holding him tight cried, "Oh God. No."

The questioning began. Deputies Faris and Upchurch learned more about Hokey. About the day-long drinking spree. About the girlfriend, and

Hokey's jealous rage against Fats. They learned where Hokey's car could be found. They heard about the braying horn.

Faris and Upchurch jumped into their squad car. Upchurch put out a radio call giving their location and detailing what they had learned. He reported that he and Deputy Faris were hopefully closing in on Hokey. This call was picked up by Missouri State Highway Patrol Officer Jeffery M. Hickman, who responded to the Caruthersville Sheriff's Office that he was near Pascola and was familiar with the area. He said he was going to assist.

At 9:50 p.m., Deputies Faris and Upchurch headed for the Plank bridge, splashing water and mud up into our yard as they raced by. Approaching the bridge, they saw the darkened log cabin and a black car backed into the short driveway by the cabin. Their heartbeats quickened from the adrenalin rush.

Faris turned the squad car into the parked car, bumper to bumper, blocking any attempt by Hokey to leave. He flooded the area around the log cabin with his search light. The beam danced across the field of brown stalks, the ditch-dump and into Feeder Ditch 68.

"I'll check the car, you check under the bridge first then the shack," directed Faris. Deputy Upchurch, although a communications officer, was every inch a lawman. Both knew they were hunting a killer. There would be no warning shots.

Deputy Upchurch, after clearing the space under the bridge, kicked the door open to the log cabin. After a few moments, he yelled out, "No one in this place. I don't believe anyone has lived here in years, it's a dump."

Deputy Faris, gun drawn, finger on the trigger, eased up to the black car. "Donald," he hollered out. "If you're in there, raise your hands and come on out." Faris peered inside, shining a beam of light from his heavy flashlight into the dark interior.

"Damn, Junior, he's here!" hollered Faris. "Donald's here in the car!"

Hokey's black motorcycle jacket was open. Thick blood saturating his shirt had begun to gel. Bright red bubbles of blood in Hokey's mouth were, at least for the moment, proof of life.

"Looks like he's dying." Faris hollered out to Upchurch.

Deputy Upchurch from behind the log cabin had climbed to the top of the ditch-dump and in doing so, walked directly into a bloody trail. Deputy Upchurch called out, "CF, I just ran across a blood trail."

"Check it out" yelled Faris, "There might be someone else out there."

Upchurch followed the blood-soaked trail west, away from the car, toward the Floodways, for about forty feet. "Whoa," he yelled. "I found the spot where somebody got it. Damnation!"

"What'd you find?"

"A bloody mess and a shotgun. The shotgun's broken down and some shells are scattered round."

"Bring it with you and help me get him outa this car."

Upchurch hurried over the path to the squad car. He placed the shotgun into the trunk of the squad car and slammed it shut then hustled back to help Faris. With mud and blood covering all three, the deputies carried Hokey to the patrol car, opened both of the rear doors and gently laid him in the back seat with both his feet hanging outside the car. Upchurch ran to the driver's side of the car, reached across the back seat and placed his hands underneath Hokey's arms. He pulled Hokey across the heavy plastic seat covers, then lubricated with blood, until his head of blonde hair was near the edge of the back seat, directly behind the driver's seat. Hokey moaned as Upchurch lifted Hokey's knees, enabling his feet to be totally inside the car so that the door would shut. Hokey's form seemed small and fragile, like a child, as his labored breathing weakened.

"Let's go, let's go," Faris said.

With both deputies in the squad car, Deputy Faris' driving expertise was put to use in this daring race to get Hokey to the Hayti Hospital—fifteen miles away.

They raced back the same way they came, south past the Walker and Busby houses, the Johnsons' and the Strothers' to the blacktop, State Highway A, south through Bragg City to Highway 84, then east to Hayti. Deputy Upchurch made radio calls to the Sheriff's Office, asking them to contact the Hayti Memorial Hospital emergency room with an expected travel time of twenty minutes.

Missouri State Trooper Hickman, traveling north from Bragg City, monitored Deputy Faris' call of having Hokey who was in bad shape and would probably die, and that they were heading to the Hayti Memorial Hospital as fast as possible.

Both Faris and Hickman, traveling at high rates of speed, met and passed each other on State Highway A, between Bragg City and gravel road 228 leading to the farm. Neither recognized the other's car that rainy night.

Hickman advised Troop E Headquarters of his location and further advised that he was going to stop at the Busbys' and take them to the Hayti Hospital.

Hickman knew the Busby family. He remembered the day he went to get Hokey, with no thought he was dangerous, just wild from drinking too much. Troopers and deputies alike worked alone except in extraordinary circumstances. He wondered if things could have been changed had he found Hokey that day.

Deputy Faris whipped through Bragg City, headed south on the gravel road that dead-ended at Highway 84. Deputy Upchurch tended to Hokey, speaking to him, telling him, "Hang on, we'll be at the hospital real quick, just hang on." He also questioned Hokey: "Why'd you kill Harry?"

Hokey was long past any ability to respond. He could only moan at the deep pain caused by the hole in his left lung. When he moaned, fresh blood bubbled up from his wound and oozed in small bubbles from his mouth.

The smell of fresh blood was overwhelming. Occasionally, Hokey would kick the door in an awkward spasmodic manner. Blood splattered the ceiling of the squad car and up the side of the door, causing Deputy Upchurch's stomach to heave. Trying to stop his need to vomit, he placed his hand over his mouth. The vomit spewed through his fingers and onto Hokey.

"Damn, Junior, don't vomit on me," hollered Faris. "We'll be there at the hospital in a few more minutes."

Upon the deputies' arrival at the hospital's emergency entrance, a team of doctors and hospital employees in white coats were waiting with a gurney.

The tires of the patrol car slid to a stop and Deputy Upchurch's door flew open. It was 10:20 P.M.

Upchurch slung open the door to the back seat. One emergency room helper reached in to pull Hokey out and reflexively stepped backward, turning his head away and covering his mouth, his last meal now on his hands. Blood spatter was all over the back seat, mixed with vomit and blood clots oozing out of the hole in Hokey's lung.

Faris jumped from the squad car and began speaking to a doctor, telling him what he suspected. "There's a hole in his left lung made by a shotgun, and there's not much life left in him. It's either a suicide attempt or the attempted murder of a murderer, by someone. My bet is he tried to kill himself after having killed his best friend over a sixteen−year−old girl."

"Ain't it always," the doctor said.

"Women or money, it never changes."

Hokey was placed on the gurney and rushed into the operating room through double doors directly off of the check-in area and waiting room. There were a few folks in the emergency waiting room, one of which was Naomi Riddick, a friend of Mom's, who was there with a family friend. She recalled that the doctor, when picking steel shot out of Hokey's lung, was asking him over and over, "Who shot you, boy?" But there was no intelligible response from Hokey.

The Busby family arrived with Trooper Hickman, who stood near them, his Smokey Bear hat in his hands. Ruth, Raymond, and Li'l Joe stood near the big double doors that swung back and forth as medical personnel ran in and out in a race to save Hokey. They could see the table on which Hokey lay each time the doors swung open. Tears ran down their cheeks. Ruth, in a kind of chant, said over and over, "Oh my God, oh my God." Li'l Joe held onto her dress. Raymond stood mostly mute, his eyes glassed over with tears.

Bill, still feeling the effects of his day-long drinking spree, sat in a plastic chair, his left elbow on the arm of the chair, his left hand bracing against his cheek, his unruly graying hair spilling over his hand.

At 10:30 P.M., the shuffling of feet and the hurried nature of the operating room became quiet. The doctor walked out and spoke briefly with Trooper Hickman, and then moved to the Busbys. A moment of quiet. Some soft spoken words. Then a scream and sobs. Hokey had just died and Jimmy Osburn was called.

* * *

After hearing the whole story, or the story as Dad knew it that night, I had to ask, "Since no one saw Hokey get shot, exactly how did Hokey die, by suicide, by accident, or did someone kill him?"

Dad responded in a short burst. "You saw the ditch−dump, the car, and the blood up there, didn't you?"

"Yes, but did he kill himself or did someone kill him? No one actually saw it happen, did they?"

"Ruth said the deputies insist it was a suicide, and that's how they're going to report it."

"But," I said, "Hokey'd never commit suicide. They're wrong."

"That's enough," Mom said. "You don't know what Hokey would do or not do, do you?"

"But, Mom."

"No 'buts', young man, its bedtime. Try to get some sleep. You've got to go to school tomorrow."

"Mom's right," Dad said. "It's time to get some sleep, now go."

"Yes, Sir." *Dammit.*

26

"Get up, get up, get up!" rang in my ears from a source deep within my psyche, an internal clock I couldn't ignore. The bedsprings squeaked as I rolled over, pulled my feet from under the homemade quilt, and forced myself to sit up. Stretching, I wiped the sleep from my eyes, trying to clear my thoughts. Then I remembered.

The enormity of recent events flooded back into my mind, punctuated by cold linoleum. It was early, 5:30 a.m., Monday, December 9, 1957. Even worse, it was a school day.

The volume on the family radio was, as usual, set just above comfortable as Mom conducted her cacophony of sound, intended, I believe, to wake me without her having to say a word. It was something Dad could do with just the sound of his voice. On a normal day, I'd eat breakfast, do some chores that included pumping water into the six-foot water trough, and then get to the school bus at the railroad crossing.

It was a school day, but it was also viewing day. The weather was seasonal, chilly, but the sun came out and the roads were drying out. The mud had begun turning into a crust, following the weekend rains. The quarter-mile walk to the railroad crossing was a welcomed stroll.

The past two days ran together and had my mind spinning. Before leaving my bedroom, I walked to my window on the world, the one I gazed through at night when the stars shined bright and I dreamed of things to come; the window through which I admired the northern lights or watched for signs of reindeer. But that was an earlier time, a time before the killing. On this day I stared into the morning darkness toward the plank bridge hoping to see something.

Although I knew Dad had said he was going to move Hokey's car to our house, I didn't know if he had already done it. Throwing on my jeans, I padded barefoot into the living room and out the front door. I welcomed the cool morning air and I walked the few steps to the north edge of our porch. I began to see through the purple mist of the early morning. The car was gone.

I hurried back into the house and through the kitchen past Mom to the back door. Opening the door, I saw it. About 40 feet from our back door sat Hokey's car. "Wow, it's here." I blurted out. "Mom!" I yelled, as Buddy yawned and rose to greet me.

Anticipating my question, her response came in a loud, stern voice so there would be no mistake in what she was about to say. "No. You're going to school."

"Damn," I grumbled to myself, cringing at how close I came to saying the word loud enough for Mom to hear. We never said "damn" in my family; no curse words were ever used by my folks. It was simply not allowed. Yet, it perfectly fit the situation and, while I would maybe say it at school, I never would at home, not intentionally.

"Has Raymond been here?" I hollered.

"No," Mom said.

"Is he going to school today, do you think?"

"I don't expect him to go today."

"Do I hafta go today?"

"Yes, and that's the end of it. You're going."

"Damn," I again grumbled to myself. "What's Dad doing today?"

"You never mind, you're going to school. And don't get lost on your way home 'cause we have to go to the viewing tonight. We're taking the Busbys. And be quiet about all this at school. It's nobody else's business."

Hustling through my chores of feeding and watering the livestock, I couldn't help but walk up to Hokey's car once again and peer inside. The car had a magnetic appeal I couldn't understand. I wanted to touch it, but a slight chill came over me like the first time I looked into the bloody interior. It was as if it were alive. I backed away, deciding to leave it alone for now.

The school bus turned around about a quarter-mile down the road. My path would take me past the Busby house and the McMahan House, the folks who had recently moved onto the Gill farm that bordered our farm on the south. Raymond would normally wait for me at his house and we'd walk together to the railroad crossing. This day, Raymond was not in front of his house and I couldn't go on by without at least checking on him.

As I climbed the wooden steps and walked across the porch, the front door began to open before I could knock. I guessed they heard my footsteps. It was Raymond. I breathed a sigh of relief because I hadn't seen him since he left our house the night of the killing. He wouldn't come out on the porch but he briefly spoke to me while holding the door partially open.

"Hey, how're you doing?" I said kinda quiet like.

"All right I guess," his voice low, his eyes darting.

"Are you gonna go to school?" I asked even though I already knew the answer.

"No, I got important things to do today."

"What're you doing today?"

"I gotta clean up the car and get Donald's jacket." I don't believe I ever heard him call his brother anything but Hokey before this.

"You mean the motorcycle jacket?"

"Yeah."

"Was he wearing the motorcycle jacket when he...?"

Raymond thought for a moment, looked away, and then turned back toward me and answered, "Yes."

At the moment I asked the question, I wished I hadn't, not wanting to talk anymore about the jacket, or the killing, because I felt awful bringing up such things.

"Okay," I said, "I gotta get to the bus. See you after school?" As I walked away from the door across the porch to the steps down to the ground, Raymond called after me.

"Harold!"

Stopping, I turned toward him. "Yeah?"

"I didn't go across the field."

"I know," I said. "I wouldn't't've either...see ya after school?"

"Yeah, I'll be here or at the car. I think Fred's taking Mom and Dad back to the funeral home today."

"Gotta go, see ya later."

"See ya," he said, closing the door.

I hurried on down the road to the railroad crossing, knowing that if I missed the bus, I'd be in for it. Mom would never believe I didn't miss the bus on purpose because Raymond and I did one time. If I missed it for any reason now, I'd have to walk the four miles to school along the Cotton Belt tracks. So I'd just have to make the best of it, and maybe I could learn more about what happened the night of the killing from the Robinson girls.

I was the last to climb on the bus behind the McMahan and Marchbanks kids and some kids who were there with their folks living on the Marchbanks place that was across the railroad tracks from our farm. As I climbed aboard the bus, Mr. Dozier, wearing his ever present brown fedora cocked to one side, and with a Camel cigarette hanging out the side of his mouth, gave me "the look." He'd as soon leave me if given the chance. His feelings about me went back a ways, ever since Dad had a word with him about leaving me behind once. The feeling was mutual. I didn't like him either.

The bus sat on the railroad crossing that was higher than the gravel road, so you had to hang on to the seats while you walked down the aisle. The chatter was loud and irritating. No one seemed to notice when I moved further back, looking for a seat as close to the rear as possible.

Then I saw them. Alma Faye and Helen Robinson were sitting together, looking forward when I passed by them, quiet as could be. I detected Helen looking briefly at me before ducking her head as I looked at her. She didn't want to talk, or even be noticed. After all that happened, they were here. All the way to school, I relived the weekend in my mind and wondered what they saw that awful night. I hoped at some point they would tell me.

Alma Faye was in the eighth grade. Raymond and I were in the seventh grade and Helen was in the sixth grade. First graders through sixth graders went to school in the elementary building about three blocks away from the high school. The seventh and eighth grades were in the high school building, attached to the gymnasium. Alma Faye and I got off the bus. Helen went on to the elementary school building. Alma Faye walked fast and disappeared into the building with her friends before I could talk to her. It was apparent that she didn't want to talk about what had happened. I was immediately approached by a couple of my friends in school, Don and Wayne. I learned they had heard nothing about the killing. I also learned that I couldn't keep a secret. Forgetting what Mom warned me about, I began immediately.

"You ain't gonna believe what happened this weekend," I spouted.

"What?" Don said, his eyes big and questioning. Don was a big, tough guy. We had been friends ever since I could remember and our dads were also good friends. Wayne was from North Island, an area west of the Floodways that required a two-hour bus ride to get to school. He was familiar with the people who lived on the Floodways, like that old grizzled bum, Elmer, who hid out in his stinky old log cabin on Swift Ditch with the dead critters. Nope, it didn't surprise him at all, nor should it have, that someone was killed there this past weekend.

Wayne didn't even blink, he just said, "Who got killed?" like he was talking about nothing more important than whether it was raining or not.

Throughout the remainder of the day, Don wanted to know more details until I almost had to start making stuff up. "Why'd he kill Fats?" he asked over and over. I hated to say I didn't know, so I just said, "It's under investigation." That satisfied him for the time being. Don had cut through all my blather to the question I pondered the most.

Not knowing the answer, I changed the subject. I decided to talk about my visit to the funeral home.

"Did you really go into a funeral home and see dead people who were shot?" Don asked.

"Well, I almost saw dead people." I spoke of the casket store and the burial clothes.

"Did you really see all that blood in the car?"

"Sure did, a whole lot."

"Gee Whiz!" He repeatedly said.

I had experienced more than Don or Wayne could imagine, or that I could have imagined and I talked about it all day long. Mrs. Shipton, the math teacher, certainly didn't want to hear any of it and quieted me down by slapping a ruler flat against the table where I sat with Don and Wayne.

What I recall most about that day was the silence. Not one teacher asked me about it. No one knew about what happened and those I told about it didn't seem to care.

No one except me and the Robinson girls knew about the killing, even though it was supposedly reported on the radio on Saturday. It was as though it didn't really occur. There was no bevy of grief counselors. There was no school nurse asking how we felt, or teachers exhibiting any concern whatever.

I saw Alma Faye at lunch. She seemed okay.

"How's it going?" I asked, trying to start a conversation with her.

"Okay," she said, turning her head slightly away from me.

"Are you going to the viewing tonight?" I asked, like it was going to be a night at a cotton carnival.

"What's that?" she said, kind of stunned.

"Hokey's viewing, at the funeral home, they call it a viewing. You know. Him all laid out and all."

"No!" she blurted out, her face turning pale. She hurried away from me like I had lice.

I knew I shouldn't have said anything, and it was plain she wasn't going to tell me anything. The bell rang for afternoon classes. By the end of the school day, I was tired of talking about it and ready to go home. But the thought of the viewing revitalized and excited me. At the same time, I began to have some questions. I might not be so sure about this viewing thing. For a bit, the idea of going to the funeral home again kind of gave me the creeps.

Soon I was getting off the bus and walking home. The other kids were busy yapping about this or that as I walked off by myself. I considered my options, to go or not to go. Again, I stopped by the Busbys'. Bill was sitting on the porch, the first time I'd seen him since the killing. He sat in an old rocking chair that had been on that porch for as long as I could remember. Looking much older than the last time I saw him, he wore a light barn jacket with holes in the sleeves. The red and black plaid flannel lining showed through at just about where his elbow should have been. He stared off into the fields and, for a moment, he reminded me of a picture I had seen in the history books of Abraham Lincoln sitting in his chair, all worn out.

"Hey, Bill" I said.

"Hey there, Harold Gene." His voice was barely audible. He always called me by my first and middle name. I felt bad for him. I figured he had sobered up and wasn't sick anymore and I didn't want to bring up the obvious and ask him anything about Hokey.

"Is Raymond home?"

"Nope, he's up at your house, working on the car."

"Yeah? Guess I'll go on home. See ya later," I said. After walking a few steps toward home, I turned and said, "I'm awful sorry, Bill." I would have felt real bad if I didn't say something.

"Thank you," he muttered, "much appreciated." He spoke with an unnatural calm and dignity. I didn't understand why he wasn't crying or anything, because I wanted to.

"See you later," I repeated. Rocking slowly back and forth on that porch, Bill nodded his head and slightly raised his left hand in a wave-like gesture. A breeze blew his graying hair just enough to notice. I walked on. Reaching home, I headed directly to the car.

The doors on both sides were open. A wash bucket full of sudsy water and the water hose lay on the ground by the car. Raymond hunched over in the back seat, scrubbing the old cushions with a sponge he'd borrowed from Mom. He was soaked from head to toe.

"Hey Raymond!" I yelled to get his attention over the volume of the car radio blasting rock-a-billy. Stopping the scrubbing, he looked up.

"Hey," he said.

"How's it going?" I asked, even though I could see how it was going.

"Okay," he said with a slight grin. "I got the car started this afternoon. Out of gas was all that was wrong. It runs good now. I cleaned it out, threw the trash and bottles into the barrel, and burned it all. The blood ain't coming out very easy though." He talked quietly, almost to himself. I didn't know what to say. Raymond wasn't his old self. He didn't want to talk, he wanted to scrub.

"Well, can I help?"

"Naw, I gotta quit soon. The viewing's at seven."

"Yeah, well, okay, I gotta get into the house."

"Okay," he said, "see you later."

"Yeah, see ya later." I looked back at Raymond. I didn't know what to make of him crawling all over that car when I could hardly bear to touch it.

But I had learned one more thing. Hokey couldn't start the car because it was out of gas. This proved to me he had acted without any planning or forethought. Of course, he was drunk and that was part of it. It also showed me that Hokey had acted upon his immediate feelings, spontaneously, with no regard for his own safety or route of escape. He acted just like a moc, standing its ground and attacking headlong, never turning its back to you. He truly had been a dangerous man, the kind who would kill at the slightest provocation, satisfied only when his quarry was dead.

27

As I bolted through the back door, the screen door slapped hard against its frame. The house seemed to cringe at the unmistakable sound of my arrival. "Hello, I'm home! Is there anything to eat?"

With a shrug and without breaking stride, I tossed my jacket into the air with a practiced eye. It billowed momentarily before settling onto one of Mom's ladder-back, cane-bottom chairs. "Yes! Two points and he never lost a step!" I said, mimicking a phantom sports announcer as I rounded the kitchen table, heading for the refrigerator.

As I placed my hand on the refrigerator's door handle, Mom's voice came from the living room. "I'll be fixing supper in a little while," she said.

"Yes, ma'am!" I called out, scanning the shelves for familiar shapes such as a plate of fried chicken, or sandwich sliced ham, or anything edible. There was a quart bottle of Cragmont Cola and some fried chicken was visible through plastic wrap. I grabbed a couple of pieces of chicken and poured some Craigmont into a water glass. I then assembled what I thought was the best snack ever, with some leftover biscuits I found in the breadbox.

"It's four-thirty," Mom called out. "What're you doing home so early?" A brief pause brought the following question. "You didn't skip any classes did you?"

"No, ma'am, sure didn't," I said as I walked into the living room. "For some reason, Mr. Dozier drove the bus a little faster than usual today. He must've had to get back to school for a ball game or something." What Mom didn't know was that this day I hadn't stopped to chat with the Busbys, spending an hour or so listening to Bill's yarns about cowboys, motorized bicycles, and his days as a muleskinner like I normally would have done. Mom had become so used to me getting home at a later hour that she never started missing me until about 5:30.

The living room looked like a Sunday morning. The ironing board was set up, taking up most of the walking space, what with Mom ironing Dad's white dress shirt. Seeing me with my plate of chicken, she snapped, "What are you doing? I told you I'd be fixing supper in a little while. Don't eat that in here!" Then, almost in the same breath, she said, "Well, I'm just not going to make any supper today."

"I'm sorry," I said, backing into the kitchen.

"The viewing starts at seven," she said. "We hafta leave here no later than six or six-thirty."

Glancing out of the kitchen window, I saw Raymond leaving the car, heading to his house. "Mom, was Raymond working on the car all day?"

"Most of the day," she said. "He started about noon, asked me for a bucket and some detergent."

"Why do you think he's doing it, working so hard in that car, in his brother's blood and all?"

"I just don't know. Your dad was out there too, working on one of the tractors." She paused for a moment, then said, "Raymond's got a lot to think about."

"Like what?"

"He's now the oldest son and he probably feels the responsibility."

"I don't understand. What responsibility?"

"You can't understand if you haven't experienced it. You're the youngest. If something was to happen to Johnny, heaven forbid, you might think differently about it. There's a difference and you gotta respect Raymond's feelings. This is such a tragedy and after the funeral most folks'll forget about it. But Raymond'll never forget, and for that matter, no one on this farm will ever forget. Until that car is gone from here, we won't be able to think of anything else either. Goodness knows I dread having to see it each time I look out the window."

"Have you looked inside it?"

"No, and I won't. Your dad and I remember when Bonnie and Clyde were killed in the 30's. It was on the front page of every newspaper. That car was shot all to pieces and so were they. It gave me the creeps, and every time I look at Hokey's car, it brings those awful pictures to mind. I want it gone.

Now, go on. Don't bother me anymore. I gotta finish this ironing and your dad'll be here any minute."

I didn't ask any more questions and finished the snack that was now officially my supper. Time seemed to fly by. Dad came in and, as the clock approached 6:30 we were about ready to go. It was already dark. Mom and Dad were all dressed up, and I had changed into a freshly ironed shirt and jeans that Mom had laid out on my bed. Soon we headed for the Busbys'.

I found myself becoming more curious about the viewing, but out of respect for the Busbys I kept my mouth shut. When we picked up Ruth, Bill, Raymond, and Li'l Joe, all seven of us crammed into our car like squashed apples. There was some small talk, but not much, and nobody talked about the killing.

Ruth, while looking out the window, said softly to nobody in particular, "I told the director today we'd like to have the service at the Tatum Chapel with Brother Crane preaching the funeral."

"Oh," Mom replied, "When?"

"Tomorrow, but I don't know for sure what time yet. Probably in the afternoon some time."

"I spoke to the director, too," Dad said. "He said Fats will have a wake at his mother's house in Clarkton tonight and he'd be talking to them about where they want to have the service." No one said much after that; we were all plain uncomfortable after Dad brought up Fats. Dad didn't follow up on his comment either. Instead, he concentrated on driving. Bill didn't say anything. He held his Zippo cigarette lighter in his closed fist, flipping the lid open and then closing it, then opening it and closing it, making that clicking noise. It about drove me crazy.

"Stop it," Ruth commanded after enduring the clicking sound as long as she could.

"Huh?" Bill said with a start, looking down at his hand holding the lighter. "Oh, sorry." His voice turned quiet and distant. Everyone was trying to be extra polite but soon Li'l Joe began complaining about having to sit on Bill's lap, and Raymond stared out into the darkness. It was going to be one of those blue-black nights in more ways than one.

We arrived in Gideon at almost seven. Dad drove real slow when we got close to the funeral home. He always drove like that in town, afraid he'd hit some kid darting across the road. The funeral home was slowly coming into view on the left.

Two or three cars were already there. What I had been looking forward to all day was happening, yet beads of sweat formed on my forehead. I began to have second thoughts about the night ahead.

Dad pulled our car into the graveled parking lot, the tires making that distinctive crunching sound. Once parked, we unfolded like an accordion as the doors opened. I looked at the cars already parked and noticed their occupants. The side windows were cracked a little on one of the cars and whiffs of smoke formed outside the slightly fogged windows.

We gathered on the sidewalk and began walking toward the funeral home's front door. I hesitated after a few steps, standing to one side, not wanting to be the first to go in. I stretched some, looked at my feet and said, "Well, I'll be doggone, my shoe came untied." Dad continued to lead the group to the door. Mom and Ruth followed close behind with Raymond and Li'l Joe in tow. Bill, however, remained behind the others with me. He paused and looked down the street where lights began to flicker from house windows and headlights outlined the coming traffic. I noticed his head was slightly bowed as he instinctively pulled a red tin of Prince Albert out of his coat pocket, along with some cigarette papers. In a few moments, he had himself a decent roll-your-own. I'd seen this ritual a thousand times and found it an extraordinary example of dexterity. Bill was a true artist when it came to roll-your-owns. However, on this occasion, I noticed his fingers seemed to shake more than normal, and his large eyes were sad and reddened. "Oh my God," he whispered, lowering his eyes to the sidewalk. Tears began to glisten on his cheeks as he softly wept.

I could taste the grief and couldn't make myself leave him alone. He took one more deep drag on the cigarette, letting the smoke drift gradually from his nose. It had that recognizable sweet aroma of Prince Albert. Ruth, about that time, appeared at the door, looking at him and not saying a word. He looked back, dropped his cigarette to the ground and placed the toe of his shoe on it, pressed down and twisted it into the sidewalk. He sighed, wiped his eyes, paused, and like going through that door was the last thing in the world he wanted to do, began to move. I followed a few steps behind. As Bill opened the door, I heard the doors of the other cars in the parking area opening and closing, and voices I didn't recognize. The viewing had begun.

That overwhelming stench of flowers met me again when I entered the door behind Bill. The funeral director, tall and lean, dressed in a crisp black suit, his silver-gray hair glistened and his shoes were as shiny as anything I had ever seen. He was shaking Dad's hand like a politician, placing his left hand at Dad's elbow. They seemed to have become fast friends as Dad nodded his head in approval at whatever the director was telling him.

Bill and I entered the door and I saw the director abruptly move from my Dad to greet Bill. He glanced at me and moved on as if to say I wasn't getting another Coke out of him, which I didn't want anyway, not then anyhow. Dad gave me that "come on" look. But I wanted to hear what was going on and waited a moment or two longer while Dad glared at me. The director spoke to Bill and Ruth in a whisper so low, I could only see his mouth move. I don't believe Bill could hear him at all, but Ruth could. She had good hearing.

I followed Dad into the large viewing room that looked like a church. The lighting was soft, created by floor and table lamps. The lampshades formed shadowy circles on the ceiling.

Several rows of folding chairs were lined up in the center of the room, with sofas and a couple of easy chairs situated in small areas in the rear of the room. It seemed fancier now than it did the day before. A small light lit up a book placed on a waist-high table just inside the entrance to the room. Mom said it was a guest book and signed it while I watched. "Everyone who comes in is supposed to sign the book," Mom said. Soft music floated through the air, sounding like angels, soft and pretty, like nothing I ever heard before.

Looking farther into the room, I saw the casket sitting on a table covered with a greenish-looking tablecloth. Floor lamps situated at each end of the casket spawned circular shadows on the ceiling above. It looked like the same casket Ruth had picked out the day before, the one covered by the insurance.

The big lid was open, but I couldn't see anything from where I stood in the back of the room, even when I stood on my tip toes. Once we all gathered in the room, Bill and Ruth began making the long walk to the coffin. Raymond and Li'l Joe, who had been standing at the rear of the room with Mom, followed along with Bill and Ruth. They all seemed so scared to look in that box, and the closer they got to the casket the more they seemed to be holding each other up.

Ruth's shoulders drooped as she and Bill approached the casket. A muffled sob escaped the small white handkerchief she held to her mouth. Bill, with his right arm around Ruth's shoulders, spoke softly into her ear and he reached out, placing his left hand into the coffin, his head slightly bowed. Bill supported Ruth while they looked upon the body of their first-born male child. "My boy," she said, "my little boy." Bill softly patted Ruth's shoulder. I was startled, unprepared for such tenderness. Raymond stood straight, eyes set, his hands at his side. Li'l Joe with one hand on Ruth's dress, tip toed, stretching his neck as far as he could. Bill stooped down and picked up Li'l Joe, holding him tight as they both looked into the casket.

Mom walked to Ruth's side, adding her strength to Bill's. After a bit, Bill stepped aside and, along with Ruth and Mom, they moved to some folding chairs in the first row nearest Hokey. Raymond moved aside but didn't sit down. He remained standing near the casket like a centurion, assuming his new role as the oldest son, his heartbreak and hurt evident to all those paying their last respects.

Dad left the side of the funeral director and beckoned me to come with him. I nodded and walked at his side to the casket. There seemed to be no one else on earth as we approached. I hesitated. Dad said, "Come on, it's okay." I continued walking, keeping close to Dad. Nearing the casket, Hokey's profile came into view, his head resting on the cream-colored pillow. A step farther and I was within a foot of the casket, about chest high on me. Dad stayed for twenty to thirty seconds, stepped back and turned toward Mom, Ruth and Bill. I remained.

I no longer felt uncomfortable. This seemed to be the first time I ever really looked at Hokey. I could see him clearly, his features sharp and handsome. His blondish hair was combed in that rock-a-billy style he liked.

His face was so calm, as if in a deep, peaceful sleep. I believed he might rather have been dressed in his motorcycle jacket, cowboy shirt, and Levis instead of the fake gray burial suit. His hands, folded across his stomach, looked hard yet delicate. He had the hands of a working man, hands that picked cotton and pulled bolls, hands now clean with neatly trimmed fingernails yet still nicotine–stained. The same hands that had killed Fats, an innocent who had done him no harm.

I stared at Hokey's hands so intently that the fingers on his right hand appeared to twitch. The same chill I felt when I first saw his car flowed over me again. My legs felt heavy. I found myself unable to move or to look away. Maybe this was a sign from him, kind of like a good-bye. His calm facial features showed no indication of the horror he caused, no sign of the grief and terror he spread. He gave no hint of what he must have looked like when he was lying in that bloody wallow, or in the back seat of his car, kicking and thrashing about while bleeding to death. I couldn't resolve the difference, the absolute disconnect between his appearance and his deed.

I felt a tug on my sleeve. It was Dad. "Come on, son" he said. "Others are waiting their turn."

"Huh?" I said, as if I were waking up. "Sorry."

"Come on, it's time to move on." I nodded, forcing myself to move away. Still, it seemed a spell had been cast over me by Hokey's form and by my knowledge of what he had done only two days before.

"Dad," I said softly, not wanting to draw attention to myself.

"What?" he said quietly.

"Where's Fats?"

"Come on, let's go outside and get some air."

Raymond had taken a break from his position at the casket and took Li'l Joe with him outside. Upon seeing Raymond outside, I said, "Raymond!" He turned and walked to me. I said, "I don't know what to say. I feel so bad for y'all."

With tears in his eyes, Raymond said, "He was my brother."

"I know."

"No matter what he did, he was my brother and I loved him."

"I know. I liked Hokey, too." I don't know why I said it. I talked without thinking. Maybe I wanted Raymond to know I didn't hold a grudge against Hokey. But I was still trying to figure out how I felt. Dad and Mom said Hokey was bad and it was just a matter of time before he killed someone, if he hadn't already done so. Yet lying in the casket, he didn't seem to be a stone killer. But he was.

"Guess I better get back in there," Raymond said.

"Yeah," I said. "I'll see you a little later."

I had to admire Raymond, watching him head back in. He was standing by his brother no matter what. It was the family thing to do, and no one expected anything less.

The night dragged on. At one point, the crowd stretched out the funeral home door almost to the street. Most stayed only long enough to view Hokey, then left stone-faced or sobbing. Some remained outside the funeral home in the shadows, swigging from a pint bottle of Four Roses and passing it around. I heard the term "Hell-Raiser" used more than once, talking about Hokey, and several other words used that I wasn't allowed to use. Were they Hokey's friends or Fats' friends? I began to question whether the ones in the shadows were the good guys or the bad guys. Dad said I had to know the difference between the good and the bad. I realized I really couldn't tell the difference, except for those I knew of course.

The 9:00 p.m. hour was upon us when the director put out a sign that shook me. "Services for Donald R. Busby and Harry L. Shell will be held at the First Baptist Church, Clarkton, at 2:00 p.m. Tuesday, December 10, 1957." This was a surprise. I didn't know both were going to be at the same funeral service. Hokey's funeral was supposed to be held at the Tatum Chapel, an old community church south of Peach Orchard. What happened? I wondered.

The deep thunder of heavy engines and squealing tires filled the air, causing some attendees to look on in disgust as they left the funeral home. Loud music flowed from the windows of some of the cars and shouts and hurrahs resonated in the air. I knew then that these were Hokey's friends, the ones we never saw. They were saying their farewell in the only way they knew, by living life to the fullest. By 9:30 p.m., the director started clearing the funeral home of attendees. Mom was talking real quiet-like to Ruth and Bill. Dad stood back and jingled his car keys, ready to go. I wandered back into the viewing room as small groups formed and left. I wanted to see him again.

The funeral director's assistant came out of the double doors in the back of the room, the double doors marked private. He had dark hair cut into a flattop and he looked like a basketball player at the local high school. He wore dark trousers and a white shirt, no tie, and he looked about Hokey's age. He walked in a deliberate and respectful manner to the casket and went about his work. The lining of the casket, laid open for the viewing, was tucked back in with care. The burial shroud, a white, soft–looking cotton–like material, was placed over Hokey's face and the lid gently closed. I stared at this ritual, lost in this scene, not done for the family or for any kind of audience, but as a showing of respect for the dead.

The assistant used a small crank to tighten the lid, to protect Hokey's body. Dad stepped back into the quiet funeral home, waiting patiently for me, then, placing his hand on my shoulder, he said in a soft voice, "let's go home."

28

Barely audible yet familiar voices seeped into my consciousness, distant, vague, and indistinguishable from a dream. Moments passed. I could hear my heart pounding, competing with the dream-like mutterings for supremacy. The night's cold December breath still enveloped the farm. Gusts of wind rattled the windows. Clear plastic, placed over the windows by Dad before each winter, snapped and popped against the panes of glass. The reassuring smell of freshly brewed coffee drifted through the house, adding to my awakening, making me feel safe and secure.

The normal sounds of breakfast, gospel songs, and rattling pots and pans were absent. The quiet bestowed upon that morning created a rare sense of seriousness. My mind slowly began to focus. Mom and Dad were having one of those talks about important things not discussed in my presence.

"Well," Mom said. "What are we going to do today?"

An odd question, I thought. Of course, we're going to the funeral today.

"I just don't know," Dad said. "This funeral has the makings for some real trouble. I've been uncomfortable with this since I learned of it. I never heard of a double funeral where the killer and the victim are side by side in the same church and, to top it off, two preachers, one for each family. Ought to be quite a show."

"Or a big fight," Mom said, finishing Dad's sentence. "The preachers couldn't be more different." There was a longer-than-normal pause. "I'm worried about Harold."

What? Why? I thought, turning to my right side and propping my head up off the pillow with my right hand, while remaining as quiet as possible. The whoosh of the wind against the windows drowned out my parents' words. I decided that holding my breath would offset the disadvantage caused by the wind. It had worked before. The trick was to take a breath between their words and hold it as long as possible, then to gulp another, like when taking careful aim. It worked. Their words were distinguishable as long as the wind didn't worsen and my gulps of air remained in cadence with their conversation.

"He's so involved in this thing," Mom said, her words heavy with tension and anxiety, like she was scared of something.

"That's understandable," Dad said in his matter of fact manner. "I used to have a pretty vivid imagination, too."

"I know. We all did when we were his age. But I was up late, just couldn't sleep, and I could hear him talking in his sleep."

"Harold was talking in his sleep? What'd he say?"

"He mentioned Hokey and something about his hands."

"Whose hands?"

"Hokey's hands," Mom said, raising her voice in volume and octave. "All this—the killing, the funeral home and the viewing—has deeply affected him."

"Yes, but death is a part of life, and we can't protect him from life."

"This is different. I don't think he should go to the funeral," Mom said with a familiar firmness in her voice when she was sure of her position.

"I'm not so sure about that," Dad said, quietly but not subdued, making me believe there was still hope I'd be going.

I wanted to jump out of bed and run into the kitchen. Mom couldn't mean it. Me not go? I had a stake in this and wanted to see it through. As for me talking in my sleep, what's wrong with that?

Mom continued. "Why should he go? He was one of the first to see the car that morning and he's been through the funeral home and the viewing. He's already seen too much."

"Well, now," Dad said, sounding like he was in my corner. "He went to the car without us knowing and I took him with me to the funeral home because I didn't expect Bill to go with Ruth. I needed him, for propriety."

"But, I'm just saying. He's been to everything and he's starting to have bad dreams, and furthermore, if he goes he'll miss school. And God forbid, what if there's trouble?"

Trouble? I thought. What kind of trouble?

"What if he gets hurt, or there's another killing, what then? We don't know Fats' family. Hokey killed Fats with no more feeling than swatting a fly, which everyone seems to have forgotten since they're having the funerals together. Everyone becomes a saint when they die. And friends, huh?" I could just see her eyes rolling. "But, pardon me," she said sarcastically. "It's worth the risk 'cause they were the best of friends? My foot they were! And maybe, just maybe, Fats' family also has a 'Hokey' in it. What's to stop their 'Hokey' from doing the same thing as our Hokey did...at the funeral?"

Dad was silent to Mom's rant as he most always was, but he wasn't subdued, he was thinking. I heard nothing from either Mom or Dad for several moments. I could feel the tension. In a few moments Dad said, in his slow Mississippi drawl, "I don't know that anything on this earth could stop what you think could happen. I mentioned to the director last night after seeing the sign put out about the funeral that there could be trouble with a double funeral. He agreed, but dismissed the idea saying it couldn't be helped because the families wanted it that way, and he promised to talk with the Clarkton police." Dad sighed, put some cream in his coffee, stirred it a bit, and took a sip. Sitting the cup back down into the saucer, he said, "The Clarkton Police Department has a full-time constable and a part time-deputy, not too reassuring if things get out of hand. My hope is that Fats' folks, who do have a legitimate grievance and might want to take revenge see this killing as having nothing to do with the Busbys or the Robinsons—that it was more of a squabble between two friends that just plain got out of hand."

"Friends, huh," Mom said. "Or it could be like the old feuds you've told me about in Mississippi, where the saying goes something like 'He who sheds the blood of our family must suffer the same fate, by the hand of our family.' A blood feud."

"Well," Dad said, changing the subject. "About Harold...let me think about it."

"Okay, but we gotta be together on this, either way and real quick."

"We will be." I heard Dad's footsteps leaving the kitchen, heading to the back door.

Dad won't go along with Mom on this, I thought. It'll be okay.

The radio came on as Mr. Rudy was introducing the next song, "Gimme That Old Time Religion," sung by Gentleman Jim Reeves. The melodic sounds of Gentleman Jim mixed with the rattling and banging of pots and pans; it was time to rise and shine.

29

I rushed to the bathroom, brushed my teeth, threw some water in my face, combed my hair, and made my way to the kitchen table. I tried to dismiss the earlier conversation I had overheard between Mom and Dad, not allowing anything to disrupt this day. This day, I wanted to get up early. This day would end it.

I yawned and stretched before sitting down at the kitchen table. "What time are we going to the funeral?" I asked Mom.

Mom was standing at the kitchen sink with her back to me, staring out the kitchen window into the chill of early morning. "You're not gonna be going today."

"What?" I kinda yelled, forgetting myself. I could not believe what I was hearing. Perhaps I shouldn't have dismissed the earlier conversation I had overheard.

"Your dad and I have talked it over," she said as she turned to face me. It took a few moments for this to sink in. I was stunned. I instinctively knew that as far as she was concerned, the decision was made. She was unyielding. Yet for the first time in my life, I couldn't accept a dictate from my mom.

"Why?" I bellowed. "I've seen it all! I knew them both! I liked them both! Why can't I go?"

Her eyes flashed with temper as she threw the dishrag into the kitchen sink. Her hands shook. "We don't want you to miss school. This thing has been eating us all up, especially you. You're just too involved," she said, "and this funeral won't help, believe you me. It may even be the beginning of something worse."

Her explanation that I was "too involved," just couldn't be the last word. I couldn't believe I was going to be forced to miss this funeral, the main event, the end of it all. I couldn't stop myself. I ran out the back door into the cold, early morning air, barefooted, in jeans and t-shirt. I ran past Buddy, who whined and trotted along behind me, past the death car and the barn, to the tractor shed where Dad was working. He was kneeling down, working on a piece of equipment. Hearing the screen door slam, he glanced up to see me sprinting across the yard toward him. He grimaced then looked back down at his work.

As I came closer to Dad, I called out, "Dad! Why can't I go?"

He stood up, removed his cap, wiped his forehead with the back of his gloved hand and said, "You're 12 years old. The answer is no." He paused, took a deep breath and continued. "You're barely 12 years old and you've been too torn up about this thing. Did you know you were talking in your sleep last night about Hokey, something about his hands? Can't you think of anything else?" he asked, barely suppressing his angst.

"I thought I saw his hand move when I was looking at him in the casket."

"That's just your imagination playing tricks on you, showing you're too involved in this."

"No I'm not," I said, gasping for air as my chest tightened up like I was going to have an asthma attack, which sometimes happened when I breathed cold air.

"But you did!" he stated. "Look, your Mom and I don't even want to go, but we have to. It's our duty to go. It's gonna be hard on everyone. I don't know Fats' family and just about anything could happen. The wrong look, the wrong word, from one family member to the other, could start something. I talked to the funeral director last night and asked him if he was sure this double funeral thing was a good idea. He said he had handled double funerals before, but nothing like this. This is something no one has seen before. He said it was the wish of both families, but believe you me, he's worried about it, too. Beats anything I ever heard of."

"Do I really have to go to school today?" It was my last plea.

"Yes, you do have to go to school today," Dad said with that flash in his eye, which I learned was a definitive response.

I knew then and there, there was no hope. I had never argued with my parents, never any back talk. Such behavior would never be tolerated in my house. Still, this was different. My stomach tumbled and my heart pounded in my ears.

Turning to walk away, I made a last, desperate attempt. "I'd a lot rather be alone on the Floodways than in school today. Please...I don't want to go to school. They're so ignorant there. They don't care. No one cares, but I do, I care."

Dad listened, but it was apparent the decision had been made and I had been told more than once. There was no hope.

"We all care," Dad said. "You're not being fair to your mom and me. If you don't go to school, you'll be over on those Floodways, with Buddy, doing nothing but thinking about everything that's happened. You need to get your mind off this. Going to school today will help you do that. Don't you see?" he said, pulling me to him and placing his hand on my shoulder. "You're just too young for this."

"But Dad, Raymond and Bill are expecting me."

"Well, I'll be taking you to school today, and that's that. I want to make sure you get there."

"This ain't fair," I said. I made a fool of myself. I had played this all wrong. Now my fate was sealed.

"Fair has nothing to do with anything. Nothing much in this life is fair," Dad said with a flash of anger.

Farmers are realists and no one was more of a realist than Dad. Some would call it being negative. He had a hard life, full of toil and desperate times, and it had left its mark on him. It was my second lesson during this killing. Life is not fair.

"This ain't right!" I fumed.

"That's enough now. You go ahead and get ready for school. I'll be in the house in a bit."

The trip to school with Dad was a slow, embarrassing ride. I kinda slid down in my seat on the passenger side of the car while Dad drove past the bus turnaround. The kids were waiting for the bus and there I was, being driven to school to keep me from running to the Floodways.

Dad seemed to be driving extra slow to ensure maximum humiliation to me. My punishment was complete as all I wanted to do was disappear. The

drive took us by the Busbys' and the McMahans' houses, past the bus stop
where the kids were gathering, past Parnham Johnson's place, past the place
where the old Nylow Church once stood and the Strother's place to where
the gravel meets the blacktop, with the Cotton Belt tracks running alongside
us all the way to Bragg City.

Arriving at the school, Dad let me out at the entrance door, in direct view
of my friends, Don and Wayne. Their open mouth stares required an
explanation.

Trying to take the trip in stride, I said to them, "The funeral's today and
I can't go," I said to both at once.

"You ain't going to the funeral?" Don asked as we all three walked into
the school building.

"Naw," I said, trying not to show how much it hurt.

"Where's it at?" Don asked.

"Clarkton," I shot back.

"I know where Clarkton is," Wayne said, grinning big.

"Everyone knows where Clarkton is," I said. "But do you know where
the First Baptist Church is there?"

Thinking about it for a moment, he said, "No, I don't." I had one on him.

Classes ground on and, as lunchtime neared, I told Don I was thinking
about leaving and making my way to Clarkton. Don advised in a whisper,
"If you leave, they'll send the sheriff out to your house to find you and you'll
probably be locked up for a day or two. But that wouldn't bother ya, would
it?"

"I guess not," I said. "Didn't Bilbo get locked up last year in Kennett?"
Bilbo was a notoriously nasty guy in our class who came to school on and
off. He was prone to get in trouble, big trouble, cause he wasn't civilized.
But I liked him okay. One time Bilbo got locked up in Kennett by Sheriff
Scott for who knows what. On one of those occasions Don and I were in
town with our dads and we went to the jailhouse a couple of blocks south of
town square on Kennett Street to visit. We never got past the door. They
wouldn't let us in because you had to be family.

"Yeah," Don agreed. "But it didn't bother Bilbo any, being in jail."

"Nope, don't nothin' much bother Bilbo," I said.

"Yeah," Wayne said. "He's always in trouble and it don't seem to bother him at all."

"Well," I said, "if I go, I gotta take off during lunch, before the bell rings for afternoon classes, 'cause the funeral starts at two."

The lunch bell rang precisely at twelve noon. It was time to walk the few blocks to the lunchroom next door to the elementary school. But that was not the only option. Some students went to town and ate nickel candy at Gill's, Napier's, Curtis' or Shipley's grocery and general merchandise stores, or at home if they were townies. Yet, many stayed in the gymnasium, eating a lunch they had brought to school from home, after getting a dime soda from the school store called the Wigwam, because the school mascot was the "Indians".

I walked to the door to see my friends off to lunch and to think about the reality of it all as they looked back at me and waved goodbye. "Good luck," they said, leaving me standing in the doorway of the school as they both began laughing and talking to other students about other things. All hundred or so of the student body from seventh through twelfth grades headed in different directions, like a gaggle of geese scattered by a fox. The doors on the metal wall-lockers clanged and banged as the students threw their books into their lockers and some grabbed their lunch bags, already wet with grease from the biscuits and bacon.

It was decision time for me.

30

My parent's decision not to let me go to the funeral hit me like an unexpected thunderstorm on a clear summer day. While dealing with my disappointment and anger, I made plans to react. I could choose to go to the funeral by myself. The very beginning of my plan seemed easy, just walk away from school and take the Cotton Belt tracks north or hitchhike north on the blacktop, County Road 228. But, after giving this some thought, I realized it would not be that easy. I then decided to forget about hitch-hiking, which Mom always preached against, saying either the hitchhiker is killed by the driver or the driver by the hitch-hiker. I would simply wait till the lunch bell rang and take my chances walking to the Cotton Belt tracks and head north to the Floodways.

When the lunch bell rang, the kids not waiting to be dismissed sprang from their seats and swarmed into the halls heading in different directions. I eased away from the group I normally ran with and made my way to the southwestern edge of the school, just outside the windows of the science room. My heart pounded like I imagined an escaping convict's might. Doubt and fear gave rise to a slight tremble. I had to think. During all my thinking, I could always come up with a way that it wouldn't work.

Wallowing in uncertainty and self-doubt, I concluded that my ill-devised plan would have ended in failure. Recalling Mom's warnings, hitchhiking would likely result in getting me killed. Staying on the Floodways all afternoon would probably result in me freezing. And, if I survived either of these two scenarios, a Pemiscot County deputy sheriff truant officer would be coming for me for skipping school. It would be a no-win situation all the way round.

Although I decided to remain in school, I couldn't overcome the nagging resentment I felt toward my folks' decision to not let me go to the funeral. I had lost all interest in school. The things I considered important before the killing I now considered trivial. I suddenly became detached from classmates because, to me, they just didn't get it.

I was absorbed with my thoughts of the killing, and to my way of thinking they didn't have to deal with reality, an absurd thought. Everyone in this tiny rural school dealt with his or her own harsh reality on a daily basis. It was my turn to learn how to deal with an ugly intrusion into my tranquil life.

The next worst thing about remaining in school that day was that this was basketball season, the most important time of the year for schools without a football team. Some of these schools were so small they struggled to meet the bare minimum of five starters for basketball with only a couple of substitutes on the bench.

The season called for an acute eruption of pep rallies, normally held during the last class period of the day. This day was no different. Yes, our Indians were on the warpath. The rumor of a rally leaked out early and was greeted with delight by everyone but me. The fact that I was going to have to endure a pep rally made me sick to my stomach.

As I removed my books from the wall-locker I shared with both Don and Wayne, Don said, "I thought you'd gone to the funeral."

"Naw, I thought about it, but decided to stay here."

The classes began. I watched the clock and time dragged. The funeral would start in about an hour, the same time as the pep rally. My anxiety increased as the time drew near.

The last period bell finally rang. The funeral had begun as teachers herded us toward the gym. I walked along with the crowd, unresponsive to the chatter circling my head.

As I sat in the bleachers, my anger at being in school this day overwhelmed me. I wanted in the worst way to scream, shut up...just shut up! I wanted to grab them each by their faces and say, to hell with basketball! I wanted to scream, Hokey killed Fats, you idiots. Don't you get it? He did it with a shotgun, at a range so close the whole family got powder burns and nosebleeds and went deaf for an hour or more, maybe for the rest of their lives. It was Raymond's brother who did it! Don't you care? They're being buried today and there'll probably be more blood on the ground today at the funeral and I'm here listening to this bullshit pep rally? That's what I wanted to say. I wanted to scream it. But I didn't. I never screamed anything. I just moved along with the herd and hated myself for doing so.

I made a decision right then and there never to do this again, never to go along to get along. I never did again go along to get along, to my detriment on many occasions, but that's the way I wanted to live my life.

I endured the pep rally and impatiently waited for the bus ride home, carefully avoiding the bus bully, whose brother was in prison. This was a reality I would soon have to address, but not now, not today.

Upon leaving the bus, I ran past the Busbys' house even though I knew they were probably not back from the funeral. I felt embarrassment and shame for not having gone to the funeral. Once past the house, I walked the remainder of the way. I fed and watered the livestock as soon as I got home. Small specks of snow swirled around the blackness of Hokey's car as the temperature seemed to plunge further. I sat on the back porch for a bit, enduring the cold while patting Buddy's head, comforted by his presence. I wanted very much for Mom and Dad to come home.

Buddy finally abandoned me for the warmth of his house, and I soon gave up the watch, retreating into the house as darkness surrounded me. Turning on the TV, I found nothing but static and turned it off. I grabbed a snack from the refrigerator, pulled the shotgun from the closet, loaded it and placed it within easy reach while I sat on the living room couch and waited. This was my new normal. When alone, never be far away from a weapon. It was now totally dark. *Where were they? What happened?* Looking south out of the big double windows in the front room, I finally saw headlights coming from the direction of the Busbys'. The car slowed and turned into our driveway. Buddy barked a greeting and I ran to the back door, careful to ensure it was Mom and Dad, before opening the door.

"It's over," Mom declared as she made her way into the house.

"Did you feed the livestock?" Dad asked.

"Yes, sir," I said, hoping I had done all he wanted but not knowing for sure. I was never for sure then, even when I was sure. Dad began walking directly toward the barn. He never trusted me to do what I was supposed to do because one time I had forgot. He'd always checked. I deserved that. I seemed to live in a perpetual wheel of Dad checking and re-checking my work.

"How was school?" Mom asked, surprising me as to how she could ask such a benign question as I followed her into the house.

"Fine," I said, the response that means nothing. I didn't want to push too much. She was obviously tired. I had learned that by holding my upper and lower lips between my upper and lower teeth, I could prevent myself from making an ill-advised, spontaneous outburst. It worked. It was absolutely the best way for me to keep my mouth shut. Mom's casual question exhausted my patience, but I couldn't show it. Who cares how school was today? What happened? I screamed inside my head.

"It's all over," Mom repeated. She walked toward me and hugged me with her don't say another word look. She then gently whispered while drawing her hand over my head, like petting a dog, or soothing a horse by rubbing the side of its neck. "It's really all over, and I hafta get some rest." She walked slowly away from me into the front room and to their bedroom. I stood transfixed.

I wanted to ask, was anyone else killed? What did Raymond say? What did Ruth and Bill say? Who was there? What was the funeral like? Was there any trouble? But I didn't. I was all alone with my thoughts.

31

The story of the funeral on December 10, 1957, came out little by little, piece by piece from Mom, Dad and others, speaking only after years passed, when they were ready. It was entirely appropriate that such a funeral would be in the final days of a historically poor year that brought out the worst in man.

On that cold, gray day, Mom, Dad, Ruth, Bill, Raymond, and Li'l Joe all crowded into our four-door Chevy. Raymond, sullen, sat next to the door behind Dad, who was driving. Bill, pale and nervous, sat in the middle with Li'l Joe on his lap. Ruth sat next to the door behind Mom on the passenger side of the car, stoic, absorbed in thought.

The trip to Clarkton, in addition to taking them through some of the most majestic scenery of the Bootheel, also covered more of the same stark winter landscape, an endless expanse of withered, gnarled, and twisted cotton stalks that never reached their full potential. Tired–looking cotton trailers with faded paint sat in the distance. The scene, bathed in a vaporous mist, was reminiscent of Civil War battlefields seen in fading lithographs.

A few hardy boll-pullers worked in the fields in which there was only a hint of cotton remaining. Their forms, bent and distorted by the heavy sacks they pulled through half-frozen mud, blended into the distance. Like apparitions, condemned to work the fields forever, they squeezed every penny out of the fields before the stalk-cutters arrived. They could have been Hokey and Fats.

The people, as tough as the land, took pride in saying they were born to work the fields. In the Bootheel, the poor lived in a perpetual depression, even in good years, with only backbreaking work and meager pay, their faces reminiscent of the same high character captured years before in grainy black and white photos depicting survivors of the Dust Bowl and Great Depression.

Dad's route to the funeral in Clarkton would take them over the Floodways, through Peach Orchard and then Gideon, passing by the funeral home. Approaching the funeral home, Dad slowed the car. "Ruth, do you need to stop here for anything?" he asked, even though he felt there was no more need to stop.

In response, Ruth placed her right hand on the back of Mom's seat, grimaced, and pulled herself forward just enough to see, to her left, around Bill, Raymond and Li'l Joe. The hearse, visible from the car, was backed up to the large rear door of the funeral home, its back hatch standing open, ready to receive its grim cargo.

"No," she said. Then, as an afterthought, in a soft voice, she added, "There's nothing more I can do there." Easing herself back into her seat, she turned her head away from the scene and stared out of her window, once again absorbed in thought.

Dad gauged his speed in order to bring them to the church in Clarkton at about 1:00 p.m. This would provide some time for him to speak with the funeral director and the preachers before the service commenced. As they continued north through Gideon, the only traffic light in town turned red. Dad brought the car to a smooth stop and, holding the clutch in, shifted into first gear to await the green light, the deep rumble of the powerful engine somehow reassuring.

The intersection was the exact center of Gideon's business district where each corner brought forth memories while they sat. On the southwest corner of the intersection grew an old maple tree in the front yard of the historic Gideon Hotel, where businessmen from all across the country doing business with the big landowners and Gideon-Anderson stayed. The tree, wrapped in dark bark, stood bare, having lost its leaves to fall. Heavy branches twisting upward and outward ended in spindly dark fingers, appearing all the more ominous that day in sharp contrast to the brilliant white, wood-frame hotel and the darkening sky.

On the northwest corner stood the Gideon-Anderson Box Company where large, yellow Ross straddle-carriers moved about the lumberyard like giant insects repositioning lumber taken from a recent train delivery. These same movers were operated by Hokey when he worked there not that long ago. The operators, wearing heavy coats and baseball caps, some with ready-made cigarettes clinched in their teeth, representing someone well paid, wheeled the behemoths around the yard.

On the northeast corner loomed a two-story grocery that touted a pharmacy, a rarity. Gideon had three doctors, two general practitioners, and a chiropractor, a necessity for a place where so many saw-blades screamed throughout day and night.

On the southeast corner operated one of the fanciest department stores in the Bootheel. Some say it was as good as could be found between Memphis and St. Louis, a store for the landed gentry, the monarchs of this land. Its large display windows rose from the sidewalk to near the same height as the building. Mannequins in various poses, dressed in the latest styles, stared soullessly out those windows. Simple working folk stared back into a world they could never know.

About fifty feet east of this intersection, the town constable in a marked police car took notice of the goings on. He parked in such a manner that would allow him to give chase at the slightest infraction. The light turned green. Dad, aware of the constable's presence, glanced at the constable before accelerating through the intersection. In one smooth coordinated motion between brake, clutch, and accelerator, he eased the car through the intersection, the deep growl of controlled power billowed from beneath the hood, struggling to be unleashed like my brother allowed it to be when he was home.

Less than a block north, the car approached the familiar Cotton Belt tracks that crisscrossed the Bootheel. The car shuddered and shook as it lumbered over the double set of steel tracks. Dad turned west at the next intersection (North Main and Railroad St.) near the El Morocco Club, leading to State Road (SR)162 west to Clarkton.

The El Morocco Club, a well-known and infamous honky-tonk, sat north of the railroad tracks on the northeast corner of the intersection of North Main and Railroad Street. A large porthole window, an uncommon architectural feature, sat high on the west wall of the joint. The club ran near twenty-four hours a day, except on Sunday in strict observance of Missouri's

Blue Laws. Many Gideon-Anderson employees cashed their payday checks there and went home broke after shots and a beer and paying last week's tab.

Hokey, Fats, and their friends were known to hang out at this watering hole where the smell of stale beer, Prince Albert cigarettes, and deep-fried catfish were accompanied by deep bass sounds coming from a 1940's era art deco Wurlitzer. It belched out the latest country standards and rock and roll twenty four hours a day, including the latest releases of Jerry Lee Lewis, Johnny Cash, and an upstart from Tupelo, Mississippi—Elvis Presley. The club was a raucous, dangerous place full of smoke where the abrupt screeching of chairs being pushed back from tables, accompanied by screams and curses, signaled that blood, beer, and whiskey would likely once again stain the plank floor.

Leaving the city limits of Gideon heading west, travelers found Clarkton coming quickly into view, as there were only a few miles between the two towns. Gideon's location along the western border of New Madrid County placed the town within close proximity to both Pemiscot and Dunklin Counties.

Many exciting high-speed, alcohol-induced car chases occurred between Gideon and Clarkton on SR 162 and secondary gravel roads. If a runner could reach the county line between Gideon and Clarkton before being forced to a stop by city or county authorities he was home free, provided there were no Missouri state troopers lying in wait. That short stretch of ground between Gideon and Clarkton was a regular cotton–country thunder road where wrecked cars were a common sight. Hokey, no stranger to this deadly game, often spoke of his hair-raising high-speed antics and of, 'leaving the law behind at the county line.'

As they turned south off SR 162 onto Clarkton's Main Street, SR 25, the center of town was a couple of blocks away. Stately old homes lined the brief approach to a downtown that included a magnificent two-story brick mansion that had seen its best days some fifty years earlier. Clarkton, situated midway between Malden and Holcomb, was once home to many of the most prosperous pioneers of the Bootheel. Like most small enclaves, it was also home to a cotton gin, grain elevator, honky-tonks, cafés and several churches along with a variety of general stores and feed stores.

Merchant buildings along Main Street were, for the most part, on the west side of the street and exhibited some of the oldest architecture in Missouri. High awnings ran from the storefront to the street. Plank walkways and hitching posts were long ago replaced by concrete but, with a little imagination, one could readily envision the heyday of Clarkton.

Some fifty or sixty feet farther south on the east side of the street was a small stand-alone concrete-block building, not unknown to Hokey. Two small, barred windows on both the north and south sides near the rear of the building were covered with wire mesh similar in appearance to chicken wire and set higher than a man could reach. The words "City Jail" stood out in bold black letters high above the front door and overwhelmed the whitewashed frontage, hard to miss and fair warning to those inclined toward ill behavior. Many an itinerant cotton-picker going astray in Clarkton woke up in jail the following morning, smelling of urine and stale beer, with a busted head and nothing but lint in his pockets.

A block or so farther south, a set of steel Cotton Belt tracks lay across the road. Further on the east side of Main was the Clarktonian Café, a favorite coffee and sandwich spot. A service station and Greyhound station were also attached. Setting due south of the Clarktonian was the church parsonage where the Baptist preacher and his family lived.

At Main and Commercial Street, stood the First Baptist Church that claimed to have the largest attendance of any of Clarkton's many churches. It was located some fifty yards or so inside the southern boundary of the town limits. The church stood out what with its unique outward appearance.

The outer walls were covered by large flat stonework, irregular in shape and in various hues from pale pink to soft rose, with heavy, dark tuck-pointing that stood out in relief against the stonework. A spacious, graveled parking lot enclosed the front and each side of the church. Three concrete steps led up to the large double door entry into the vestibule. Six additional steps were required to navigate through the second set of double doors that opened directly into the sanctuary.

When Dad arrived, he parked the car. The engine settled into an idle. Everyone remained inside for a moment, silent, as though struggling to exhale.

32

Wayne Wood, thirty one years of age, was Pastor of the Clarkton First Baptist Church. He was a well-known and respected member of the Southern Baptist clergy and an educator of repute. He lived in the parsonage next door to the church with his wife Ruth and their daughter, Maria. In later years, he would complete his doctorate degree in Education and serve as Superintendent of Schools for the Gideon School District while also pursuing his pastoring and preaching career. Brother Wood was selected by the funeral director, on behalf of Fats' mother, to conduct Fats' portion of the funeral. Wood knew little of Fats, but the pastor's reputation and eloquence of speech and manner placed him high on the director's list of preachers to be called upon in circumstances requiring special warmth, compassion, and understanding.

Brother Wood's preaching was of the more conventional style, given his mild manner and impeccable elocution. He provided insight into the teachings of Jesus. He was revered by his congregation and held in great esteem by the Bootheel Baptist Association and fellow protestant denominations. A strong attendance, in concert with a procession of baptisms, provided ample evidence of his ecumenical success.

The Busbys' first choice of church couldn't have been more different in tone and delivery. It was the Tatum Chapel, or just plain Tatum, originally a one-room schoolhouse built by a large landowner of the same name. It was in a remote area about two miles southwest of Peach Orchard in the heart of cotton country.

Tatum was known as a geographical landmark as much as it was known as a school or chapel. In 1941, church services began in the one-room schoolhouse on Sundays, a common usage for such remote locations during that era. Furthermore, it was typical for those living within close proximity of a school, a church or a big oak tree of some repute to identify where they lived by reference to such landmarks. Actually, hardly anyone spontaneously knew the county road numbers, nor cared to know. Numbers and routes were for the post office and county officials.

The pastor of the Tatum Chapel General Baptist Church in 1957 was Herbert Junior Crane, known affectionately to all as "Brother Crane," "Preacher," or just plain "Junior." Brother Crane was 39 years of age, a tenant-farmer/share-cropper and a hellfire and brimstone preacher. He had no classical theological training, but it was said he could 'preach the varnish off of a church pew.' Through determined study and a literal interpretation of the King James Bible, Junior became well-versed in his faith, showing great promise as an evangelical fundamentalist preacher at an early age. He first became a deacon in the church, and then its first full-time pastor. He was both revered and controversial. He believed in the healing power of prayer and practiced what he preached. The traditional Baptist rituals observed at Tatum Chapel were communion and full immersion baptism with occasional added symbolic rituals of the washing of feet and the laying on of hands. Baptisms traditionally took place during the hottest days of the year in the Floodway ditch next to the church known as Two Ditch.

With his coat off and the sleeves of his white dress shirt rolled to about mid-way between his wrists and elbows, Junior preached the Word of God at Tatum Chapel and at rousing Brush Arbor revival meetings, to thousands during the sweltering liquid-heat of the long, hot summers. His passion for the Word of God grew from an evangelical fervor seldom seen except in the most charismatic of preachers. With sweat on his brow and his right hand curled into a fist, his index finger pointed toward Heaven or Hell, depending on the topic, Junior drove home the Gospel like slamming a railroad spike through solid oak. There were no half ways or nuances in his world. The end of life brought either Heaven or Hell, and there was only one way to get to Heaven, which was to have been 'washed in the blood of the lamb.' Love him or hate him, everyone who knew Junior knew where he stood in matters of faith, and he was the Busbys' choice to preach Hokey's funeral.

The Gideon Funeral Home requested the loan of a hearse from a Piggott, Arkansas funeral home with whom they were affiliated. This was common practice if there were two independent funerals taking place. However, the circumstance of two hearses for the same funeral for a killer and his victim was not only unusual—it was unheard of.

The driver of the Arkansas hearse was making his way from Piggott along SR 1, through Holcomb to SR 25 north to the home of Fats' mother in Clarkton, where family and friends of Fat's gathered. The driver and his assistant were passing through the barren landscape, sipping coffee from thermoses and smoking Lucky Strikes while listening to local radio stations along their route. They'd be picking up Harry's casket and transporting it directly to the church, then to the cemetery.

Hokey's casket would be loaded into the hearse at the Gideon funeral parlor by the driver and a helper. The Busby family and friends would gather at the church.

Pastor Wood finished a fresh cup of coffee, kissed his wife, and told his ten-year-old daughter, Maria, to have a good day at school. He then walked the short distance from the parsonage to his office in the church. There, he began making preparations for the funeral.

After having written several notes through which he would weave a funeral sermon for Harry "Fats" Shell, he wadded them into a ball and tossed them into the wastebasket. He knelt in solitary prayer, as was the manner of this humble man, to ask God for guidance. Furthermore, he wanted to learn more of Harry. He had never before co-preached a double funeral, especially not under these circumstances. And, in a showing of respect, he decided not to refer to Harry as "Fats." It wasn't right, he believed, to refer to him so casually as his life was so brutally taken from him by Hokey. He asked why did this brutal affair happen? He had to learn more about Harry and Hokey. He thought he should speak to some people who knew Harry and his family. He left the office to speak to some of the church volunteers. Also, he hoped to have some time to spend with Junior, to discuss church business, if possible.

* * *

Meanwhile, Junior Crane, deep in thought, was being driven to Clarkton from his home near Tatum by J.C. Joyner, a church deacon. "Why do you think they're having their funerals together?" asked J.C.

"The funeral director drove out to see me yesterday. He said the families, the Busbys and Ms. Huddleston, Harry's mother, wanted Wayne Wood and me to preach the boys' funerals in the Clarkton church because they were best friends. The director said he didn't believe the Chapel was a large enough building for the crowd expected, could be that more than a hundred folks'll show up for this. So, we all agreed to have the funeral in Clarkton. As to why they wanted to have the funerals together, guess they just want to show everyone there's no hard feelings between the families." He looked out the window and added, "Probably hoping there won't be no more killing."

"Think that'll work?"

Junior sighed and turned his head to look out the window into the barren fields, then back at J.C. and said, "Just don't know, only God knows and only time'll tell."

"Yep," said J.C., "but it don't seem right, have'n their funerals together like this."

Junior said nothing in return, tightening his grip on his Bible, finding reassurance in the dog-eared pages, yellowed with age. All the answers are here, he thought as the pickup truck bumped and bounced along the rough gravel roads leading to the blacktop that would take them to Clarkton. Junior knew the words as well as anyone and better than most. His favorite passages were underlined with notes scribbled in the margins. His thoughts turned to Romans 6:23: "The wages of sin is death." And Romans 8:10: "If Christ be in you, the body is dead...but the spirit is life because of righteousness." This may work with Harry, he thought, but not Hokey, 'cause Christ had never been in his body. He also considered Psalms 51:1-17 regarding the remission of sin. It also didn't fit with Donald. It seems there was only one that fit: Romans 6:23.

The coming service weighed more heavily on him than he thought it would. Normal funerals were for older folks whose lifetimes of hard work have taken their toll, or a young person brought down by some unknown fever or accident of some sort. His thoughts brought back the image of a young boy whose folks lived near Tatum. He'd been shot in the head by his brother in a hunting accident. Horrible, the overpowering grief, like a veil of darkness, hung over the whole community. Yet this was different, much different. This time, it was murder by shotgun at close range, not a hunting accident.

Junior bowed his head slightly, his eyes closed tight. He prayed in a whisper, "Dear Lord, give me strength and guidance...give me the right words..." The tightrope he had to walk was to be true to his religious beliefs and not waiver, but also be sympathetic to the Busby family without diminishing the evil Hokey wrought upon Fats. This tightrope loomed closer and closer.

* * *

The funeral director was approaching the church in his personal car, well before the hearses were scheduled to arrive. He knew the churches in the Bootheel as well as any salesman knows his customers, and he knew the preachers' styles and temperaments. He had been the intermediary who helped broker the deal between the Huddlestons and the Busbys to have a double funeral. Now, he thought, I need to talk to Wayne and Junior, to see how they want the caskets placed. Both had to approve of the plan.

The director had facilitated many funerals at the church and he knew the layout by heart. Normally one casket would be positioned perpendicular to the pulpit, at the base of the raised platform. This was what they would want. However, with two caskets, would it be different? Were the caskets to be open or closed during the service? It could be a volatile situation. If the caskets remained open throughout the service, it could inflame passions on one side or the other. Fats' family and friends could be a rough bunch if they wanted. He personally preferred the lids closed and the caskets placed perpendicular to and centered on the pulpit. He'd speak to the preachers as soon as possible.

Parking in the graveled parking area, the director got out of his car, took a deep breath, and looked at the angry sky and what appeared to be micro–specks of snow. He opened the car trunk and removed some parking cones marked, "Reserved for Funeral." He thought for a moment that a cup of coffee from the Clarktonian would help keep him warm.

However, before the director could complete his task of identifying the parking spaces the town constable, in his police car, pulled alongside the director. There would be no time for coffee. Without getting out, the constable rolled down the car window. Dressed in regular work clothes and wearing a St. Louis Cardinals baseball cap, he looked like any other farmer save for the city constable badge pinned to his red and black plaid flannel shirt.

"Hey, Bud," the constable called out to the director. He called everyone "Bud", whether he knew their names or not. "Kinda cold for you to be working outside ain't it?" he said, with a chuckle and jaw full of chew.

"You're kidding, aren't ya? I always work outside," said the director.

"Ha! How're things looking so far?"

"Little ahead of yourself, aren't ya? We haven't got started yet."

"Well, ya can't get started too early in these kind of things. I tell you what. I'll be sitting just over there off the main road where I can see everyone who arrives. If there looks like any kind of trouble, send someone after me. If I see a problem, I'll intervene, but I don't like having to get involved in funerals...don't present the proper public image, you know."

"What's wrong? Isn't that what you get paid for?"

"I don't get paid to get killed. I knew Harry. Everyone called him Fats, but he wasn't so fat, he was just beefy-big. He was a good kid, too. From a good family and well-liked. Too bad he got mixed up with that bad seed. There are those who don't like what happened, him getting killed like that." The constable took a moment, looked up and down Main Street, pulled the collar up on his jacket and said, "I just don't know about things like this. I might be getting too old for this sort of work. Since you called me and gave me a heads up about it, I've called in a couple of my friends who have a little more horsepower than me. A state trooper friend of mine, Joe Brooks out of Kennett, you probably heard of him. He's a tough one and knows all these folks and they know him. He'll be leading the hearses to Stanfield and Sumach cemeteries. And Sheriff Scott is sending Chief Deputy Huggins up here, too."

"Yeah," said the director, "I think I know 'em both. Ain't Brooks the one who kicked the living shit out of that politician fella, somewhere east of Kennett on 84 Highway?"

"That's him," chuckled the constable. "They say that politician fella was drunk and challenged Brooks after being stopped. Ha! He told Brooks he wouldn't be so tough without his badge and gun, so Brooks obliged him by taking off his badge and gun. He drug the guy out of his car and commenced, as you said, to kick the living shit out of him, then proceeded to haul his smart ass to jail. But, hey! Nothin ever came of it. Didn't even make the papers."

"Huggins isn't no one to mess with either," said the director.

"Nope."

"Those two'll put a chill in 'em all right," acknowledged the director.

"You bet. But if there's any trouble, don't you worry none, I'll be in control."

"Well, okay." the director said, looking at his feet, shuffling them back and forth a bit, trying to warm up.

"It seems to be getting colder," the constable said. "Guess I'll get out of the way of the folks trying to park. Now don't hurt your back lifting them caskets, ya hear, ha!"

"Yeah, don't worry about me." Said the director, looking around the area. Maybe just the sight of Brooks in that state patrol car and Deputy Huggins in his squad car will cause any potential troublemakers to think twice.

The constable quickly repositioned his car, parking it across the street from the church.

Inside the church sanctuary, Kate, the organist, was busy sorting through sheet music. Flowers, purchased by church members and friends, were being placed on the raised platform by church volunteers. Two ornate carved chairs with red velvet cushions sat on either side and, to the rear of the pulpit, one chair for Brother Wood and one for Brother Crane. At the rear of the platform, behind the chairs were two flags. The Christian Flag with a white field and a red Christian cross inside a smaller blue field was on the right side as seen by those seated in the sanctuary. On the left side of the platform was the United States Flag.

The director made his way into the church, studying the available space between the raised platform and first row of pews. He stood in the large center aisle staring at the front of the church while church volunteers scurried about, ensuring each pew held the correct number of hymnals. Brother Wood saw the director standing in the center of the aisle. Walking up behind him, Pastor Wood placed his hand on the director's shoulder to get his attention. The director flinched, turned and said, "Oh, Wayne, didn't see you there."

"You're jumpy. You okay?"

"Well," said the director, shivering slightly as he turned his head to look out the tall windows in the sanctuary, "the weather's worrying me a bit. Looks like it could get stormy. But what's funny is that it don't look like snow clouds. For some reason, looks more like rain, even in this cold temperature." He hesitated a moment and rubbed his hands together. "I hate burying folks in the cold and rain, but I've done it before, a plenty, in warm rain, in freezing rain, and snow storms too. I've done most everything when it comes to burying folks," he grimaced, "but I most hate cold rain. Makes it real nasty."

Brother Wood listened intently, then, slapping the director on the back, he said, "Oh, I don't think we need to worry. Probably won't be anything, just some clouds. But I'd just as soon get this over with as quickly as possible."

The director nodded while pulling his coat tight around himself. "I better get back out there. It's getting time for the hearses to arrive and more people are coming in every minute." Walking out the door and down the steps, the director met Junior Crane coming up the steps. "Preacher," the director said, "how're you doing?" He liked Junior and seeing him arrive made him feel better.

"Just fine, sir, and you?"

"Okay, I suppose."

"What do we need to talk about?"

"Nothin' much. I just spoke with Brother Wood and everything's about ready. He's looking forward to seeing you. Seriously, just get it over with so I can get these boys in the ground before dark. I gotta get back outside to meet the hearses."

"Stay warm," Junior said.

"It's too late," he grimaced. "I'm freezing."

* * *

The hearse from Arkansas arrived at the Huddleston home in Clarkton, a small wood-frame home with gray brick siding. Fats' body had been visited by most everyone who knew him and his extended family from Zalma was there, asking questions. His casket had remained open for the entire period, from the previous evening's wake to this hour. The family, deep in grief, was subdued and, for the most part, ready to move on with the funeral. His mother, Elsie, near collapse, fought against grief and exhaustion, compounded by the tragic loss of her daughter, Mildred, who, three years earlier, burned to death in a truck accident. Fat's loving half-sisters handled the household chores. Homer, Elsie's husband, stood in the center of the room near Fats' open casket, grieving for his stepson while comforting his wife.

The driver exited the hearse to speak to Homer. The assistant stood alone by the back of the hearse, and spoke quietly with friends and relatives of Fats mulling about. Some asked questions about the Busby's, "Who were they?" and "Why?" Others questioned the advisability of a double funeral, fearing problems. The assistant, when asked, quietly dismissed the possibility of trouble.

* * *

At the church, Junior pulled open the heavy door and entered the sanctuary. He pulled off his overcoat and hung it over his left arm as he walked down the aisle to within a few feet of the raised platform and pulpit. This church is magnificent, he thought. Stained glass windows, polished pews and a strong attendance, as reflected on the church register that hung on the wall. Junior couldn't help but think of his small Tatum Chapel and his congregation of rock solid Christians.

His chest filled with pride in the simplicity of Tatum, where there were no polished pews or velvet cushions on the chairs. He could see divine providence at work in his having this opportunity to be heard by Baptists other than those from his church membership, and he quietly thanked God for this opportunity to preach to them.

Brother Wood, seeing Junior arrive, walked to meet him. He liked Junior and was always glad to see him. Brother Wood believed Junior should consider bringing his church into the Bootheel Baptist Association where there could be more cooperation between the two churches and more opportunities to expand the membership of both. However, Junior was a go-it-alone preacher cut from the cloth of pioneers, and not one to be guided by anything other than his own beliefs. Smiling, Brother Wood offered his hand. Junior grabbed it.

"Hello, Brother Wood."

Junior was of medium height, approximately 5'8" and 130 or so pounds, slim and sinewy with strong calloused hands and the leathery wind-blown look of a man who worked in the fields.

Brother Wood was also of medium height and weight, but his look was more that of an accountant, pale from working inside. His black-rimmed eyeglasses gave him the appearance of a university professor. His suit fit him like a well-worn glove while Junior was dressed in black pants, white shirt and tie with a long frock-like coat. His dark, deep-set eyes were piercing. His black hair, well groomed with mutton-chop sideburns. His appearance was the very essence of a man to be reckoned with.

"Let me take your coat," said Brother Wood.

"Thank you, Brother Wood," responded Junior.

"Please, just call me Wayne."

A church volunteer took Junior's coat from Wood and hung it in Brother Wood's office. Attendees began arriving, taking their places in the pews. Brother Wood scanned the sanctuary. "Junior," he said. "It appears everything's in order. The hearses should be arriving at any moment. Before you got here, the director and I were talking. I suggested the caskets should be closed throughout the service. What do you think?"

Junior thought for a moment. He didn't carelessly share his opinions, it wasn't his style. After weighing the options and possible consequences, he looked at Brother Wood. "I guess it all depends on the families' wants. But, whatever's decided on, both families have to be in full agreement."

"Absolutely," said Brother Wood. "Any difference between the two could be considered a slight by one side or the other and be the spark that starts something. But I also have a nagging feeling that open caskets could spark unwanted emotions, too."

"Yeah," sighed Junior, "they'll probably go along with the caskets being closed through the service as long as they're opened up for a final viewing at the end. But I'll talk with the Busbys."

"And I'll talk with Harry's mother when she arrives."

Brother Wood and Junior returned to their places near the large double doors, gently greeting arrivals while at the same time keeping an eye out for the hearses.

On the question of open caskets, Ruth deferred to Elsie. Elsie said her boy "has the rest of eternity to be in that box, so keep it open." It was thus settled, the caskets would remain open throughout the service, in accordance with family wishes.

"Ain't this just awful?" asked one attendee while yet another, with dripping sarcasm, sneered, "What a wonderful idea, having the murderer and his innocent victim's funeral together." Most however, deep in grief, simply walked in without saying anything.

As the flow of attendees slowed, Brother Wood said, "Junior, may I talk to you for a moment regarding some church business while we have the chance?"

"Sure, we got a few minutes." They walked off to the side, away from the door.

"This might be awkward and I hope you don't mind, but I don't get a chance to see you too often."

"What's on your mind?"

"What do you think about joining your church up with the Bootheel Baptist Association?"

"What?" Junior said, surprised at the suggestion. "Don't that mean taking orders from the Baptist Association?"

"There's no hierarchy in our association. We're simply a group of like-minded local Baptist churches. Many are members of the SBA, but it's not mandatory."

"Brother Wood..."

"Just call me Wayne."

"Ok, Wayne. I'm General Baptist, an independent. Some call us Free Will Baptists. I don't think we'd fit in with your association."

"I know you don't think so, but there's little difference between your church and ours. Most people can't tell the difference: General Baptist, First Baptist, Missionary Baptist, Southern Baptist, Free-Will Baptists. There are all kinds of Baptists, but we all hold the same core beliefs."

With a slight grin, Junior said, "I couldn't get along with all the professors in that group."

Brother Wood returned the smile. "The group is far from professorial. Anyway, don't you and I get along fine?"

"You're different from them others. You don't talk down to me 'cause of my lack of education. And you know I get mad when I preach. I get mad at the Devil and his demons and what they make good people do, keeping them away from being washed in the blood. I can't be nice about it like you. I don't talk like you."

"I know you, and I know you preach what you believe, and you believe every word in the Bible."

"That's right, and I don't sugarcoat it. You either accept The Word, as written, or you don't. And if you don't, I don't care how much good work you do, you're going to Hell."

"See what I mean? You have everything in proper perspective. Just gotta smooth them edges a bit for some folks."

"That's just it, I can't smooth them edges. No offense to you, but it's them edges that makes us different. Them edges are who I am, it's who my dad was and it's what I believe and preach."

"I like you and admire your passion for preaching. That's something that can't be learned, and Heaven knows your preaching sure draws a crowd. Everyone knows about your year-long tent revival, up round Greenville. I'm told the highway patrol had to direct traffic every night there. Musta drew thousands. And I've seen some of your baptisms at Two Ditch. Very impressive." Brother Wood paused, took a deep breath, and said, "Well, anyway, will you give it some thought?"

"Thanks for your kind words and your invite, I do appreciate it, but I think we'll be going it alone."

Brother Wood nodded as he and Junior returned to greeting attendees who, for the most part, were made up from their individual congregations.

At about 1:30, Mom, Dad, and the Busbys arrived at the church, parking in a spot reserved for the families near where the hearses were to be parked. After parking the car, Dad spotted the director standing at the bottom of the steps smoking a cigarette.

"Glenda," Dad said, "there's the director. I need to talk to him. Ya'll go ahead in. I'll be along in a bit." Mom looked at Dad with that what-are-you-doing look in her eye. "It's okay, Glenda, I'll be in there in a jiffy, don't worry, just save me a seat."

"Well, okay, but don't be long. You'll catch your death out here in the cold."

"I know, I know, but I'll be all right."

As Mom and the Busbys made their way out of the car, a gust of wind caught the open door and pulled it out of Raymond's grip, slamming the door on Bill as he tried to get out. "Darn it, Raymond!" Bill said, avoiding the word "damn." "Hold the door!"

"Well, get on out, why don't you?" Raymond said.

After getting out of the car, Bill made his way around to Ruth's door and opened it for her, holding on to the door with both hands. Ruth finished tying her headscarf on tight under her chin. Bill leaned into the wind. Li'l Joe scrambled out of the car and ran to Raymond's side. Mom waited on the Busbys, then walked with Ruth while Bill and the boys led the way onto the church steps.

Dad gripped the front brim of his Sunday hat to keep the gusts from blowing it off, and walked to the director who was trying to keep warm as he waited for the hearses.

"Why hello, Fred," the director said.

"Is everything going to be on time?" Dad asked.

"We'll be ready to go at two and out of here by three, if the preachers don't get carried away thinking this is a revival meeting."

"Any trouble so far?"

"Naw, not yet anyway. I gotta think there won't be any trouble. But if there is, we're ready for it."

While Dad and the director spoke, Mom and the Busbys made their way into the church. A light blue 1957 Ford Fairlane with a red dome light on the roof and a Missouri State Highway Patrol logo on both doors rolled slowly by the church. Trooper Brooks was here, dark sunglasses and all. He drove on north for a bit, ensuring everyone saw him arrive. Then he turned around at the jail and headed back south to the church, curbing the car on the right side of the street near the constable's car.

Brother Wood and Junior greeted attendees. Junior ushered the Busbys to the front row on the left side reserved for Hokey's family. Pastor Wood introduced himself to the Busbys once they were seated, then, noticing that Harry's family pews were empty, said to Junior, "Wonder where Harry's folks are?"

"Don't know," Junior said. "Wonder how many of 'em'll show up?"

"I just don't know, but I do expect a herd of curious strangers. These things can draw a lot of kooks, don't you think?"

"So did public hangings," Junior said under his breath.

"Yeah, I guess. Hope folks don't think of this as a hanging."

Once the Busbys were settled into their pew, Brother Wood said, "Junior, let's talk a bit more before the hearses arrive." They moved off to one side. "How well did you know either of these two fellas?"

Junior said, "I know Donald's folks, Bill and Ruth. They're good Christians. As far as Donald, most everyone called him Hokey. As for Harry, I saw him a few times at church. He occasionally came with the Robinsons or Busby families. They called him Fats but I didn't know much more about him than that."

Brother Wood folded his arms with his left hand under his chin. He looked at his feet for a moment like he was studying his shoes, then, in little more than a whisper, said, "I was told Harry's folks attended church every once in a while, but not regularly. Harry's mother was apprehensive about having a double funeral, but I was told by the director that she finally agreed because Harry and Donald were best friends. I wonder how much empathy she really has for the Busby family. She was real proud of Harry and he was a good person I'm told. He always brought most of the money he made to her, to help out. He was the only boy Elsie had. He had one full sister and three half-sisters. The Busbys once lived in Clarkton and were neighbors of the Huddlestons. The Busbys were contacted by the director and they were okay with a double funeral because of the boys' friendship, but were so humiliated and guilt-ridden, they didn't know what to do."

"Well," Junior said, "I wondered why there was a change, so it musta been the director's idea about the funeral plans."

"Looks that way," Brother Wood said. "I was contacted on Sunday to do Harry's funeral at Clarkton, then, all of a sudden, on Monday the director came to me and said it was going to be a double funeral."

Junior then asked, "Do you know if Harry was saved or not?"

Brother Wood thought for a moment and then responded, "His mom said he was, but I hadn't seen anything to prove he was ever baptized."

Junior said, "I'm sure Donald wasn't saved. He was a wild one." His eyes drifted away from Brother Wood toward the sanctuary.

Brother Wood said, "God has put this thing in our hands and we gotta make the best of it."

"Who goes first?" Junior asked.

Without answering Junior's question, Brother Wood turned and looked directly into Junior's eyes. "Have you ever preached a killer's funeral?"

Junior straightened to his full height, took a breath, furrowed his brow, and quietly answered, "No, we don't get a lot of them in my congregation. How about you?"

"I've preached a lot of funerals, I can't tell ya how many. But I have never knowingly preached a killer's funeral. Anyway, I'll be doing the preaching for Harry and we know he didn't kill Donald."

"That's for sure"

"How long you think this'll take?"

Junior squinted, bowed his head slightly and massaged his temples like he was getting a headache, and said, "With no special music and no eulogies, I've gone through a funeral in ten minutes or less. But that was a Potter's Field graveside service at the county."

"We're gonna hafta be fast today, 'cause it gets dark around five and it'll be earlier today, what with the clouds and all. The director's real nervous about all this and the times. If we're out by three, the gravediggers can get them in the ground before sunset, Harry at the Stanfield cemetery and Donald at Sumach."

"Okay, let's talk to the director."

Junior and Brother Wood walked outside the church and motioned for the director to come to them. The director, watching for the hearses, was standing almost in the street. Upon seeing Brother Wood wave for him to come to the church, he tossed down his cigarette and stepped on the smoldering butt. With the collar of his coat turned up and with his hands deep in his pockets, he walked at a brisk rate. He huffed and puffed from the exertion as he reached the top of the steps.

"Yes sir. What can I do for you?"

"Come in for a minute and warm yourself," said Brother Wood.

"Well, I gotta be out here to receive the hearses, but I guess it won't hurt to warm up a bit." Once inside the church, the director said, "What can I do for you?"

"What time do we have to be outa here, for sure?" asked Brother Wood.

"We have to be at the cemetery by three."

"I thought you said out of here at three."

"No, I said we need to be at the cemetery by no later than three. A storm is brewing. Now I think we should have had only a grave-side service for each."

"That's not funny," Brother Wood said, looking at Junior. "We gotta keep this short as possible. Tell you what. Junior, why don't you go first with Donald and do his in ten to fifteen minutes. Then I'll do Harry's. We'll sing a few hymns, have a prayer or two and get outa here. How's that sound?"

Junior stared at Brother Wood for a moment before saying, "That wouldn't be right. Donald killed Harry. Donald should be last, not first. Innocence before evil."

The director said, "You two work that out. We just need those boys at the cemetery by three o'clock." The director pulled his coat tight, mumbling to himself while he hustled out the door. "Excuse me, sorry, sorry," he said as he hurried through the folks coming up the steps.

Brother Wood knew Junior's idea of what's right couldn't be changed and, with the two o'clock hour closing in, Brother Wood relented. "This is not a usual service, and I agree that the innocent should be addressed first, so that means Donald goes last?" Brother Wood felt uneasy about the time issue. His primary concern was that if he went first, with Harry, and kept it short and sweet, Junior would follow and, with no one scheduled behind Junior, if he got rolling, he couldn't be held to a time limit. Junior's preaching had never been governed by a clock. He was known to have preached for hours, nearly collapsing from exhaustion, when the spirit moved him.

Junior placed his hand on Brother Wood's shoulder and said, "Don't worry none, Wayne. I can get done with Donald before long. Then I gotta get to Sumach Cemetery and you gotta get to Stanfield."

The organist began playing a soft medley of traditional hymns: "Blessed Assurance," "Rock of Ages," "Amazing Grace," and "I'll Fly Away." The sanctuary was as ready as it would ever be. There would be no choir. It was a simple setting. However, one of the church members, an aspiring vocalist, asked the organist if it would be possible for her to sing an a cappella version of "Amazing Grace".

"No," Kate said with a stern voice "No special music today."

"We'll just see about that!" In a huff, the aspiring vocalist abruptly turned and walked away. Brother Wood, overhearing the exchange between the two, shook his head, glad that the organist had held her ground.

The church provided ample seating for at least one hundred people, maybe more. The main aisle down the center of the church was about eight feet wide, leading to a raised platform upon which sat the pulpit. There was plenty of room between the platform and the first row of pews for a large wedding party, or, in this instance, two caskets placed end to end.

Pieces of black crepe, brought in by church members, somberly festooned the interior of the church. There was enough of the material to drape across the top of the piano and hang from four of the large windows, nearest the front of the church. Some church members and family friends brought in funeral wreaths, situating them on each side of the pulpit. Church members also volunteered to assist the funeral home personnel as needed. Time was drawing near.

The folks who came early to prepare the church offered their condolences to the Busbys. Footsteps on the hardwood floors echoed within the church from folks shuffling back and forth. Mom took up seats in the second row behind the Busbys, holding a seat for Dad on the aisle so he could stand, or leave, if necessary. Dad remained outside in the cold – watching.

33

At about 1:55 p.m., red lights flashed, flickered, and glared off the sides of buildings, store windows, and low-hanging clouds hovering over Main Street. The air itself seemed to be on fire as each tiny crystal of snow magnified the brilliance. The source of the phenomenon was a rotating red beacon atop the deputy sheriff's patrol car leading a procession south on Main Street at a speed no faster than a man could walk. Following close behind the patrol car was a shiny black hearse—Harry "Fats" Shell's hearse. A line of cars and trucks with their headlights on, a traditional show of respect for the deceased, snaked along behind. Onlookers edged along the canopied sidewalks nearest the street. Men removed their hats and women bowed their heads.

Inside the church, the empty pews reserved for Harry's family were all the more ominous. Outside, the director studied the coming procession, his eyes flitting from vehicle to vehicle, like a military officer making a threat assessment. Satisfied there was no outward display of hostility, he motioned to a young man standing nearby. He spoke briefly to the youngster, who immediately turned and ran into the church. All heads were turned toward the youngster as he made his way up the aisle with measured heel-toe, heel-toe steps in a cadence that demanded attention.

With the posture of a small soldier, the boy walked directly up to the raised platform, his eyes firmly focused upon Brother Wood. Brother Wood recognized the boy as a messenger and motioned for him to come forward. Junior, seeing this, redirected his attention away from his Bible to the youngster. The steely-eyed boy bounded up the two short steps from the hardwood floor to the platform and, in two long strides, was at the arm of Brother Wood.

Brother Wood leaned forward with the boy's approach, his right forearm resting on the arm of the chair, his left hand holding his Bible. The boy bowed slightly at the waist, his left hand on his knee and his cupped right hand shielding his mouth from the sanctuary. The attendees, eyes wide and curious, whispered among themselves, creating a discreet murmur. Having delivered his message, the boy made his way back the same way he came in, with the same distinct heel-toe, heel-toe cadence, while heads turned to watch him go.

Brother Wood nodded to Junior and then stepped to the pulpit. "I was just notified that Harry Shell's hearse is arriving. Please, remain seated."

Outside, groups of Hokey's and Fats' friends and family members gathered in murmurous knots, smoking and talking about the killing. Some had returned to the churchyard from inside the church or the Clarktonian café. A half-pint bottle of Four Roses whiskey was being passed among some of them, as cutting comments rang out.

"He was shot down like a dog by that son-of-a-bitch, Hokey," a hatchet-faced man snarled.

His acne-scarred friend replied, "What did Harry ever do to him to deserve this?"

"He musta did something," reasoned another voice.

"Fats never did nothin' against no one. He was a good man" was heard from another.

One person seemed to be the most enlightened when he said, "Why, Hokey knew that Fats was trying to move in on him and take his girl away from him, that's what it was all about."

Another philosopher was more to the point: "Hokey was just on a cheap wine drunk and that's all there was to it!"

"That's right, it was all about a girl, I heard that!" was raised by another voice.

"Figures. That Hokey was sure a wild one."

"What girl?" one questioned. "I hadn't heard anything about no girl. Then that's a different matter."

"I heard he was ambushed," interjected another.

"You got 'em confused. It was Hokey who was ambushed."

"That's crazy, no one could ambush Hokey."

Pushing and shoving began between the loudmouths as the procession approached the entry into the church parking lot. The deputy promptly stopped his car in the middle of the street and, with a flick of his finger, caused a low growl to emit from his siren. The rowdies were put back on their heels and a silence fell upon them. The constable adjusted his gun belt, spat out a chew of tobacco, wiped his lower lip with his hand and, with all the authority he could muster, walked to the gathered crowd. Seeing the whiskey bottle in the hands of one of the men he knew, he said, "Art, seeing this is a funeral, and that I'm here to keep the peace, I'll just take this hooch from you rather than arrest you here and now, if you promise to behave yourselves. If not, then turn around and put your hands behind your back." Art remained face to face with the constable and, holding the whiskey bottle in the air for a moment, he dropped it in the constable's outstretched hands.

"There you be," Art said. "I forgot I had that hooch, boss," Anyway, Fats was a friend of mine." He grimaced, "And he was shot down for nothing. Why can't a man have a drink over that?"

"You can, Art, but not in the churchyard. Now just get along with yourself before I change my mind."

Art grumbled and glanced back at the constable as he walked away, his feet moving in tiny steps.

"Now go on with yourself and quit looking back at me like that before I lose my temper, ya hear?"

Trooper Brooks, seeing the potential disruption, got out of his patrol car. Tall and tough, he paused a moment to adjust his uniform coat, gun belt and Smokey-Bear hat, then joined with the constable. Brooks' presence, in the familiar state trooper uniform, with its polished black over-the-shoulder (Sam Brown) gun-belt and his military style sunglasses, was the embodiment of head-busting authority.

"Any trouble here?" asked Trooper Brooks with an eye on the man walking away.

"Naw, nothing I can't handle," said the constable, both thumbs hooked on his sizeable gun-belt, wrapped around a great belly. "Art's okay, just a little tipsy, that's all." Looking toward the man, who had once again stopped at the edge of the crowd, the constable said, "Dammit, Art, now go on, get. I don't wanna hafta tell you again. Go home."

Art's eyes narrowed as he tried to focus on both the constable and Trooper Brooks. He began to waver, then limped toward the café. His uneven gait revealed a probable case of jake leg, brain damage caused by drinking bad moonshine.

Dad, who was standing at the edge of the crowd, was disgusted with the constable's ineffective way of handling Art. However, he was relieved upon seeing Trooper Brooks moving in to back the constable.

The constable nodded toward Sheriff's Deputy Huggins who was still sitting in his patrol car and called out to him. "It's okay. Bring 'em on, come on." The deputy drove past the entrance, clearing the driveway into the churchyard. He again stopped his car in the middle of the street, his red light still flashing to stop any traffic that might be coming from the south. However, there wasn't any other traffic.

The county's permanent population was small enough so that this funeral was common knowledge. No one in the vicinity of the funeral would have knowingly driven into this activity, not today. The hearse turned ever so slowly into the entrance, stopping briefly to receive instructions from the director.

The driver lowered his side window some six to eight inches, wisps of cigarette smoke escaping. After giving brief directions, the director backpedaled away from the car while pointing to the spot he intended the hearse to back into. He nodded in approval as the hearse pulled forward past the parking space, and began to slowly back into it. The cold gravel crunched and crackled under the weight of the hearse, coming to a stop within 20 feet of the church steps.

The director moved to the car in line behind the hearse that still sat in the street. It was the car in which Harry's mother and stepfather were riding. He directed the driver to park in a reserved spot next to Harry's hearse. The remaining vehicles in the procession parked in whatever spots were available in the church parking lot and along Main and Commercial Streets.

The driver of the hearse and his assistant jumped out and moved to the large back hatch. They needed volunteers to act as pallbearers. Four men from Harry's procession volunteered. The driver spoke in a low voice with the volunteer pallbearers, while flipping a cigarette butt to the ground and grinding it into the gravel with a twist of the toe of his shoe. Grabbing hold of the large chrome handle on the great rear door with both hands, the driver set his feet and, looking over his shoulder, said, "Ready?" Then, with a twist of the handle, he threw his weight into pulling open the heavily curtained door. As the door swung open, the casket was revealed. A spontaneous yet barely audible lament rose from those gathered.

The director paid close attention to the volunteer pallbearers. He had experienced occasions when volunteers who appeared to be strong and steady faltered under the unexpected weight of a full casket. Therefore, reassuring himself that these volunteers possessed the physical strength to be of assistance, he announced to the crowd, "Please go inside the church and be seated."

"There ain't no more seats," called out a voice in the crowd.

Dad, unable to accept that all was well, remained in the churchyard with the certainty that Mom was holding his place. He would wait until Hokey's hearse arrived.

The people in the churchyard continued milling about, mostly unresponsive to the director's request that they enter the church. One person spoke out, "We'll stay with Harry until he's in the church, then we'll go in." These friends and relatives of Fats were dressed in pressed bib overalls and jeans with heavy work shoes, or in business suits with white shirts, ties, and polished shoes. The women wore long print dresses, little makeup, and their hair was loose, falling down to their waists. Others did their hair up in buns, and all wore hats or headscarves. They were a hard-working lot, sons and daughters of the land, wearing dark colors with little difference in their appearance and actions compared to those bereaved already seated inside.

Appearing tired and bent, Harry's stepfather, Homer, and his mother, Elsie, along with Harry's half-sister, Sallie, made their way from their car to the hearse. Sorrow hung on them like a heavy sack, evident in each measured step. As they approached the hearse, Harry's mother, who had been leaning on the arm of her husband, paused for a moment. Then, she walked alone to the casket still resting in the hearse. The pallbearers and funeral personnel stepped back, heads slightly bowed in a mutual showing of respect and tribute. She laid her hand upon the bronze-colored finish, steadied herself for a moment and patted it tenderly, as quiet sobs escaped her lips.

Harry's stepfather took her right arm as she slumped, whispering to her, "Come on Elsie—it's time." The pallbearers stood mute, some wiping away tears as Elsie moved slowly through the crowd toward the steps leading up to the church. The director stepped forward, making his way to the couple, taking Elsie's left arm. They proceeded toward the church door where Brother Wood, Bible in hand, was now standing.

The pallbearers waited patiently for one of two casket-carts now inside the entry to the church to be set up before they carried the casket up the steps. With a strong pull, the casket slid about one foot out of the hearse. Each pallbearer took hold of a handle as they came within reach. In a few moments the casket was free of the hearse, the pallbearers taking the full weight in unison. Carrying it ever so gently to the steps of the church, they grunted and groaned as muscles and arteries bulged with blood under the weight of Harry's casket. The director, having helped Harry's mother to the family's pew, hurried back to hold open the church door, allowing the casket to pass into the sanctuary.

The sounds of struggling pallbearers flooded the quiet church along with the cold westerly wind. Wisps of delicate snow crystals dissolved immediately upon settling on the casket and hardwood floor. A couple of babies made their presence known. Their mothers covered their heads with small blankets, held them close and whispered into their ears. The pallbearers set the casket upon the heavy, chromed casket-cart, and the door closed. The director walked around it, ensuring it was properly seated and safe to move. With a quick nod from the director, the hearse driver and his assistant took charge of the casket and pushed and pulled it up the aisle to the front of the church.

The sight of the casket brought muffled sobs of grief and anguish from many of those present, some near collapse. The casket rested in accordance with the director's instructions. Harry would be to the right of the pulpit, in front of his family. The director then used the small crank-like tool to unseal the lid and open the casket for viewing. Following a brief moment or two during which time the director removed the shroud and adjusted the lining, Harry's full face, somber, with a touch of sadness, came into view. In the fake, light-gray funeral suit, white shirt, and tie, the violent nature of his death was undetectable.

Brother Wood's hands trembled and he began to pale. He looked upon the families, so fragile, the inescapable signs of sadness, anger and guilt all mixed together in their reddened, pleading and sleep-deprived eyes. The pain they were suffering at this moment could also be seen in many of the attendees.

He whispered to Junior, "This is gonna be difficult. Let's just get through it as soon as possible." Brother Wood then moved to the pulpit. "Dear friends and families of the departed, the hearse bearing the remains of Donald Ray Busby will be here shortly. Please remain seated." A lady of the church walked quietly to Harry's casket and gently placed a spray of flowers on the lower portion.

A funeral home employee standing outside the church opened the door and nodded to the director. The second hearse had just come into view. No police car or sedan led it. There was a small caravan of five or six cars, friends from his days of wilding. Flecks of snow whirled around the hearse as the director rushed to direct the driver to back into the open space beside Harry's hearse.

The pallbearers for Hokey jumped from their cars parked in front of the church. The groups for Harry and Donald intermingled with little differentiation among them. Cigarettes were lit, jackets drawn tight, and collars pulled up against the wind, and eyes nervously darted about the parking area. The air felt alive, like the moments before a fight. The director once again spoke to the driver of the hearse as Dad carefully watched the throng. The constable, Trooper Brooks, and the deputy took up prominent positions.

Bill and Raymond left the family pew, making their way outside. The director attempted to hurry the process. Brother Wood, sensing restlessness in the attendees, nodded toward the organist. In response, she adjusted herself on the bench and began to play a solemn hymn, "Old Rugged Cross." This seemed to have a calming effect on the attendees.

The same familiar sounds, the grunts and shuffling of feet, brought attention to the open door. The temperature inside the sanctuary once again dropped with the rush of cold air. Donald's casket looked just like Harry's, but weighed much less due to Hokey's lighter frame, making it easier for the pallbearers to carry. It now rested on the second casket-cart. Moments later, the casket was pushed and pulled into position on the left side of the pulpit. The sound of the cart was like distant thunder as it rolled over the hardwood floors. The director went about opening the upper portion of the casket lid, drawing a slight groan from some and a wail from others along with muffled curses. Here was Donald, "the provider of the feast," his looks still strong, his deed still fresh.

With the opening of the caskets complete, the director and his workers moved to the rear of the church. The director centered himself in the doorway. The drivers left the church, moving back to their posts in the hearses. The director nodded to Brother Wood and Junior Crane. It was time for the service to begin.

34

Despite the cold temperature, at about 2:10 p.m. small groups of people lingered about the churchyard.

The Constable sat with Trooper Brooks in his patrol car. Deputy Sheriff Huggins sat alone in his car, reading the Daily Dunklin Democrat, sipping coffee out of the orange-colored cup-lid of his ever-present thermos. He looked at his watch every few minutes while occasionally eyeing the weather and the churchyard.

Inside, Kate softly played old time gospel favorites. Brother Wood and Brother Crane were seated in the cushioned chairs on the raised platform. Soft sobs echoed off the church's ceiling and intermingled with wind gusts rattling the windows. The heat in the sanctuary barely kept the chill off and the windows began to slowly fog from the combined breath of the mourners. Kate nodded toward Brother Wood as she finished playing, "What a Friend We Have in Jesus." All eyes shifted toward the open caskets, and Brother Wood and Brother Crane.

In keeping with their agreement, Brother Wood rose first to preach Fats' portion of the funeral. He straightened to his full height and walked the few steps to center himself on the pulpit with his Bible in hand. Alongside his Bible, he placed a small notebook of ruled white paper, on which he had scribbled notes.

His words were strong and reassuring to Fats' family: "Jesus said, 'I am the resurrection, and I am life: those who believe in me even though they die, yet shall they live and whoever lives and believes in me shall never die, I am Alpha and Omega, the beginning and the end, first and last. I died and behold I am alive for evermore and I hold the keys of Hell and death. Because I lived you shall live also.' We are gathered here today in heart-breaking grief to remember Harry, lovingly known to friends and family alike as 'Fats,' whose life was cut short in a most hideous manner. Harry, a good man, a good son and step-son, departed this life on December 7, 1957, 23 years 11 months and 7 days following his birth, cut down in the prime of his life by someone he considered a friend, a friend driven to madness by drink."

The attendees were wide-eyed, leaning slightly forward in their seats, yearning for any words of solace. Brother Wood's words were soothing and fatherly as he continued in his measured pastoral manner. He spoke of the short life of Harry, who grew up in difficult circumstances without his father, yet under the watchful eye of a loving mother and stepfather.

Brother Wood expounded on Fats' cheerful nature and trusting ways. "He worked hard at various jobs requiring muscle and stamina, and no matter his state of exhaustion he always had an easy smile for those around him, and he never refused help to others with what little he had to offer. He attended church when he could with his mother and sisters. However, he came more and more under the spell of someone he thought to be a friend." Eyes began to roll, quiet sobs grew in intensity, babies grew restless, and feet began to shuffle.

Brother Wood, like a skilled attorney before a sympathetic jury, wove together a case for Fats' redemption. "Repentance, faith, and baptism are stalwarts of our faith, but only God knows the heart of a man, and God's decision is made at the pearly gates. I believe Harry is now in Heaven, having been judged by his maker and found worthy of admittance into that celestial city." The familiar echo of "Amen" from several voices rang out in the sanctuary.

Brother Wood ended his comments with, "In the name of the risen Christ and with every head bowed, let us pray." Every head did bow, some more than others, some with one eye open trying to see what was happening. Brother Wood's prayer beseeched God to have mercy on Fats and his family, finishing with the Lord's Prayer: "Our Father, who art in heaven, hallowed be thy name, for thine is the kingdom, the power, and the glory for ever and ever. Amen." He never once mentioned Hokey's name, a conscious decision on his part to avoid any suggestion that he was placing blame. Yet the implication was apparent and couldn't be ignored, not with Hokey's body lying there. Turning from the pulpit, Brother Wood walked slowly to his chair, nodding his head ever so slightly to Junior.

Recognizing a need, the church choir director, seated in one of the pews, voluntarily rose from his seat to conduct the singing from the center aisle. His spontaneous actions drew a grateful nod from the organist and Brother Wood who mouthed the words "thank you" to him.

The organist played "I'll Fly Away" while the choir director led the singing. Some toddlers, bored with it all, managed to break away from their parents and began to run up and down the main aisle. Their shoes banged against the hardwood as parents grabbed up their children, shushing them.

In a smooth tenor voice, the director sang with the attendees. During this interlude, Junior scooted forward in his seat and nodded back to Brother Wood, like two prizefighters touching gloves, acknowledging the last round. The congregation seemed to collectively take a breath.

Junior walked slowly to the pulpit, like a defending heavyweight champion making his way to the center of the ring, a ring he knew well. Dressed in black, he seemed much larger than his 5'8" frame. His trim, leathery good looks along with his dark hair and piercing eyes, gave him the appearance of someone of authority who demanded attention. His pulse quickened. Beads of sweat formed on his forehead. His empathy for the families and the desire for a speedy service were foremost in his head. Don't compound the tragedy, he thought, but also, don't stray from the gospel, don't condemn or redeem. The service is for the family.

"You can't make a stinker into a saint," Junior said. This odd comment drew confused looks from some and muffled chuckles from others. Junior didn't use notes; he knew the Bible and could quote it forwards and backwards. He had mulled over and over what he might say since learning he would be preaching Hokey's portion of the funeral. He grappled with the delivery, substance, impact, and his own beliefs as a hush fell over those gathered. He continued, "The Ten Commandments forbid murder, killing out of hate, or without just cause."

Suddenly he knew he had no choice but to preach the gospel as he had always done; there was no middle, there were no edges. Holding his Bible to his chest with both hands, he paused for a moment, his head slightly bowed as if in a moment of prayer. His eyes closed, his forehead furrowed.

Opening his eyes ever so slightly, he remained absolutely quiet. He focused his stare above the heads of the attendees to a point on the rear wall near the ceiling. The intensity and expectation built as the church building shuddered and shook from the chilling winds.

The director, standing at the rear of the church near the door and out of sight of the attendees, raised his left wrist to eye height, pointing to his watch with his right index finger and mouthing the word "time."

Centering himself on the pulpit, Junior placed his Bible on the flat surface before him with great care and gripped the sides of the pulpit. Turning his head slowly to the right, he looked directly at the Busby family through piercing brown eyes, slightly nodding to them, showing respect and empathy to the killer's family

He placed his right hand on the Bible, curled the fingers of his left hand, making a fist, and pointed dramatically toward Fats' casket with his index finger. In a booming voice that made babies cry, he said, "Here lie the remains of Harry Leslie Shell, known to his family and friends as 'Fats'." *Thump.* Then, in a flash, he switched the Bible to his left hand while doubling up his right fist and thrusting his index finger down toward Hokey's casket. He shouted, "Here lies the remains of Donald Ray Busby, known to all his friends and family as 'Hokey.'" *Thump.* "Donald and Harry were inseparable friends until three days ago when *a demon*, controlled by *the devil*, took control of Donald and used him to murder Harry." *Thump.* "If you're looking for Donald, he ain't here. This body lying here ain't Donald, he's gone." *Thump.* "And, don't believe you'll ever see Donald in Heaven, 'cause he's not there either." *Thump.* "Donald went straight to Hell last Saturday night." *Thump.*

The thumping sound during Junior Crane's sermon was disconcerting to those unfamiliar with his preaching style, but it went unnoticed by his own Tatum congregants. He kicked his foot on the bottom of the wooden pulpit in a rhythmic manner to accent his preaching, revealing an inner passion for the Word of God.

Momentarily stunned, the director, standing in the rear of the church, cringed, shifting his weight from side to side. He nervously looked at his watch and glanced at Junior, shaking his head from side to side. No...No...No...he's gonna do it, he thought. Damn if he ain't...we're gonna have a riot. Ruth Busby broke down and buried her head in Bill's chest. Bill placed his arm around her shoulders and held her close, never taking his reddened, tear-drenched eyes off Junior. Raymond showed no emotion; he looked straight ahead, directly at Hokey's casket. Li'l Joe pulled his feet up into the pew and huddled against his mother, his eyes open wide.

Mom, not being from the Deep South, was less accustomed to this style of preaching. She squeezed a linen handkerchief in her left hand so tight her knuckles paled, while tightly gripping Dad's left hand with her right hand. Tears filled her eyes from compassion, or perhaps anger.

Some congregants of Brother Wood's church appeared stunned at this old-fashioned give-'em-Hell brand of preaching. Undeterred, Junior quoted verbatim, verse after verse, from one end of the Bible to the other, on the wages of sin and the exultation of a sin-free life when "washed in the blood of the lamb."

Junior continued. "Some say this killing was over this or that. It don't matter what it was over. It would have happened anyway to someone else if not Harry 'cause the Devil had his disciple, his acolyte in the form of Donald. Donald had every chance to give his life to Jesus, but he didn't, and by not making that decision, he made another decision, a decision that led him to follow the will of the Devil and his demons." The director made another attempt at speeding up the service by pointing to his watch.

Catching his breath, Junior paused, wiped his forehead with a handkerchief and caught the director's signal. Yet, he had one more thought, adding something that he had intended to say but had almost forgotten. "Don't believe that good works mean anything without a belief in Jesus, 'cause, if you do, you're also doomed to go straight to Hell, and no make-believe Hell, but a God-awful bed of red hot coals and sulfur Hell. I hate it when I hear people say someone was a good person and would go to Heaven because they were good, even though they were not saved." Junior kept preaching, maintaining course. a full-fledged soul-searching firestorm of a sermon equal to anything heard on the radio by the attendees who were both shocked and mesmerized.

"I'm as sure Harry is in heaven today, as much as I'm sure that Donald ain't. Now, this is no revival meeting; this is a funeral. But I'd be upset with myself if I didn't use this occasion as a perfect warning to all. If you're not saved, you better take care of that before you're wallowing in Hell with Donald." Tears, sobs, and "Amens" rose from the sanctuary.

Brother Wood sneaked a peek at his watch. It was 2:55 p.m. He looked at the director who seemed terribly distraught with a frown across his face.

Junior had sweat plumb through. As the staccato-like cadence of his delivery became stronger, the veins in his neck bulged and his face reddened in a euphoric trance-like state. He emphasized each biblical point by stabbing his finger into the air. With sweat pouring from his body and his eyes lit up like globes, he reflected a state of religious ecstasy.

An anxious look from the director, standing at the rear of the church in the center of the main isle, caught Junior's eye. Recognizing he had gone past the time allotted, Junior concluded his comments. Standing absolutely still, he calmed himself, gathering his thoughts. Taking a step back from the pulpit, he hesitated for a few additional moments, holding his Bible close.

With the church silent and only gusts of wind making a sound, he said, "Let us pray."

Junior began his prayer by saying: "'Matthew 5:9 says, 'Blessed are the peace makers for they will be called children of God.'" He paused for a moment, took a deep breath, then continued, "There is no need for vengeance in response to Donald's heinous act that was his alone. And for which, Donald will alone burn in hell." We pray, oh Lord, that there will be no attempted vengeance by any aggrieved party and that peace and love will fill the hearts of both families."

The prayer continued as sobs resonated from the attendees. Both mothers, Elsie and Ruth, shook with emotion.

Junior's prayer was more about peacemaking than condemnation, and he made the case for mending any animosity between the families. It was an unexpected turn from his main theme and much welcomed by the Busbys. As Junior signaled the end of the prayer, Brother Wood breathed easier and the music director stood and asked everyone to turn their hymnals to "Amazing Grace."

As the attendees sang, the wind outside rushed hard against the old building. It was indeed time to end it. The director stepped outside to motion for his helpers. As Junior made his way back to his chair, exhausted, Brother Wood quickly moved to the pulpit.

"Everyone please remain seated until directed by the church volunteers to form a viewing line. Family members please remain seated," he said.

The organist played softly.

35

The director's appearance at the door of the church caught the attention of the constable who was seated in his car. He placed his baseball cap squarely on his head, with the arc of the bill just above his eyes. He looked at himself in the rearview mirror and, when satisfied, crawled out of the car, zipped up his coat, stretched a bit, and walked the short distance to where Deputy Huggins and Trooper Brooks were parked.

Hearing muffled talk and noticing movement of people through their fogged windows, Deputy Huggins put down his newspaper after draining the last of the coffee from his thermos cup. Trooper Brooks, ever the professional, placed aside the daily report he was working on.

As he walked, the constable hacked up chunks of brownish phlegm, spitting it out. He cleared his nostrils one at a time, placing a forefinger first to one side of his nose and blowing hard, then doing same to the other side. The process turned his face beet-red. The officers rolled down their windows and watched the constable trudge toward them.

The constable said, "Looks like the service is finally over. Thought for a while there that we might have to spend the night." Then he placed a fresh cut of chew deep into his jaw. Brown tobacco juice began to drip out the side of his mouth and down his chin. "Damn," he said, as he wiped his mouth with a white handkerchief he took from his back pocket. "I gotta quit this habit sometime."

Both Brooks and Huggins nodded, rolled their windows up, and exited their cars. Zipping up their coats, all three moved to where the hearses were parked.

"You gonna be all right?" asked Deputy Huggins. "You got quite a cough there."

"Yeah," the constable said. "Don't worry about me, just a little cold coming on."

Small groups of folks in twos and threes, the overflow crowd who couldn't get inside the church, began moving back into the churchyard from the Clarktonian and small tavern.

Huggins said, "It seems too cold to have any trouble. But those ole boys coming back into the churchyard give me a strange feeling."

Brooks turned toward the group and stared at them like a hawk staring at field mice. "I don't like it when folks skulk around wearing heavy coats, makes me nervous, even if it's winter. You could hide a bazooka under those coats." He focused his gaze on two or three of the men. "Didn't a couple of those fellas there make some pretty raw remarks earlier?"

"Yeah, they sure did," responded Deputy Huggins as he placed the palm of his right hand on the heel of his holstered .45 Colt revolver. "My orders are clear: don't tolerate no trouble here today."

"That's Sheriff Scott for ya," chuckled the constable, "'Sheriff No-Trouble,' I call him."

"Yeah," Trooper Brooks said, winking toward the deputy. "I bet you do. And I'm sure you still have that nice hard concrete floor for any peckerwood that starts anything."

"You bet," the constable said as he adjusted his holster belt. "Now, how you boys wanna handle this?"

"Well," said Deputy Huggins, "any dipshit who mouths off or looks like he might be thinking of mouthing off has got to go. I won't stand for it."

The constable responded, "Don't worry. I'll grab 'em up as quick as possible and give them a good talking to. They'll understand then. And if they don't, off to the calaboose they'll go."

"Like you did with Art, huh?" asked Deputy Huggins.

"Well, I took care of that, didn't I?"

"Did you?"

"What's that mean?"

Deputy Huggins didn't respond, but turned his head slowly from the constable to the gathering crowd. Then, looking back over his shoulder at the constable, he said, "Nothin' chief...it means nothin'."

The deputy said, "I'll be at Fats' burial, but I don't expect any trouble. If anyone gets rowdy, they'll be going straight to the county lock-up in Kennett—in the trunk of my car. Meanwhile, since we'll be driving mainly on state roads, Brooks, you gonna take the lead in this parade?"

"Yeah, I'll lead out 'cause it's on state roads and guess it'll be me going to Sumach with Hokey. Y'all remember. If there's any trouble, get a call out and I'll do the same. I can have a couple more troopers here in a few minutes." Looking at Huggins, Brooks continued, "I'd like you to be on the tail-end of this caravan as a blocker, so we don't have any uninvited guests rolling up on us from behind." He paused, thinking of a past experience when a truckload of shotgun-wielding rabble had rolled up on a funeral procession in the Ozarks to settle old scores. "Well, just stay in radio contact."

"Boys, now ya'll know I can't leave the city limits," the constable said.

"We know," Brooks said.

"So unless I get a call for help, I can't cross the city limits. Don't ya'll forget to call me."

"We know, we know," Brooks said as Deputy Huggins turned his head away from the constable.

"I'll brief the director and the hearse drivers," the constable said.

Trooper Brooks hooked his thumbs in his holster belt. "Let's stay in the open and let 'em see we're still here."

Inside the church, children who had napped through the service began to wake. The shuffling of feet, heels clobbering the hardwood, and a quiet murmur filled the sanctuary while the viewing line formed. The director stood at the rear of the church. He looked at his watch and thought, here we are, damn near dark. The diggers'll sure want more money for this.

He walked up the aisle to take his place, standing between the two caskets. Brother Wood and Junior Crane left their cushioned chairs, stepping down from the platform to lead the mourners past the caskets, first Fats', then Hokey's.

Brother Wood paused at each casket with his eyes closed for a moment, finishing with the words, "God have mercy on your soul." Junior prayed quietly at Fats' casket and then moved on to Hokey's. While looking at Donald, he said, just loud enough to be overheard, "Look what you did,

Hokey. You let the Demon win." As an afterthought, he whispered a quick, "God have mercy on your soul," before nodding to Brother Wood and the director standing nearby. The bereaved and morbid curiosity seekers began shuffling by the caskets in a viewing line that snaked up and down the outside aisles of the sanctuary. The wide center aisle was for the exclusive use of the families.

Dad stood tense, focused. Apprehensively he whispered to Mom, "This is going to be touchy after Junior's 'Give-em-Hell' sermon. Let's get in line and get out of here."

Mom nodded then patted Dad's hand and said, "We can't hurry up, Fred. We have to take Bill and Ruth to the cemetery, then home, so let's just sit here and wait until the line has thinned down some."

"You're right," Dad sighed, leaning back into the pew, trying unsuccessfully to relax.

Both day laborers and land barons filed by the caskets. Many of those who passed by barely looked at the dead friends, seemingly fixated upon the families. Young women with small babies and saddened eyes, their faces bearing the lines of hard work at an early age, gazed at the horror as if peering into a deepening storm. Most all were polite and delicately nodded to each family, uttering condolences. "I'm so sorry," some said. "If there's anything I can do," others said. One attendee, Hank, in his best field-clothes, his blue plaid flannel shirt buttoned to his chin, his broad hat brim held in his calloused hands, turned toward Fats' mother.

"Mrs. Shell," he said. "Ah, I'm so sorry..." He swallowed deeply, his head slightly bowed and his eyes tearing, "I mean, Mrs. Huddleston. You know I've known Harry ever since we went to school together in the first grade. He was a good and honest man and I just don't have the words to tell you how bad I feel about all this. There's gotta be a reckoning to make this right." Tears rolled down his cheeks into the stubble on his chin. "I never knew a man more deserving of better."

Elsie reached her hand to him and, in the softest tone, said, "Thank you, Hank, I appreciate you coming." As she touched his strong, calloused, work-stained hands, she added, "Harry often spoke of you in the kindest of terms. Thank you so much for coming." Hank nodded, turned slowly and then moved on, Elsie's hand sliding from his. He barely glanced at Hokey as he passed his casket, but turning his head to the left, he glared at the Busbys without saying a word and turned down the side aisle toward the door.

Sorrowful wails resonated throughout the sanctuary, coming from some folks who never knew either of the dead. Some held their kids up, kicking and screaming, so they could see into the caskets. Some said, without any thought to the feelings of the family, who could easily overhear them, "If you ain't good, Hokey'll get ya, just like he did ol' Fats there." They would go to great lengths to point out which body was which, while the wide-eyed children looked on in stark terror. "This is Harry," some pointed out to their kids. "He was called 'Fats' by his friends but not in a bad way. He was a nice person." Then moving to Donald's casket they said, "This is Donald, called 'Hokey' by most everyone. He's the demon who killed Harry."

Someone snarled through rotting teeth that it was that Floodway bum Elmer who really killed Hokey. Then he added as an afterthought, "Suicide my ass. Hokey'd never've killed himself." Some openly glared at the Busby family and quietly muttered through gritted teeth, "This is just the beginning."

The director made a mental note of the most threatening faces, patted them on the shoulder and encouraged them to move on.

Some asked, "What did Fats do to Hokey to make him want to kill him?" One chuckled, "They're yellowing up a bit, looking kinda ripe. Guess they've been out of the ground too long." This comment also drew a stern "move on" from the director. The preachers remained close to the families, Brother Wood comforting Fats' mother and Junior comforting the Busbys. Bill and Ruth accepted Hokey's descent into Hell as laid out by Junior. They lived their whole lives under words like his. They expected nothing less, yet it still hurt. Raymond remained stoic, steeling himself, showing no emotion. He took it all in, the love and concern for the family by some and the hard vicious remarks by others, accepting the weight he had to bear. Li'l Joe was exhausted and confused.

The viewing line inside the church grew shorter and the crowd outside grew larger. The men and some women already outside the church, under the watchful eyes of the three lawmen, cupped Zippo lighters, lighting roll-your-owns and store bought cigarettes. They gulped down the sweet smoke as if starved. Shifting their weight from foot to foot to stave off the cold, they looked like they were participating in some silly little dance.

Back inside the church, Mom and Dad were among the last to view the remains. Mom, hardened by life, suddenly found she couldn't hold back the tears. She whispered "so innocent," to herself as she moved slowly by Fats' casket, and dabbed her eyes with her lace-trimmed handkerchief. Then she stopped at Hokey's casket. "What a pretty boy," she whispered. "No one would think by looking at you that you could have done such a thing." She recalled him as a happy youngster with dancing eyes during the innocence of his youth. It was hard for Mom to come to grips with the evil he now represented.

Dad, walking directly behind Mom, turned from Hokey's casket, facing the seated Busby family. He spoke softly to Bill. "We'll be waiting for y'all in the car." Bill, who seemed to have aged several years in the past few days, appeared disconnected, unable to speak as he gulped a breath of air and nodded. Dad turned to Mom, saying, "Glenda, we gotta move on now." They made their way down the side aisle to the rear of the church where Dad helped Mom put on her coat and scarf. Dad, concerned that Mom couldn't take much more of this, spoke briefly to the director who had made his way to the church door from his position between the caskets.

"Be watchful," Dad said to the director. "There's a good-sized crowd out there between the church and the hearses."

The director, putting his hand on Dad's shoulder, said, "We have it covered, Fred. Don't worry."

"Okay," Dad said, "see you at Sumach."

The church stood empty except for family members, funeral folks, and some church volunteers. Elsie, with her husband and Fats' sister and half-sisters, crowded around his casket, sobbing and saying goodbyes. Ruth, Bill, Raymond, and Li'l Joe were bunched about Hokey's casket. They all appeared so weary, so fragile and frail as they said soft goodbyes to beloved sons, the indescribable sadness reflected in their faces. During these intimate moments, Ruth and Elsie happened to come face to face between the two caskets.

Seconds seemed like minutes as neither Ruth nor Elsie said anything. Elsie, clearly the aggrieved, and Ruth and Bill, sad, weary and bent, simply looked at each other.

Junior, who had been standing a few feet away, recognized the impasse. He instinctively moved between the two mothers. Holding both Ruth's and Elsie's hands, Junior served as a conduit between the two. He spoke in whispers just loud enough to be overheard by those standing nearby.

"It's in God's hands," he said. "What's done is done. We're here only to commemorate and to grieve. Both families have suffered terribly. Now let God bear the tribulation." The sadness was palpable as Ruth and Elsie raised their eyes under Junior's urging.

Ruth once again began to sob and, in a gasping moan, uttered over and over to Elsie, "Oh my God, I'm so sorry." Her eyes, nearly tearless from crying, were red and swollen. "I'd do anything to turn back the clock. I'd rather have killed Donald myself and have his death on me than for this to have happened to Harry. Oh, God, this hurts," she said in a soft, barely audible voice. Bill, in an attempt to show his understanding as a father and husband, held Ruth with his left arm and reached out to Elsie with his right hand in a beseeching manner. Homer, Harry's stepfather, looking upon the trio, stepped back, not wishing to intrude into this moment. Junior continued whispering to both mothers. He delicately joined Ruth and Elsie's hands. Startled, Elsie stepped back, instinctively pulling her hand away. Even with the symbolic act of a double funeral, a bond had yet to be sealed between them. Ruth also stepped back, from fear of offending.

Junior, in a calm, tender voice, spoke to both. "Can't we stop this thang now, right here, before it gets out of hand and involves more innocents?"

Elsie cried, "Oh my, how can I do that? How can I stop anything? If I could stop anything, I'd have stopped this, I'd have stopped Harry from hanging out with Donald. I knew there was something bad about him, but Harry was drawn to Donald like a fly to a coal-oil lamp and I didn't do anything about it. Dear Lord," she wailed, near collapse, "how can I go on living with this pain?"

Homer stepped closer to Elsie, supporting her. "It's okay, Elsie. You don't have to do anything. It's not your fault." The preachers began moving the families down the main aisle to the church door. The director recognized this opportunity to close the caskets without the family looking on, and so motioned to his assistants.

As the families continued making their way to the door, shrouds were placed over the faces of Donald and Harry. The delicate lining was gently tucked into the sides of the casket. The heavy lids were lowered into place, forever shutting out the last rays of light. A small silver-colored tool was used by one of the hearse drivers to screw the lids down tight, making the boxes impenetrable, like the funeral home advertised. Once the caskets were secure, each was slowly rolled down the main aisle behind the families, creating a thundering noise on the hardwood.

The closed caskets were held just short of the door, waiting for the families to clear. With the caskets on their carts and the pallbearers now in place, ready to assume their responsibilities, both families walked through the exit and into the cold. The area in front of the church door was full of attendees that spilled into the churchyard and around the hearses to the street.

Elsie and Ruth found themselves standing together in the open doorway of the church, silhouetted by the golden glow of the lighting from inside. Even though the crowd was making way for the families, Elsie paused.

The crowd became quiet, except for a few hard cases near the street, the same folks who'd gotten the families attention when making their hard remarks as they passed by the caskets. The constable, advised of these folks by the director, pointed them out to Trooper Brooks and Deputy Huggins. Hearing the commotion, the three officers began moving toward the rowdies who, upon noticing the officers, buttoned their lips.

Elsie, standing on the threshold of the church, heard them once again and recognized trouble. She hesitated, then sought the ear of her husband, whispering to him. After patiently listening, Homer kissed her cheek and spoke softly to her.

Elsie, sensing the power of the moment, steeled herself, turned toward Ruth and Bill. In a voice loud enough to be heard over the sound of the wind, she said, "We've all experienced an awful loss." She started to cry. "And to those who feel there must be more loss, hear me clear." She paused once more as necks craned. She took Ruth's hand in hers, pulling Ruth closer to her. Looking directly into Ruth's face as tears ran down the faces of both mothers, Elsie said, "Ruth...Bill, I find no fault in your family for what Donald did, and it must all stop here, with their burial." The words moved through the crowd like a bolt of lightning. There was no misunderstanding by those in attendance. Some were stunned, while "Amen!" resonated from others.

Elsie continued. "The fault lies only with Donald, who will pay for his sins throughout eternity. There'll be no trouble between our families from this moment forward and I curse anyone who commits any offense against you or anyone else on behalf of my dead son. Harry wouldn't want that to happen, and neither do we." Ruth spontaneously hugged Elsie for several moments without saying a word. The only sound was that of the wind, upon which her words traveled.

The director, standing near Dad, whispered, "I truly have never seen anything like this," as he used the cuff of his sleeve to wipe away a tear.

36

Ruth and Elsie, at the gentle urging of the preachers and the funeral director, began moving forward and down the steps. They were careful to place each foot with care until reaching the churchyard. The hushed crowd parted for them. The constable and Deputy Huggins waved their arms at the rowdies as if they were shooing away a group of pesky chickens. No one went to jail.

Dad whispered to Mom as they picked their way through the crowd, "Do you believe that? Elsie forgave 'em."

Mom said nothing.

"Glenda, I'm just gonna start the car and get the heater going. You stay in the car and get warm. I'll wait for the Busbys outside."

"Okay," Mom sighed as her strength waned.

Dad positioned himself at the outer edges of the crowd, near the street, where he could see the entire crowd. He noticed a teenaged girl crying uncontrollably. He wondered which one she was crying for, Hokey or Fats.

The first casket to leave the church was Harry's. The pallbearers, now experienced with the weight of Harry's casket, worked in unison, clearing the casket from the chrome cart in one synchronized lift. They moved with precision through the doorway and onto the concrete steps as delicate flakes of snow swept into the church through the open door, some settling onto the caskets. What little warmth remained in the painted metal surface dissolved the crystals upon contact, leaving small beads of water, as if quiet tears were falling from Heaven.

An almost imperceptible layer of snow accumulated and made the steps more challenging than before the funeral. The pallbearers again strained under the extra weight of Harry's casket; grunts, groans, and shuffling feet bore witness to their efforts.

Donald's casket traveled the same route as Harry's, back to its hearse. As the pallbearers shoved his casket into place and the heavy rear door closed, the crowd began making their way to their cars.

The hearses appeared more ominous as they sat beside the church, their grim cargo now safely aboard. The black polished surfaces reflected a distortion of the mourners as they made their way to their cars, creating a bizarre mish-mash of ghostly images flowing like a slow mountain stream around dark boulders.

Dad opened the door and slid in behind the wheel. Before the Busbys arrived at the car, Dad asked, "What do you think about what Elsie said?"

"What?" Mom said.

"Fats' mom forgiving 'em, what do you think of that?"

"Very meaningful since Elsie said it."

"I don't know. There're some folks out there who seem to want more blood."

"For what?" Mom asked. "Hokey getting wine-drunk and killing Fats over a 16-year-old girl because of some stupid sense of jealously? He was just crazy drunk. It's awful that Fats had to die but that's all there was to it. Now, thank God it's over with."

"Glenda," Dad sighed, "the Hatfields and McCoys fought over a hog for fifty years, killing most of each other's family. Things like this mean something. It can't be stopped by a few words at a funeral, it can only be accelerated or postponed."

"Okay...okay, I give up," she said, rolling her eyes. "I guess we'll all have to start lying out in the road ditch with our shotguns for the rest of our lives."

"You just don't understand these people like I do. I've seen it up close and personal in Mississippi where it was a way of life. Feuds are for real and there's plenty of ornery folks out there that'll not be so forgiv'n and forgett'n. Some folks are always looking for something to fight about."

Mom sighed, closing her eyes.

Ruth and Bill, holding Li'l Joe with Raymond following along, made their way to the car. The hearses moved in behind the state patrol car, as directed, then, entered onto State Route 25, headed south. Dad took his place behind the car carrying Elsie and her family, and with headlights on, the other vehicles moved into line.

* * *

The gravediggers at each cemetery, Stanfield and Sumach, anxiously eyed the weather and the clock, thinking something had gone dreadfully wrong. "I ain't stayin' if it gets dark. I ain't gonna be in no grave in the dark with a ha'nt; it ain't Christian."

"You'll stay if you want to get paid," growled the straw boss. "The director don't cotton to being left with an unfilled grave. It's bad for business. I've buried folks in the dark before, many times, and it ain't hurt me none. Anyway, there ain't no such thing as a haint, only ignoramuses believe in haints."

* * *

The wind from the west erupted in random gusts near gale strength, as if nature itself was becoming angry. The treetops were pushed and pulled by the wind, looking like the anguished wringing of giant hands. The abundant dried remains of cattails in the roadside ditches whipped to and fro in wave-like motions. The landscape, if possible, appeared more drab than before the funeral.

The cortege traveled south at a steady speed of thirty miles per hour. There was very little automobile traffic, but a few big M-model International Harvester farm tractors were headed north at the same time, pulling heavy four-row discs on large hydraulic-operated wheels. The tractor drivers slowed and pulled to the side of the road, their right wheels off the blacktop. They doffed their hats as the trooper's car and the hearses passed. This show of respect for the last ride was a common courtesy in the Bootheel, even in the foulest of weather, no matter the person. At about a mile out of town, the Stanfield cemetery came into view on the right side of the road.

Brooks slowed the caravan, allowing Harry's hearse to turn into the cemetery while Donald's hearse continued on behind him. Hokey and Fats' separation was now complete as the somber parade split, depending on relationships with the deceased.

37

Hokey's hearse continued on behind Trooper Brooks making a looping turn west, then, just before getting to the Holcomb drive-in, they took a left turn onto county road M/153, due south. In a few miles, Trooper Brooks slowed as he approached tiny Sumach Church on the east side of the road, enclosed on three sides by fading fields.

Sumach Cemetery was small as were most in this isolated land. A five hundred gallon propane tank sat on the north side of the church, separating the church from the cemetery. The grave markers varied in shades of gray and gleaming white. The oldest leaned awkwardly to and fro. Some lay on the ground, broken, like bizarre jigsaw puzzles, the result of a century of wind, rain, ice storms, sweltering heat, and vandalism. Greenish patches of lichen and moss and the unmistakable mark of windswept time smoothed the names of long-lost loved ones into obscurity. Some graves were marked by no more than a length of rusting pump pipe or an old metal fence post, or both, revealing no information as to the identity of the poor soul resting there.

The unmistakable sound of crunching gravel and the reflection of headlights off the wood-framed church and headstones heralded their arrival. The hearse driver positioned the rear door as close to the canopied grave as possible. The gravediggers stood quietly under a catalpa tree near the open grave.

Mom and Dad parked as close to the hearse as possible. Then Mom, Dad, and the Busbys, began slowly making their way to the grave. They moved between graves, careful not to step on them. The hearse driver and pallbearers again gathered at the hearse's large rear door. Mourners leaned into the wind as they walked toward the grave. More cars arrived, providing additional illumination to the darkening area by leaving their headlights on, creating long, eerie shadows.

The pallbearers struggled with the casket, its broad, flat surfaces pushed and pulled by the wind, like the sails on a sloop, as they made their way among the stones. The green canopy stretched over the open grave threatened to pull away from its moorings with each gust of wind. One of the gravediggers dove at a wooden stake about to pull free. He strained to hold the tether as another digger rushed to his aid, the canopy flopping and popping. Together, they reset the stake. A worn artificial green-grass-carpet had been laid out on the south side of the grave for the family. Four metal folding chairs were lying upon it.

The dug dirt, mostly sand, was piled on the north side of the open grave. A wooden frame of rough planks had been laid around the open pit, forming a base upon which sat a heavy iron-frame lowering device. The gravediggers set up the four metal folding chairs as the Busbys approached. One of the chairs was immediately blown over and had to be reset.

Junior, driven to the cemetery by J.C., jumped from the pickup truck and walked briskly to the grave, hatless, the biting wind blowing his hair askew, his long coat flapping behind him. The Busbys were seated in the metal folding chairs as mourners encircled the grave about them.

Upon reaching the grave, Junior pulled his coat close and braced himself against the wind blowing against his back. He moved to Bill and Ruth and whispered practiced words into their ears.

A sudden blast of super-cooled wind blew hard against the mourners, causing the folks to lower their heads and lean into it. Some mothers with little ones summarily left the grave, hurrying back to their cars, the cold driving them away.

The pallbearers moved carefully, holding the handgrips with both hands as they moved in unison, sidestepping along the edges of the open grave. They carefully placed the casket on the heavy straps, making sure it wasn't offset at any point assuring a clear passage when making its downward descent. As the weight of the casket was fully accepted by the straps, a small piece of earth at the edge of the pit gave way with the weight of the pallbearer and casket.

Slipping into the grave up to his knee, the pallbearer called out for help and a mourner let out a shriek. "Get me out of here," he cried out. Almost immediately, he apologized to no one in particular. "I'm sorry," he said, "I thought this was more solid." A mourner grabbed hold of the pallbearer's jacket, pulling him upward and another grabbed hold of the casket handle, steadying it.

The pallbearer, having recovered his footing, took back the handle of the casket from the man who had stepped in to help. The casket was re-positioned upon the straps. The director arrived just in time to see the pallbearer being helped up. He rushed in to inspect the corners of the casket, ensuring unrestricted clearance into the grave. Once satisfied, he nodded toward the pallbearers who then faded into the crowd, awaiting the conclusion of the graveside service.

Junior positioned himself at the head of the grave, his Bible in his right hand. His lean frame appeared larger than life-size. The headlights of some cars from the parking area silhouetted his form as flecks of snow floated about his head. It seemed that had he wanted, he could have called down thunder and lightning.

Junior fervently believed in the literal meaning of the Bible and never cut corners, as was evident in his funeral sermon. However, here, outside the church, standing over this gaping wound in the earth, he came face to face with a familiar foe, the evil he had so fervently fought against his whole life. Junior paled and his throat moved as if unable to utter a word, as if he were in the presence of the old deluder himself, on unhallowed ground.

Looking down at the casket, poised above the hole that was to serve as Donald's final resting place, Junior's hands trembled.

He couldn't put the family through any more grief. This is for the grieving family, he thought, as he looked at them in such obvious pain. I can't forget, he thought, thus steeling himself and silently praying, Dear Lord, give me strength, as he searched for the right words. Remembering the basics, he recalled what he had learned as a new preacher years and years ago. Use words of strength and comfort to the bereaved. Even though he hadn't done this during the service, he stayed true to the gospel he lived his life by.

He asked, "Everyone, please bow your head." The cold turned his words into puffs of gray. "In our sadness, our loneliness, our grief, our deep sorrow and regrets, Donald's actions cannot be understood or explained. In our anguish, we place our trust in you, O Lord. May you look kindly upon Donald and give him peace. In Jesus' name, we pray, Amen." There was plenty of doubt in his mind that God would look kindly upon Donald, and the prayer was a departure from his sermon, yet Junior felt it the right thing to do for the family.

A deep chill came over him from what he perceived as a direct challenge from a biblical evil, an all-encompassing evil, one he had dedicated his life to defeating. He felt the familiar burn of unseen eyes when his preaching was at a fever pitch. Is this the Demon, he thought. Is it the same Demon that entered Hokey, now writhing in the grave? Shaken, Junior moved from the grave to the family, nodding his head to the director who had assumed control of releasing the handbrake of the lowering device. There would be no more ceremony. It was time.

The director released the brake. The casket jumped, jerked, and began its slow descent only to begin squeaking, stopping its descent after only a couple of feet. One wide-eyed mourner said, "I know he ain't going to Heaven, but maybe the Devil don't want him neither. Maybe he's doomed to walk the earth."

The wind swirled around Junior when he unexpectedly mumbled, "Dust to dust." Sweat beaded his forehead and soaked his dark shirt. His heart raced. Exhausted and weakened, he turned away and, without again speaking to the Busbys, picked his way through the ancient stones to where the pickup truck was waiting.

* * *

"Are you feeling okay?" asked J.C. who was sitting in the warm cab of the truck. You don't look so good."

Junior, sitting in what seemed to be stunned silence, stared into the darkness of the cemetery, unresponsive.

The gravediggers watched and, with a renewed vigor, grabbed their shovels and went to work. The mourners, including Mom and Dad, walked briskly to the car as the Busbys remained, not wanting to leave, lost in their thoughts and grief.

Ghostly shadows, created by the movement of mourners and gravediggers, danced about in the headlights of the remaining cars moving about. While Li'l Joe was being carried back to the car by his dad, he noticed a lone, shadowy figure that appeared standing in a far corner of the cemetery, silently viewing the burial party. The lights seemed to pass through it.

Sitting on his dad's lap in the car, his eyes reflecting his exhaustion as he yawned, Li'l Joe whispered into his father's ear, "Who's that?" He pointed a small index finger in the direction of the shadowy figure.

"Who?" Bill whispered in response.

"That person standing over there."

"Where?" Bill strained to see into the darkness.

"Right there," said Joe, pointing. "Don't ya see him?"

Bill squinted, staring into the darkness. Suddenly, he turned ashen and his eyes widened. He bowed his head and turned away. "No, no," he whispered, and he patted Joe's head. "I don't see nothin'"

"Yes you do, right there!" Li'l Joe placed his small hands on each side of Bill's head and turned it in the direction of the apparition.

"No, I don't," Bill said emphatically. "I don't." Tears welled in his eyes. He pulled Joe close to him. "I don't see nothin'."

Postscript

A few days following the funeral, Mom took me to visit Hokey's grave under the catalpa tree. On a sandy mound covered in brown, wilted roses and a couple of plastic wreaths was a metal funeral home marker identifying the interred as Donald Ray Busby, 1935-1957. It was a stark cold inventory, suitable for the crime.

The day was cold and wintry, the skies steel gray, as Mom and I stood together in that cemetery of lost souls and sorrow. Holding my mother's hand, I could not see or sense any signs of redemption. I could only imagine what torment Hokey was experiencing in Hell, surrounded by my memories of what life was like before the killing.

"Come on, it's time we left," Mom said.

"Okay." I said, then paused. "Mom," I said.

"Yes."

"Tell me about the funeral. Tell me everything that happened."

We made our way to the car in the church parking lot. We sat there for most of an hour. I listened intently. She told me about the extraordinary funeral service: the preachers, the attendees, and the sorrow Hokey's brutal act had wrought.

"Mom," I said, "I want to go to Fats' grave."

"I don't know where his grave is. Your dad and I went to Hokey's burial, because we couldn't go to both and the Busbys' are special people to us."

It would take a little longer to learn the location of his grave, some 50-plus years. Additional information came out in hushed tones over the years with old friends and acquaintances whose recollections had to be mined from deep within like precious stones. Eventually, far into my retirement, I believe that maybe, just maybe, I had learned it all.

For years there were rumored sightings of two men walking on the ditch-dump road, laughing. Others would swear that, late at night, on cold, rain-soaked evenings, they saw a lone figure dressed in 50's garb looking forlorn, standing near the site where Hokey's car was found. Occasionally, during my years of discovery on the Floodways, I remained on the trestles until darkness enveloped me and, with Buddy by my side, I hoped to see them. I think I might have...once.

Epilogue

During my research for this book, I again visited Hokey's gravesite, which I first visited more than a half century before. Still, there was no gravestone, just a piece of rusted pipe and a rusted metal fencepost marking the grave's location. The catalpa tree that shaded Hokey's grave has grown older and taller. Curiously, an upstart cypress tree has inexplicably interwoven itself with the Catalpa tree, an unusual occurrence.

Fats' resting place in the Stanfield Cemetery was also unmarked, and during the past half century has been lost to time. As a result of an inquiry by Harry's relatives, it was determined that Harry's unmarked grave rests in the vicinity of the caretaker's small white tool shed. However, no exact location has been identified, adding to the undeserved indignities suffered by this innocent man.

Following the funeral, the death car was relocated to the Busby house where Raymond continued to clean it. One day, when Raymond and I came home from school, the car was gone. Ruth couldn't bear to look upon her dead son's car and the bloodstained seats that no amount of soap and elbow grease could clean. She sold the car back to Charlie Thompson, a local used car dealer near Wardell, for forty dollars. The final disposition of the car has been lost to time.

Elsie Shell Huddleston, mother of Harry "Fats" Shell, passed away in 1965. Her forgiving of the Busby family and her strong condemnation of any thoughts of vendetta calmed the waters. Her loving kindness was evident to all who knew her

The Busbys eventually left our farm and, sadly, never visited California. Yet Betty, their only daughter, who lives in California, traveled back to Missouri to see them before they died. An answer to their prayers.

Bill Busby, teller of tall tales and homespun philosopher, passed away in 1985. His wife, Ruth, the rock of the family, passed away in 1991.

Li'l Joe lives with his wife in Southeast Missouri, his memory of the killing vague, due to his young age at the time.

The Robinson family left the Walker farm in 1959, moving to another farm in an area west of Wardell called "Flag Land." The killing couldn't be ignored or washed away by time. The memories were too difficult.

Martha, the mother of the Robinson family, was bedridden with a flu-like illness and grief following the killing, a condition that might nowadays be diagnosed as Post Traumatic Stress Disorder.

Martha passed away in 1969 and Ernest in 1979. Their large family has remained close-knit unlike many large families.

Arlena, mother to five daughters and a spry grandmother to numerous grandchildren, recalled those days with teared eyes.

Alma Faye a cancer survivor and mother to five girls and a boy is a loving grandmother many times over.

Charles, the patriarch of the family, following the deaths of his older brothers, married and has two daughters and two sons. He became a master tractor driver like his father and, with great pride, reflects on the day he picked 650 pounds of cotton.

Violet, called "chew-tobacco," died in a car accident in 1966 at fourteen years of age.

Bobby, the baby that Fats set down just before he was killed by Hokey, took his own life at age fifty-two. He was twenty-two months old at the time of the murder.

Earnest Dale "Buddy" who was seven years old at the time of the killing is father to a son and daughter and grandfather to five.

In 1963, Verlan Raymond Busby married his sweetheart, Helen Robinson, in the parlor of Junior Crane's home. For more than fifty years, through thick and thin, sickness and health, they never left each other's side. They had no children and lived in a small town in Southern Illinois where Raymond was known as "The Shotgun Man," due to his prowess with the weapon he favored. He was a hunter and fisherman.

On March 6, 2014, Raymond passed away, in as gentle a manner as he lived. Helen was with him that morning while he sat on their living room couch. She was worried...he said he wasn't feeling well. He asked her to call an ambulance. Trying to control her concern, she turned to him and told him they'd be there soon.

He told her of things he wanted her to know and things she should or should not do in his absence. He told her he had loved her forever. She tried not to be scared, but she was. He was as soft-spoken and gentle as he had been throughout his life. She held his hand, and whispered of things only a wife could know. She told him that her love for him would never dim and she would see him one day before the living God they worshipped together throughout their lives. As she stroked his brow and held his hand, he turned his head to one side and quietly slipped away. The trials and tribulations in this world were over for this kind and gentle man.

I was honored to be a pallbearer for my friend as he was interned in Gilead Cemetery, alongside Highway 25, north of Clarkton. Helen, his true love and partner in life, carries on with loving support from that close-knit family of brothers and sisters.

Dad and Mom eventually retired from farming, auctioned off all the farm equipment, and rented out the land. They moved to a small white frame house in Clarkton, "On high ground," Dad said, where he and Mom couldn't be marooned by floods. Dad passed away in 1988 at eighty-two years of age. Mom passed away in 2003 at ninety-four. Both are at rest in Memorial Gardens, Kennett, Missouri. Better parents no person ever had.

Herbert Junior Crane passed away in 1989. His two sons, Jerry and Lanny, are elders at Tatum Chapel. Jerry is a deacon and Lanny, is the song leader who, with his guitar and his grandson's accompaniment, make good gospel music at Tatum Chapel. Junior's grandson, Scott Crane, is now the preacher at Tatum Chapel, a very special place.

Wayne Wood, later in life, earned a Doctorate of Education degree from Memphis State University and eventually became head of the Education Department of Southwest Baptist University, Bolivar, Missouri. Much heralded in both the ministry and public education, he passed away in 2013 following a long illness.

Both of these good men, Herbert Junior Crane and Wayne Wood, were giants in their time.

My brother, Johnny, married his high school sweetheart, Helen, and remained in the Bootheel where they became the parents of four daughters and are now doting grandparents and great grandparents. He was the first gauge reader on those trestles that allowed access into our wonderland and blazed the trail that Raymond and I followed.

Hokey and Fats quickly faded from memory as the killing went mostly unnoticed outside the farm despite both radio coverage and newspaper articles. It was seldom mentioned again, except in whispers.

Yet, for many years, when Dad still tilled the land, he would tell me, "I saw Hokey's boots again today, up on the Earl's place." Those were the rubber boots Hokey pulled free of when he and Fats were pulling bolls in the half-frozen mud during that winter of 1957, only days before the killing.

The hordes of migrant workers who once flooded into cotton country to chop and pick cotton are long gone. The permanent population of Pemiscot County is now a gaunt likeness of its former self.

Elmer Harness, after leaving the Floodways, did make good on his threats to kill Harrison, his brother. He got drunk and stabbed Harrison to death. The Sheriff, Clyde Orton, took Elmer into custody and, after consultations with the county prosecutor, it was rumored that rather than spend money on prosecuting and imprisoning Elmer, they'd just take him back to Arkansas. Elmer was transported back by a deputy and told never to return to Missouri. To my knowledge, Elmer was never seen again in Missouri.

I graduated from Bragg City High School in 1963, went on to college, graduated, and joined the Marine Corps. I married my college sweetheart, deployed to Vietnam as a Marine Helicopter Pilot, raised two boys, was activated for Desert Storm, and eventually retired from a career in federal law enforcement and the Marine Corps Reserve—all stories for another time and place. During all that time, the saga of Hokey and Fats and the Floodways of my youth were never far from my thoughts.

Buddy, my beautiful collie and faithful friend, died in November 1970, just days after my safe return from Vietnam. He was 15 years old and had held onto life, seeming to know I was coming home. He lay on a cottonseed sack in a comfortable spot prepared by my Dad. Upon seeing and hearing me call his name, he raised his great head and feebly licked my hand as I spoke to him in soft whispers of days gone by while patting his scarred head. He seemed at peace and soon died. I cradled him and cried the first tears I could remember. Dad and I carefully laid Buddy to rest in the shade of a large cypress tree surrounded by a spacious pasture near my childhood home and the Floodways.

I couldn't help but remember those days so long before, when Buddy and I whiled away the hot summer days as he pranced along before me, my guardian and friend.

The land itself has changed—not for the better. The supremacy of King Cotton is being challenged by rice as the main money crop. Corporate farms, for the most part, have gobbled up the small family farms. The Cotton Belt Railroad has been ripped up and the high roadbed upon which it was built has been leveled. Only the concrete structures that held up the steel superstructure crossing Canal 251, Swift Ditch, remain and can be seen in aerial shots of the region—a silent witness to what once was.

The Floodway Canals are now even more remote, more mysterious and yes, just as beautiful, as the access to their deep inner beauty has been all but stopped by the Little River Drainage District's "no trespassing" signs.

Our family farm home became so dilapidated, the new owners burned it down. Not one house, barn, shed, tree, nor plank bridge remain on this land where I once whiled away my childhood listening to stories told by Bill and fishing with Raymond as Hokey sat and watched.

So many families lived a full, happy life on and near the Floodways. Yet, in the name of "progress", the land on which we walked, worked, laughed, and dreamed of adventures has all but faded from this earth. Only dim memories remain of the Floodways and those four days in the winter of 1957, when pure evil intruded into our tranquil lives and innocence was lost.

[i] "Haint" is primarily a southern variant on the word "haunt." It rhymes with paint.

[ii] Milo is a corn-like plant that grows to an average height of five feet and rather than producing an ear of corn, it produces seeds. Prior to 1957, I had never heard of Milo. Many of the farmers who were on their fourth planting, gave up on cotton and planted Milo. Dad kept his fourth planting of cotton rather than planting Milo. Milo had an unknown quality about it to Dad and he feared that if he gave up on what cotton crop he had, for Milo, he might not have any crop at all.

[iii] Baching. A derivative of bachelor, to keep house alone, as an unmarried man.

Bibliography

Bock, H. Riley, <u>Little River Drainage District of Southeast Missouri, Celebrating 100 years, 1907-2007.</u>

Douglas, Robert Sidney, <u>History of Southeast Missouri</u>. The Lewis Publishing Company, Chicago and New York 1912

White, Dan, <u>Canalou: People, Culture, Bootheel Town.</u>Center for Regional History, Southeast Missouri State University 2013

About the Author

Photo courtesy of Chuck Bennorth

Harold Walker is retired from the U.S. Marine Corps where in 1969-70 he served in Vietnam as a CH-46 Helicopter Pilot. Following active duty, he remained in the Marine Corps Reserve, as a UH-1N "Huey" Helicopter pilot where his reserve squadron, HML-776, was activated for Desert Storm. He retired from the Marine Corps Reserve in 1996 with the rank of Lieutenant Colonel. His parallel civilian occupation was in federal law enforcement. Upon retirement, he became a licensed private investigator.

Harold has written extensively about his tour of duty in Vietnam in a non-published book, currently being serialized for the Marine Corps History Branch. "Murder on the Floodways" is Harold's first excursion into the world of literature. By utilizing his skills as an investigator, he undertook a four year investigation into a vicious killing that took place on his family's small bucolic cotton farm in Southeast Missouri when he was twelve years old. For more information, visit http://haroldgwalker.com/.

CPSIA information can be obtained at www.ICGtesting.com
Printed in the USA
BVOW06s1749240615

406017BV00015B/277/P